2014

Dear Anna,

wishing you a very (Happy) Birthday, lots and lots of love,

KATIE XXX

P.S. I hope after you have read and looked at the amazing photography you will want to visit "ULPOTHA"

www.ulpotha.com

Published by
East Pole Foundation Limited
Commence Chambers
Road Town
1110 British Virgin Islands

www.ulpotha.com

ISBN 978-0-9573383-0-2

Copyright © 2012 by Carina Cooper
Copyright Photography © 2012 by Ingrid Rasmussen

The rights of the author have been asserted.
All rights reserved. No part of this book may be reproduced, stored in a retrieval system or transmitted in tape, mechanical, photocopying, recording or otherwise, without the prior permission in writing of the publisher.

Publishing director Carina Cooper
Photography by Ingrid Rasmussen | www.ingridrasmussen.com
Design by Therese Severinsen | www.thereseseverinsen.com
The text of this book is set in Chronicle.

Printed & bound by The Westdale Press Ltd

This book is printed with vegetable based inks on paper certified by PEFC (Programme for Endorsement of Forest Certification). The Westdale Press Ltd holds PEFC chain of Custody and a ISO14001 accreditation.

ACKNOWLEDGEMENTS
Illustration on page 4 by Pierre-Alain Bertola.
Photograph of Tennekoon on page 232 by Patricia Mamelka.
Thank you to Laura Campbell, Trish Nolan and Jean Balmond for editing.

Ulpotha is collectively managed by the villagers themselves and is operated on a not-for-profit basis. All funds generated from guest visits are invested back into the village and to finance the free Ayurveda clinic run for the benefit of surrounding villages.

MAP OF ULPOTHA

*To
Ithaka, Flynn, Tuan
Sidonie, Kiara, ZaZa
Zinzi & Flynn*

CONTENTS

Introduction	11
Lore, legend & myth	15
Dawn	24
Ayurveda	39
Wedagedara	41
The kitchen	47
Rice	63
Spices	66
Coconut	68

SALADS

Rocket, cucumber & tomato with lime, basil & salt	77
Beetroot, red onion, carrot & flat leaf parsley salad	79
Salad of chickpeas with shallots, coconut & mustard seeds	81
Warm aubergine salad	83

VEGETABLES

Breaded potato cutlets	87
Roast garlic in their skins	89
Tempered green beans with wilted onions, grated coconut & cinnamon	91
Fried onion rings with mustard seed, turmeric & nutmeg	93
Roast aubergine with grated ginger & cinnamon	95
Fried potato crisps with paprika	97
Fried bitter gourd	99

RICE, LENTILS, PULSES & GRAINS

Vegetable rice pilaf	103
Parippu *dhal*	105
Pittu	107
Coconut roti	109
Wadé	111

CURRY

Fragrant curry powder	115
Beetroot curry	117
Cucumber curry	119
Jackfruit curry	121
Mushroom curry	123
Leek curry	125
Okra curry	127
Thakkali *tomato* curry	129
Carrot curry	131
Mango curry	133

SAMBOLS & CHUTNEYS

Mint & lime sambol	137
Pol sambol	139
Pineapple & chilli chutney	141

PUDDINGS

Coconut cake	145
Kiri bath *milk rice*	147
Bananas with cardamom, pistachio & coconut	149
Curd & kitul treacle	151

DRINKS

Watermelon juice	155
Ginger & lime tea	157
Coriander tea	157

Kitchen garden	175
Night	225
Thank you	230
Afterword	237

Serendipity 'The occurrence and development of events by chance in a happy or beneficial way'

The word Horace Walpole coined after reading the fairy tale *'The Three Princes of Serendip'*

Serendip is the ancient name of Sri Lanka where Ulpotha, a traditional village, nestles amidst the emerald landscape's cultural triangle while being a pure embodiment of serendipitous tales.

Ulpotha came about playfully, says Viren Perera, one of the founders of Ulpotha. He was born in Sri Lanka, moved to Canada as a young boy, and returned to his homeland in his twenties, where he now continues to live.

He chanced across Ulpotha (meaning 'water spring') on a road trip in the early 1990s with two friends, Mudiyanse Tennekoon and Manik Sandrasagara. The land and crumbling manor house (Walauwwa) were for sale and on a whim and a chance encounter with an old man's smile, Viren found himself the new guardian of the land.

Viren restored the Walauwwa house but chose to leave it without electricity or modern appliances. A fridge could not be entertained after Tennekoon dismissively described it as a means "for keeping unfresh food". He then suggested they start a village that embraced indigenous farming practices. They would grow a variety of crops including heritage red rice, which was becoming harder to find, and use buffalo to work the fields and thresh the crops. The embodiment of their credo was a traditional lifestyle, living with nature and natural laws.

Thousands of trees were planted and diverse crops cultivated, including an assortment of rare heritage red rice. Mud huts were built using the traditional wattle and daub method, and even the murals were created using a mixture of coloured earth and ash. The village had now grown to a population of 40 and a way was needed to fund the project. One serendipitous moment led to another and to meeting Giles Scott, an Englishman, who then teamed up with Viren and Tennekoon.

Giles introduced yoga as a bridge to the West, which subsidises the village and brings in guests for six months of the year. Tennekoon's philosophy, 'Leisure, Pleasure and Rest' took on the order of the day while Viren's overview was there would be no dogma.

Ulpotha's food is based on a mélange of curries and traditional Sri Lankan food, but with a Western palate in mind. The use of chilli has been lessened and so the subtle flavours of the spices, vegetables and herbs are more prevalent.

All food is based on the Ayurvedic principle of Vata, Pitta, and Kapha. Produce from the kitchen garden is cooked in terracotta pots on open fires with different regulating heats, or sometimes just on burning embers and ash.

This book is not a replica of Ulpotha recipes but an inspiration and expression of Ulpotha food that I have interpreted and can be cooked in the West. I have synesthetic tendencies – I can smell and taste colours - so when I've cooked these recipes, Ulpotha has been in my heart, mind and spirit, and marked on my mental taste buds. Although some of the recipes might seem a little daunting because of the quantities of spices used, most of them are simple, easy to cook and don't take much time.

As I sit here at home in Devon, there are no mangoes falling off my trees or clay pots on open fires infusing curries with smoky aromas and mineral flavours. The supply of tropical ingredients and spices from my larder have clocked up many air miles and I don't have fresh coconuts to squeeze out the white flesh. I'm lucky enough to use vegetables from our biodynamic garden, so they are full of flavour.

If you can, buy the best organic ingredients possible. I find oriental shops often have fresher, tastier food than the big supermarkets. If you live in a city, find your local Asian supermarket or farmers' market. You can buy some dry ingredients and spices online.

If and where possible use terracotta or clay casserole pots. Replenish your spices regularly as they can become musty and lose their flavour quickly. If you feel more chilli or other spices are needed use your gut feeling; cooking is not exact, so be instinctive.

The rice I have found most similar to Ulpotha rice is red rice from my local health food shop and available in most Asian grocery shops.

I've used organic tinned coconut milk, which works well, but if you come across a fresh coconut, jump at the chance to use it.

If you've been an Ulpotha guest, I hope the recipes will transport you back to this magical place – and if you've never been I hope it inspires you to visit.

CARINA COOPER

LORE, LEGEND & MYTH

Deep in the jungle, surrounded by the Galgiriyawa Mountains, nature remains in her full magisterial glory. Nestled under the sheltering palm trees, a small group of huts circling an old manor house look like upside-down birds nests with their dung floors and cadjan roofs. Ancient elephant paths criss-cross through the village and there have been sightings of a rare white cobra on the path by the lake.

Rebuilt on the layout of a deserted traditional village Ulpotha's foundations are laid on the timeless grounds of nature, history, ritual and myth. Ulpotha refers to the springs feeding the system of five ancient reservoirs that irrigate the surrounding paddy fields. The area has a history dating back over 2,500 years to when roaming ascetics first inhabited the mountain caves.

According to local legend, pilgrims travelling from India in search of Lord Kataragama (son of Shiva) believed that Ulpotha, set within the seven hills, was the sacred site associated with the deity.

Ulpotha is also thought to have been the playground of Prince Saliya, the son of Sri Lanka's most legendary king. Myths abound that the prince escaped with his outcaste gypsy wife, Asokamala, from the ancient city of Anuradhapura through a secret tunnel and came to live in a cave above the lake at Ulpotha. In the ancient text of the Mahavamsa, she was described as being possessed of a beauty so rare as to be seen in the 'realm of the divine'.

To visit Ulpotha is to step back into the land that time forgot; it's a rare place where all the influences of our technological age evaporate – no plastic, no phones, no electricity, no glaring screens or newspapers.

Guests are welcome for six months a year, which enables the village to run and to support a free Ayurvedic clinic (called the Wedagedara), dedicated to the late Tennekoon.

Neighbouring villagers come to be diagnosed and treated by Dr Srilal Mudunkothge, Ulpotha's resident doctor, and to be given herbs, lotions and potions that are grown and made in the Wedagedara healing area.

The Ulpotha villagers are the earth keepers, while Viren and Giles refreshingly support a philosophy that seems more pertinent and precious in this day and age and akin to EF Schumacher's "small is beautiful" ethos.

A day here is just as a day has always been for our forefathers, a symbiotic flow between the landscape and the human inhabitants and back again.

Ulpotha enables one to free the spirit, to have an uncluttered mind and follow a butterfly, while contemplating the depth and mystery of a flower or feeling the smoothness of a pebble.

After a few days, presence settles in, the past becomes another country, the future a distant land. And when it's time to re-enter the punch bag of city life, you will find the beauty and peace of Ulpotha will have taken up a part of your heart.

DAWN

When the distant bell of the monastery tolls, stirring one's being, don't let slumber intoxicate and lull the mind into a gentle cocoon of musing. As a throaty whoop-woo from a monkey calls to others to greet and embrace the day, force yourself awake, for the pleasures of the dawn belong to the privileged.

Arise out of bed and remain barefoot, it creates more communication between the brain and feet enabling one to be present. Inhale the pale golden light and step out into the ancientness of nature as the earth breathes out in the morning full of life force. It's like watching theatre, be still and the stage comes to life.

First it's the birds that are mesmeric; they converge and trill in energetic exchange across soft refractions of light. Hear a whoosh through the air like a firework, layered with pencils being sharpened, and refined squeaks, chirps and echoes.

See a hummingbird dance in and out of the waving skirts of a scarlet hibiscus. An owl, living in the hollow next to the lake hut, tests his wings invigoratingly as a kingfisher flashes his startling blue plumage. A bird of paradise proudly flicks his tail across the verdant backdrop, watched by two golden orioles that swoop down to admire their reflection in the mercurial liquid of the tank.

An otter belts along the bund in anticipation of breakfast and play. Chipmunks, cheeky in their demeanour, scamper along branches engaging in daring acrobatics. Catch a chameleon's eyes and it is present, informed and rotates in accordance to the observer's action as he blends into his horizon.

Witness the inner life of the lotus before she wraps her petals and shies away. Frangipanis court the sun as insects nestle among the burnt orange and sulphur red of the iris plants. Lizards scuttle up warm baked mud walls. Shadows pale and sharp tease and taunt their material masters. Palm trees feather the sky to make clouds.

An alert salamander shovels the earth to bury its luminescent eggs as a lazy turtle splashes into the waters of the lake.

Follow the path to Monkey Rock, rising up from the earth. Trees provide arbour and shade. Take in the expansive, nirvanic views as a brahminy kite rides the thermals. Standing on these giant rocks is like being on dormant, monolithic creatures that are eons older than the Jurassic period. Shamans say everything has a pulse and stones do so once every 24 hours.

Look down at the boulders to the weeping edges of the tall reeds, the fluttering eyelashes to the open eye of the lake, shimmering with the reflection of all who take life from her silky depths. When you immerse yourself into the soothing flow of the tank, float on your back and merge with the sky and the water, stare at the dripping trees and count the different shades of green.

Everyone feels that Ulpotha belongs to them, because when one finds a sacred place in nature it nurtures one's own nature.

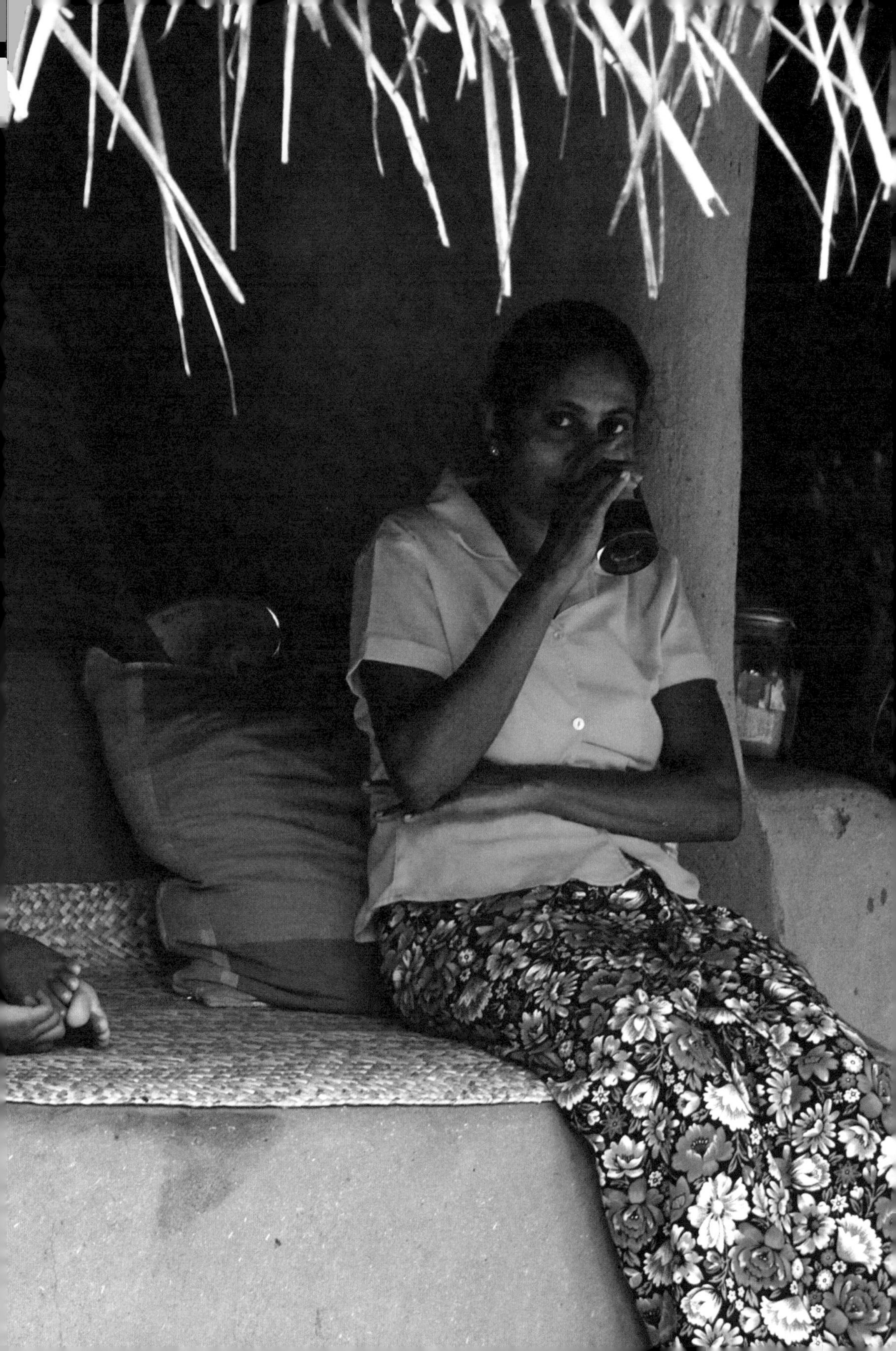

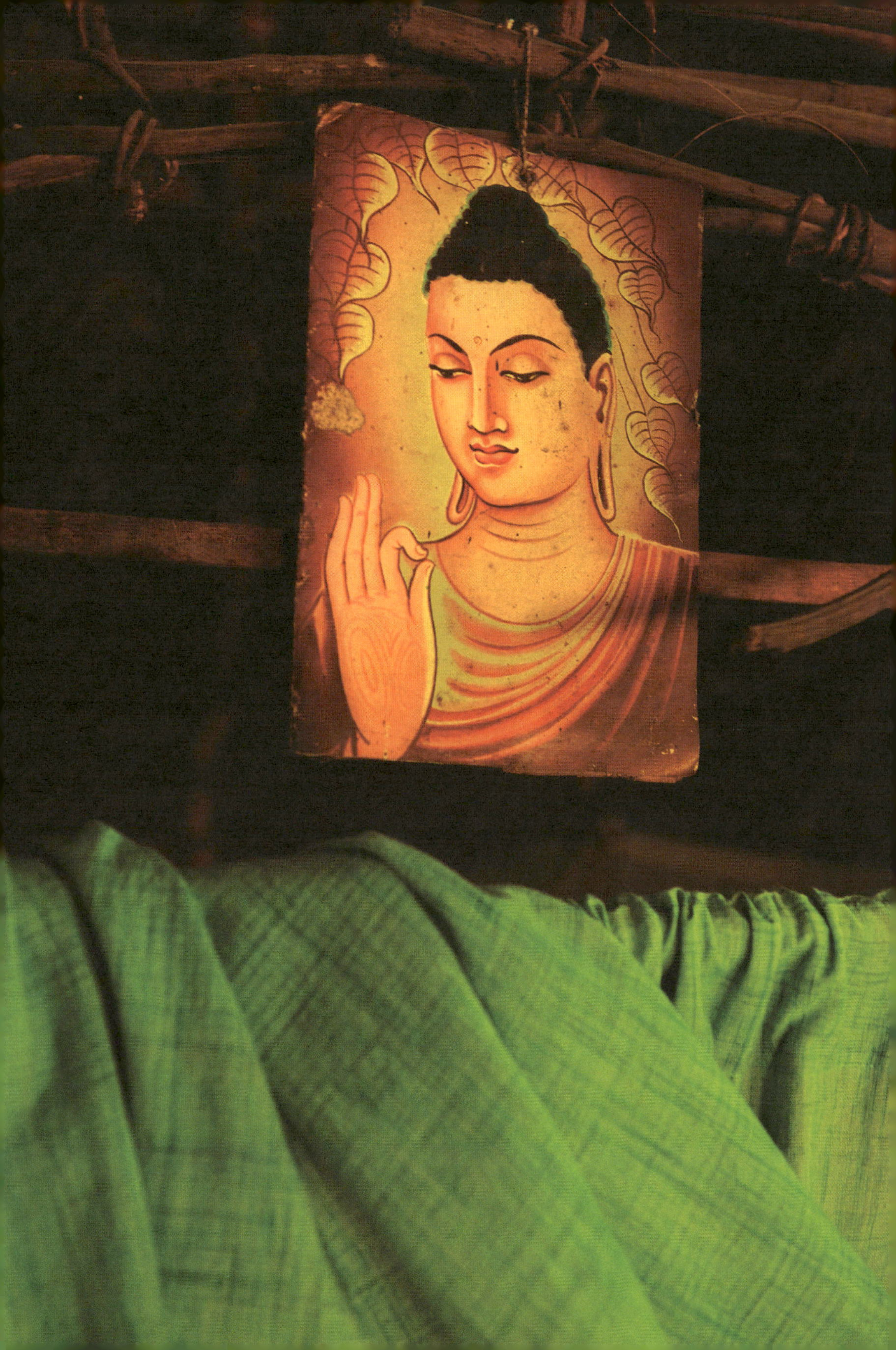

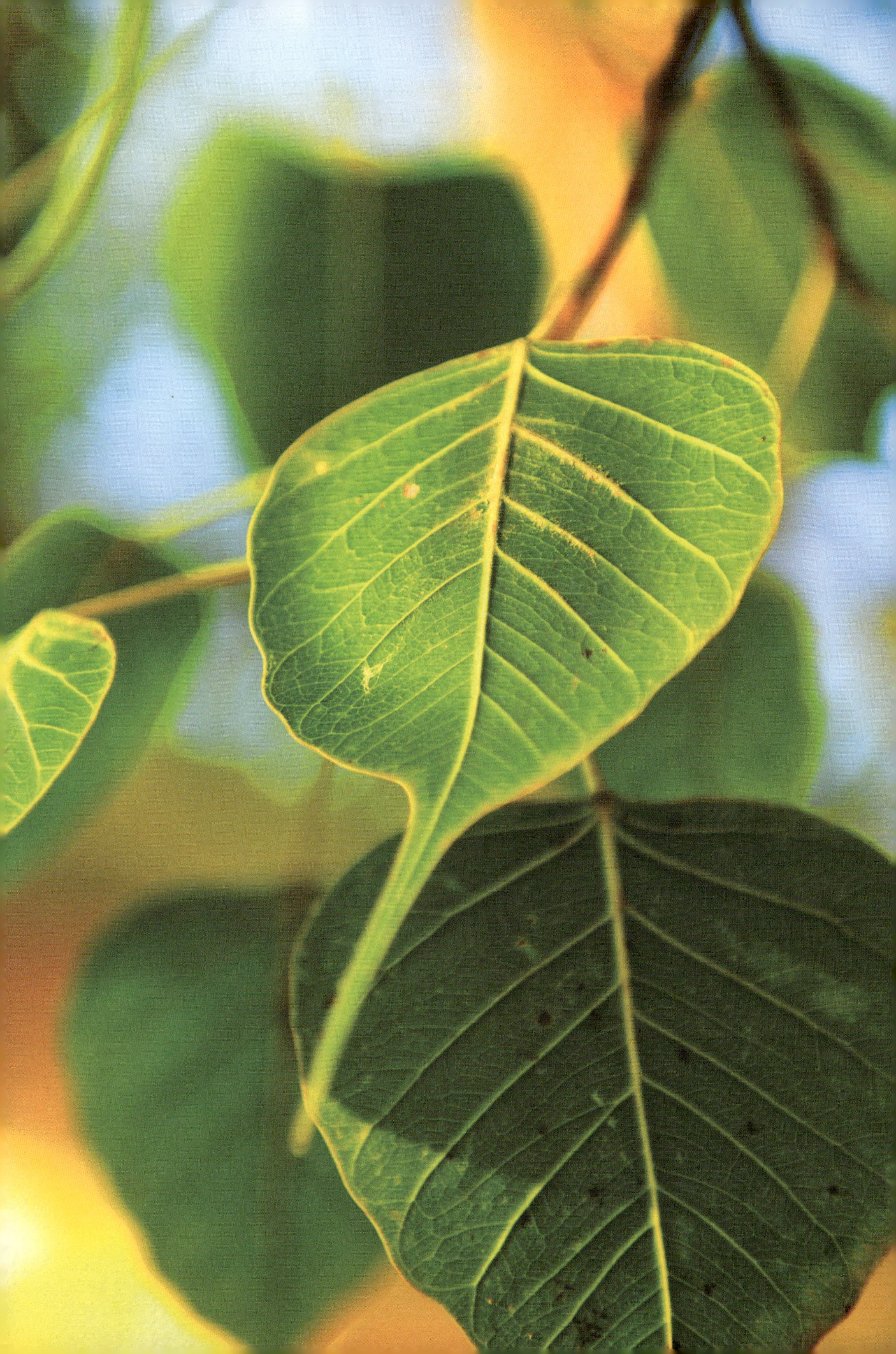

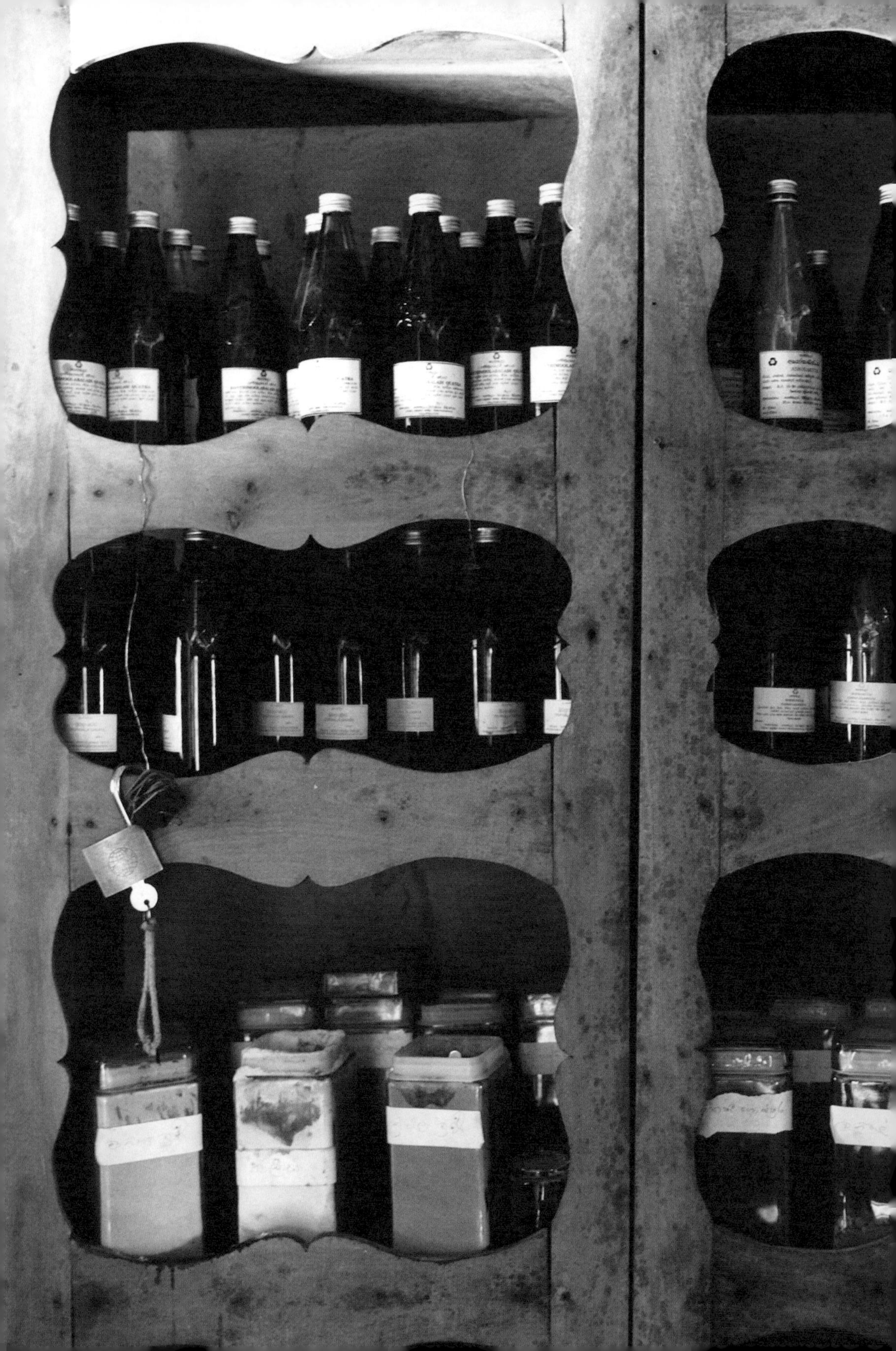

AYURVEDA

Ayurveda originated in India over 5,000 years ago. Ayer and Veda are a combination of two Sanskrit words. Ayer, which means 'life', and Veda, which means 'the knowledge of'. It is considered the world's most ancient system of holistic health care.

The principle of Ayurvedic philosophy is that humans, their health and the universe are thought to be related. The process of life disrupts the state of balance in the mind, body and spirit and an imbalance of these is thought to cause disease.

The general diagnosis of disease is done by taking the pulse points of an individual and reading their doshas in order to learn which are out of balance. These doshas are called Vatta, Pitta and Kapha.

Each dosha is associated with a certain body type, a certain personality type and a leaning towards certain types of health problems; doshas are constantly being formed and re-formed by food activity and bodily process. Each individual has all three doshas, though generally one is more prominent than the others.

Dr Srilal, Ulpotha's resident Ayurveda physician, will suggest specific lifestyle and nutritional guidelines, which include diet, steam, yoga and massage. These ideally take three weeks or longer of continuous application, until the patient's constitution is in harmony with the Universe.

According to Ayurvedic principles food is classified into six tastes: sweet, sour, salty, bitter, pungent and astringent. It's important to meet all six tastes in one's daily diet and to practice moderation in all things.

Examples of each taste are:
Sweet: cream, rice, wheat, ghee, milk, honey, ripe fruits and kitul treacle.
Sour: citrus fruits, lime, lemon, mango, tamarind and pomegranate seeds.
Salty: pickles and salt.
Bitter: greens, fenugreek, bitter gourd and turmeric.
Pungent: ginger, clove, black pepper, chilli peppers, radish and mustard.
Astringent: lentils, cabbage and cauliflower, beans and coriander.

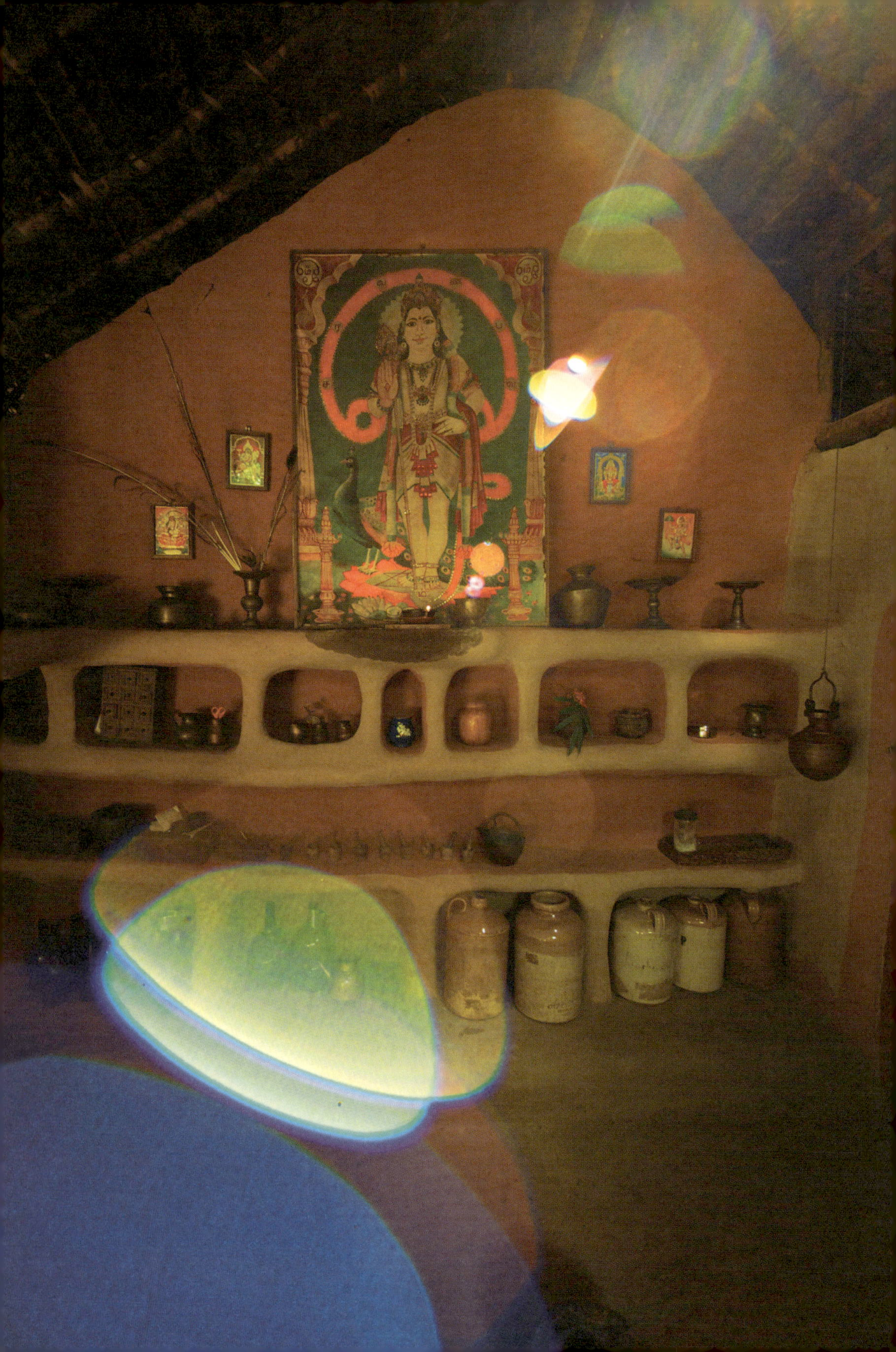

WEDAGEDARA

The Wedagedara is where Ayurvedic treatments take place to quieten the mind, soothe the body and enliven the spirit.

Dr Srilal will take your pulses and check your doshas – whether Vatta, Pitta or Kapha or a combination.

He might prescribe a treatment of being massaged with Indian gooseberry paste, turmeric and honey, or to sit in the dry sauna and breathe in the air, which has been infused with a different array of dry theraputic spices set into small recesses of a criss-cross wooden grid on the floor.

Or perhaps he will suggest that you lie in a sprung steam basket to inhale the properties of healing herbs.

Post-treatment, you will be escorted to a pink granite bath with scented oils and flowers. Looking up you will see monkeys put on gymnastic displays in the luxuriant green palm trees.

Afterwards in a state of alpha brainwaves, you will find yourself in the bathing area where velvet water will cascade over you, washing your troubles away. Finally the warm air mixed with the sandalwood incense will wrap you dry.

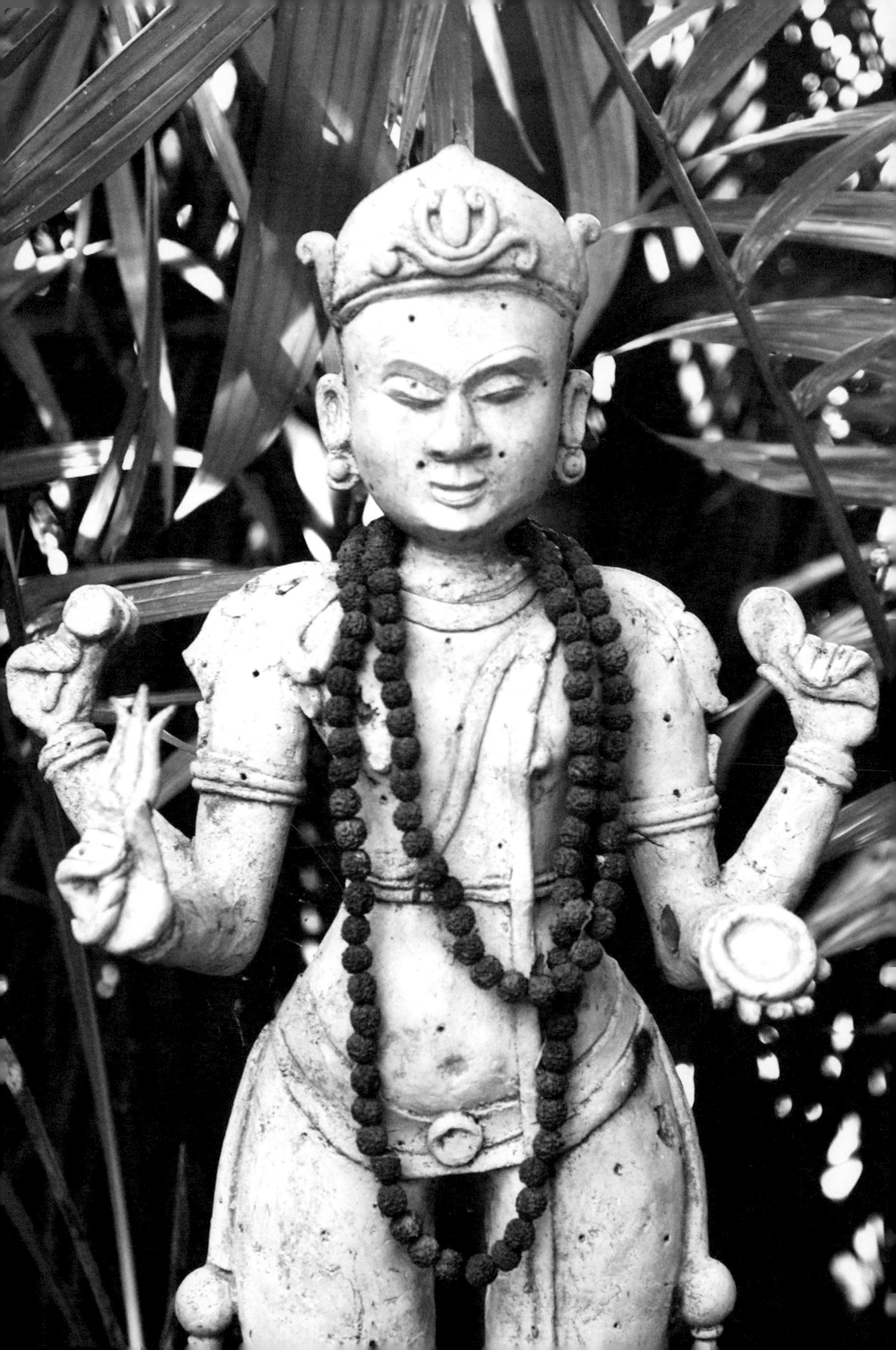

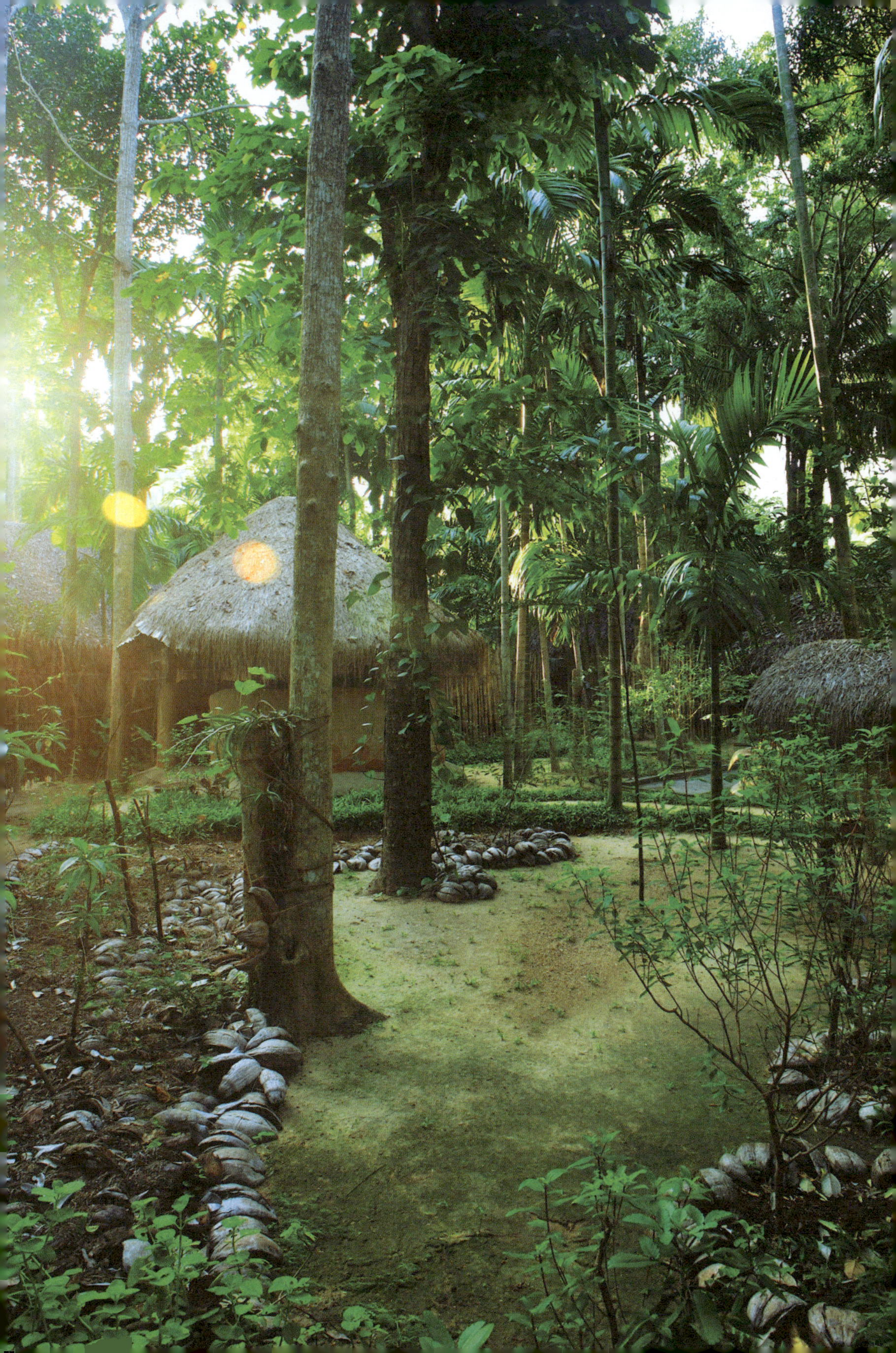

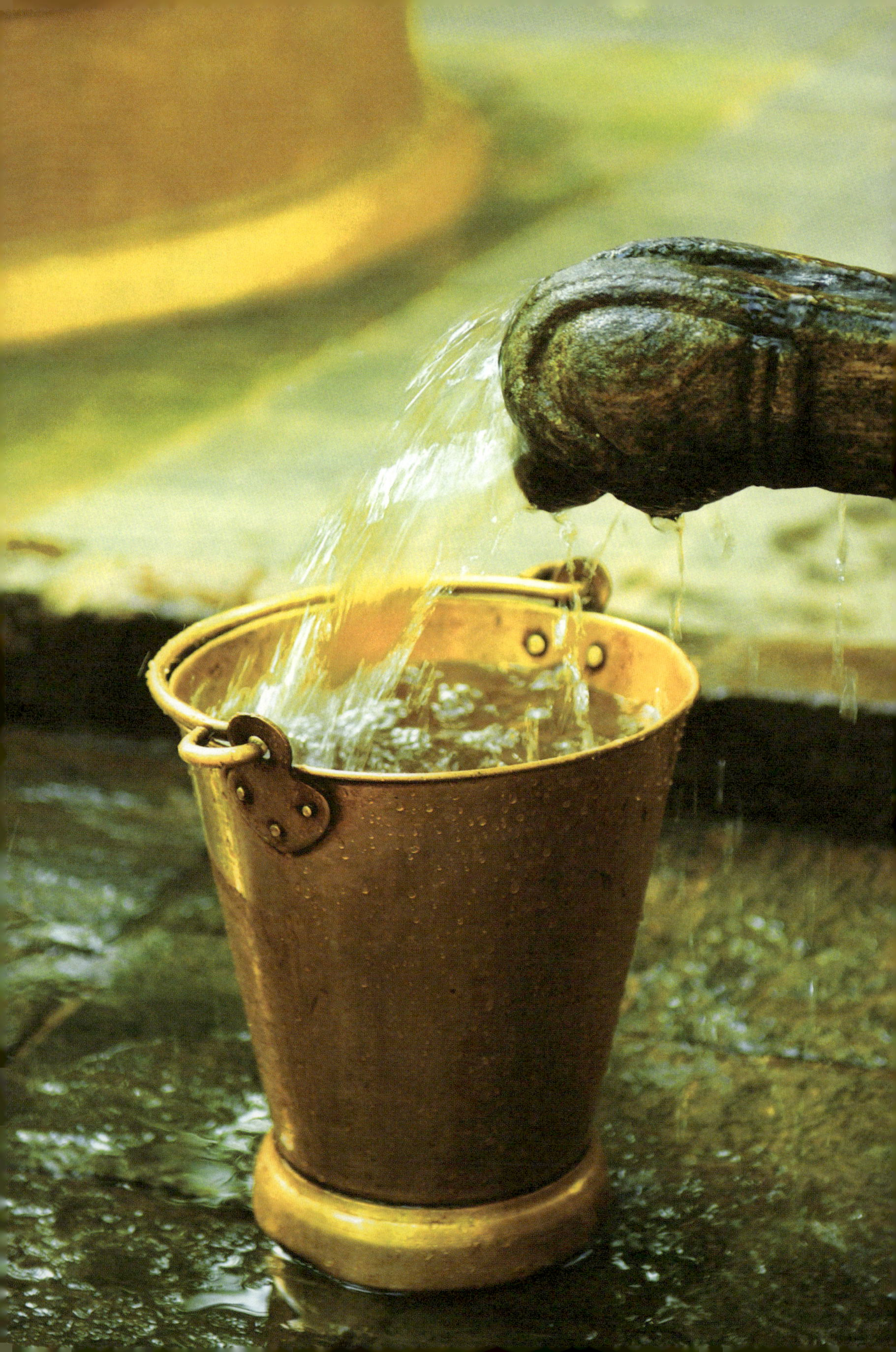

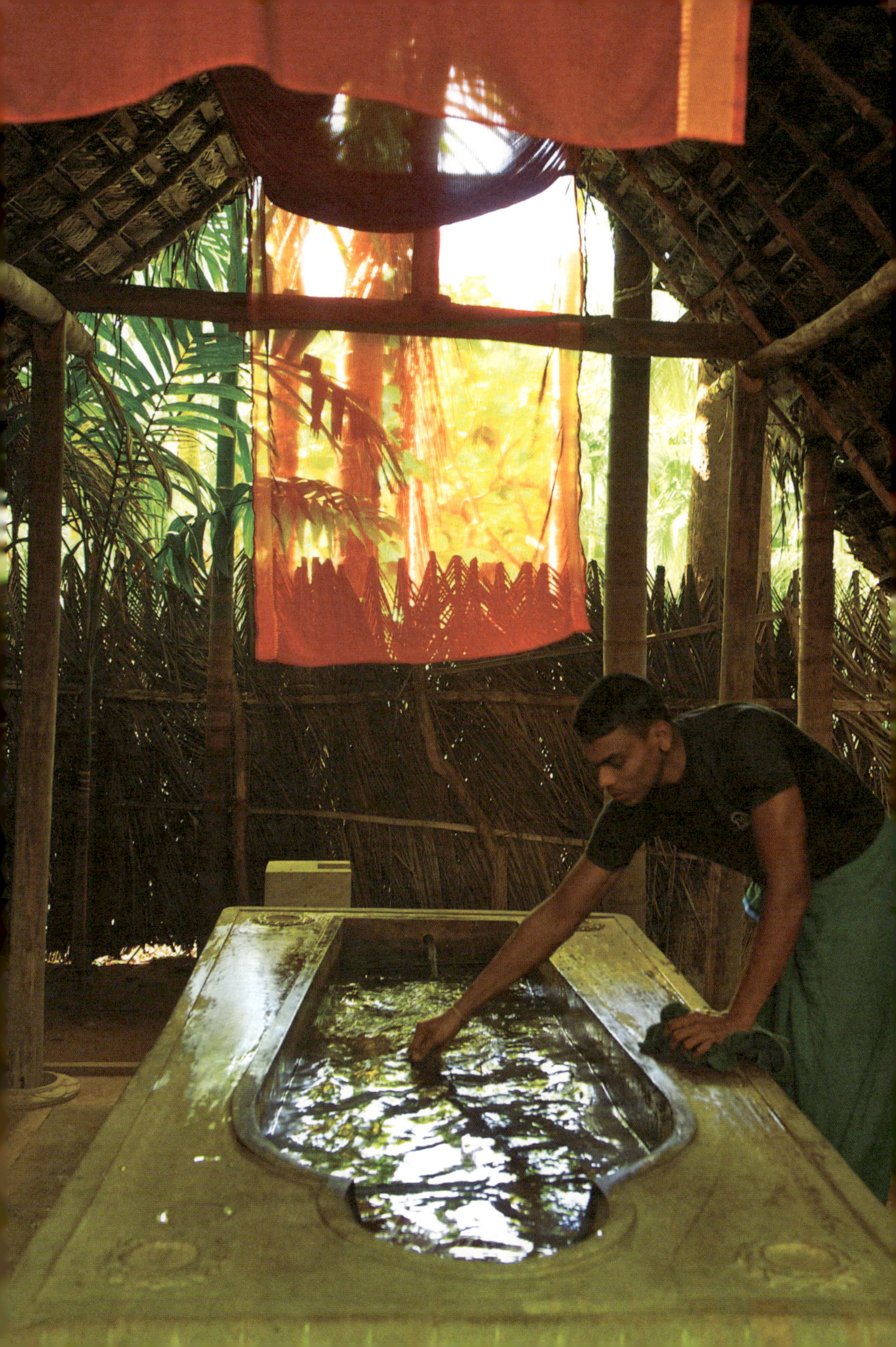

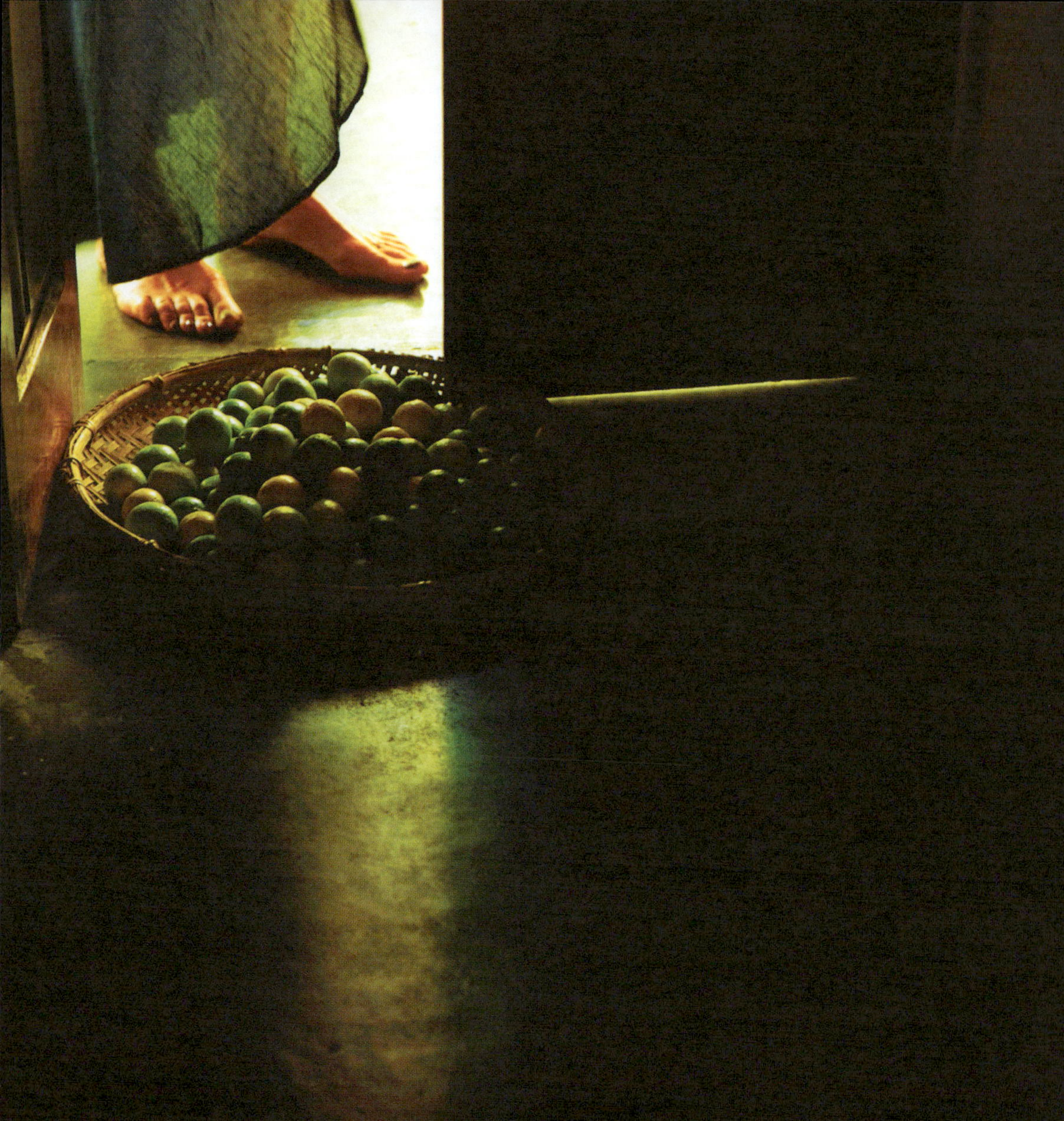

THE KITCHEN

It takes a second or two to adjust to the light as one bows one's head to enter the kitchen through its low doorway. In some traditional Buddhist cultures doorways are deliberately low to cause one to pause before entering a room, as it reminds one to be present and mindful.

Sri Lanka is known as the spice island and one is instantly alerted to the scent of fragrant and pungent spices permeating the ether: cinnamon, cumin, fenugreek, cardamom and nutmeg.

Water trickles into a brass pail, the fire crackles and a gauzy veil of smoke drifts through the kitchen. The rain splatters incessantly outside and a villager arrives in a lapis lazuli-blue sarong carrying a poppy-red umbrella.

A woman's sarong flits and flirts with the air as the rhythmical sweeping of her brush fills the room and her feet pad the floor softly.

A man sits on the floor with a huge granite pestle and mortar, grinding and scraping and crushing black beans to a milky pulp (to make ulundhuwadé), which then forms a circle on the outside of the mortar. It's mixed with onions, curry leaf and salt then fried into patties.

A woman grates fresh coconut while another chops green paisley-shaped chilli peppers, passing them to cook in a clay pot on one of the open fires. Onions sizzle, limes are squeezed.

A distant dog barks and there is a faint reply.

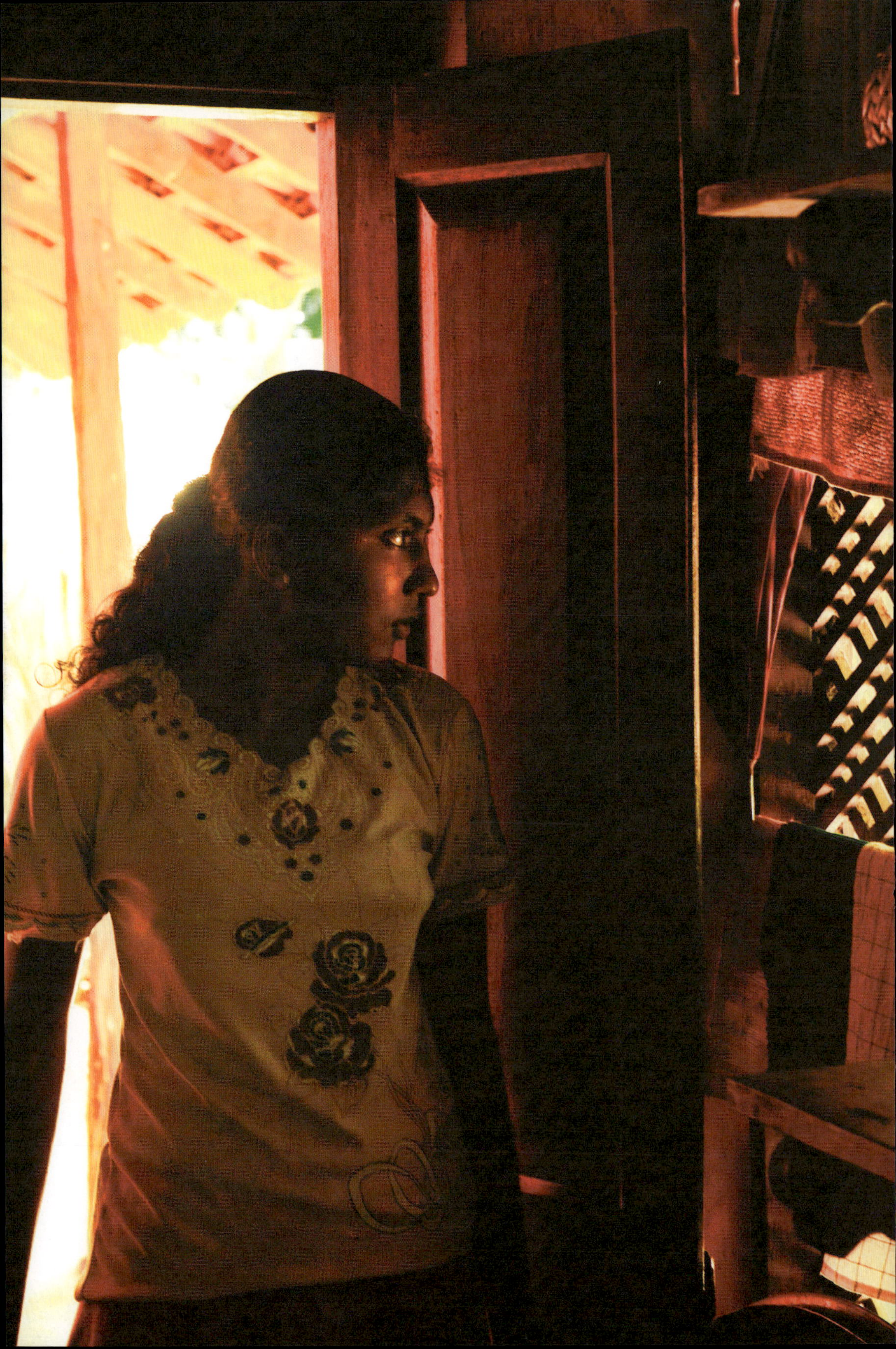

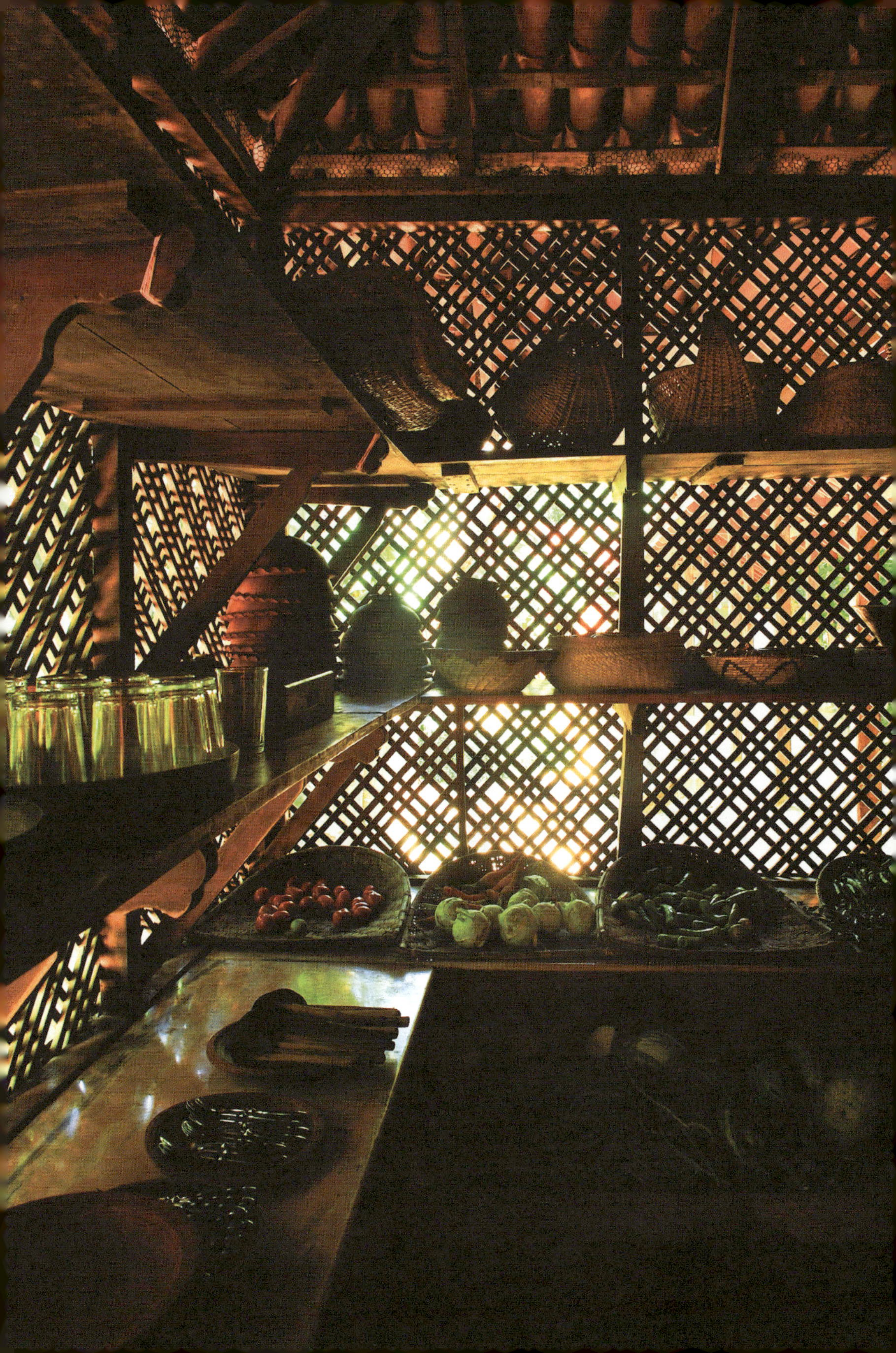

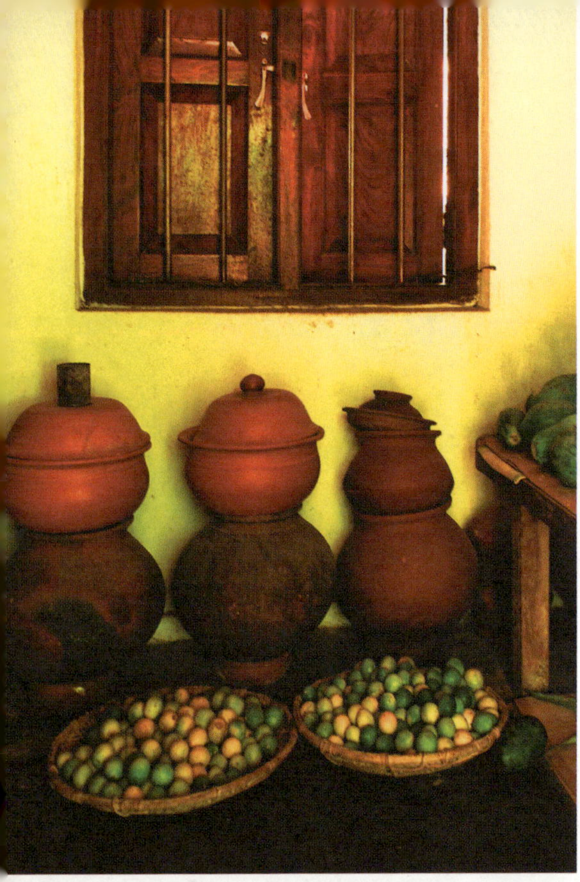
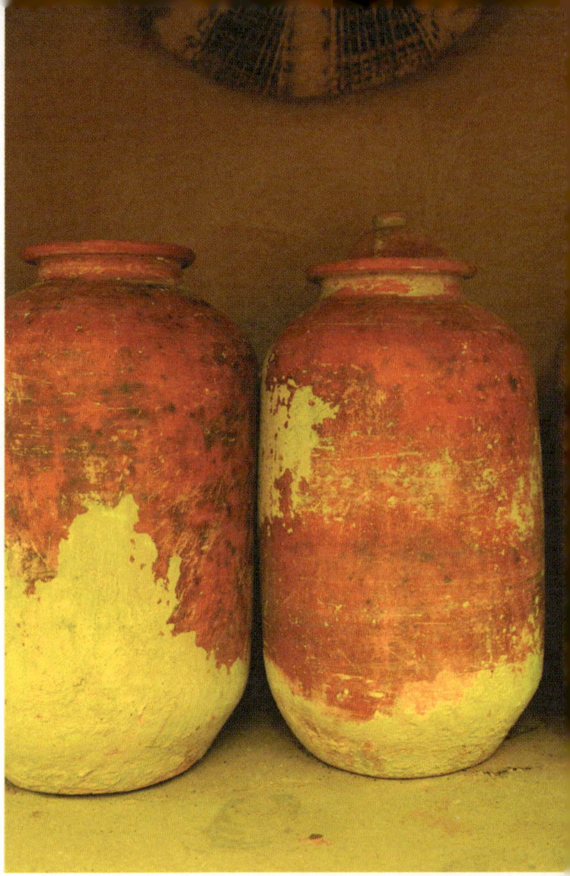
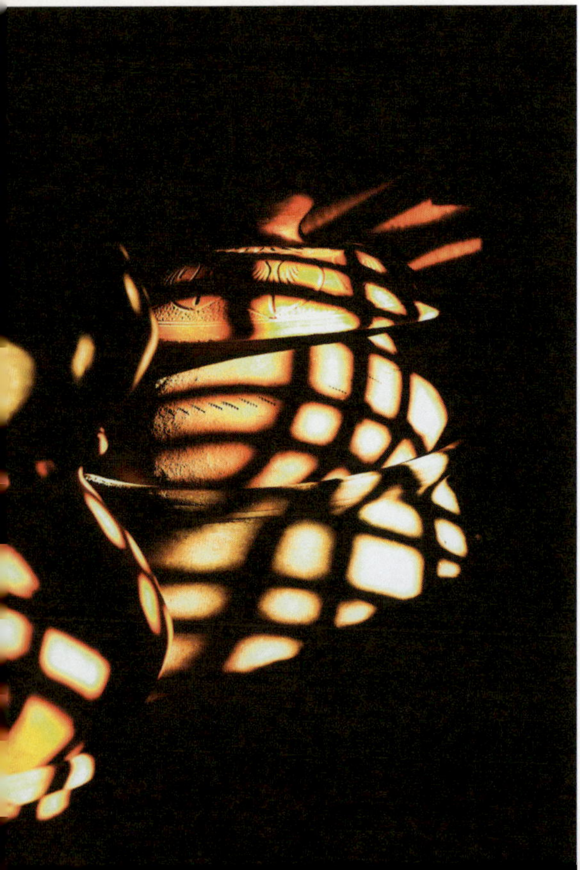
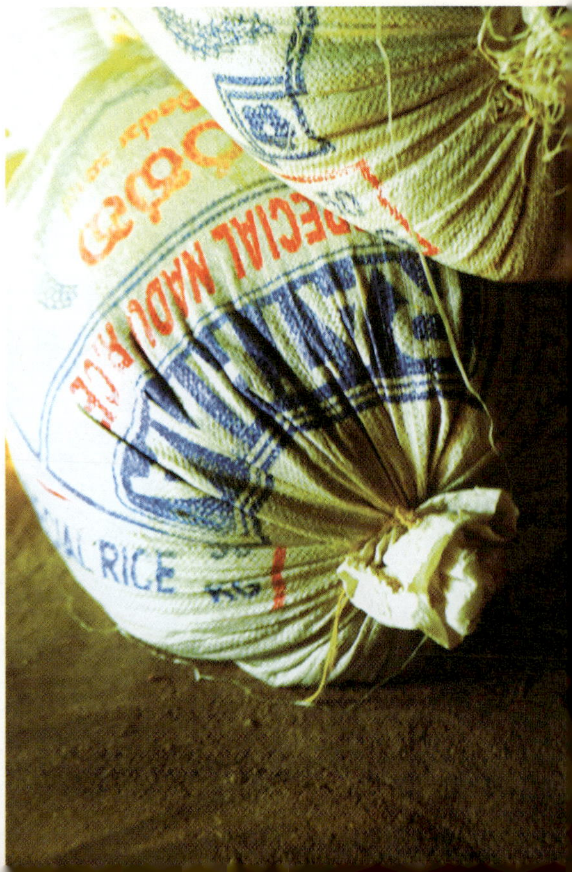

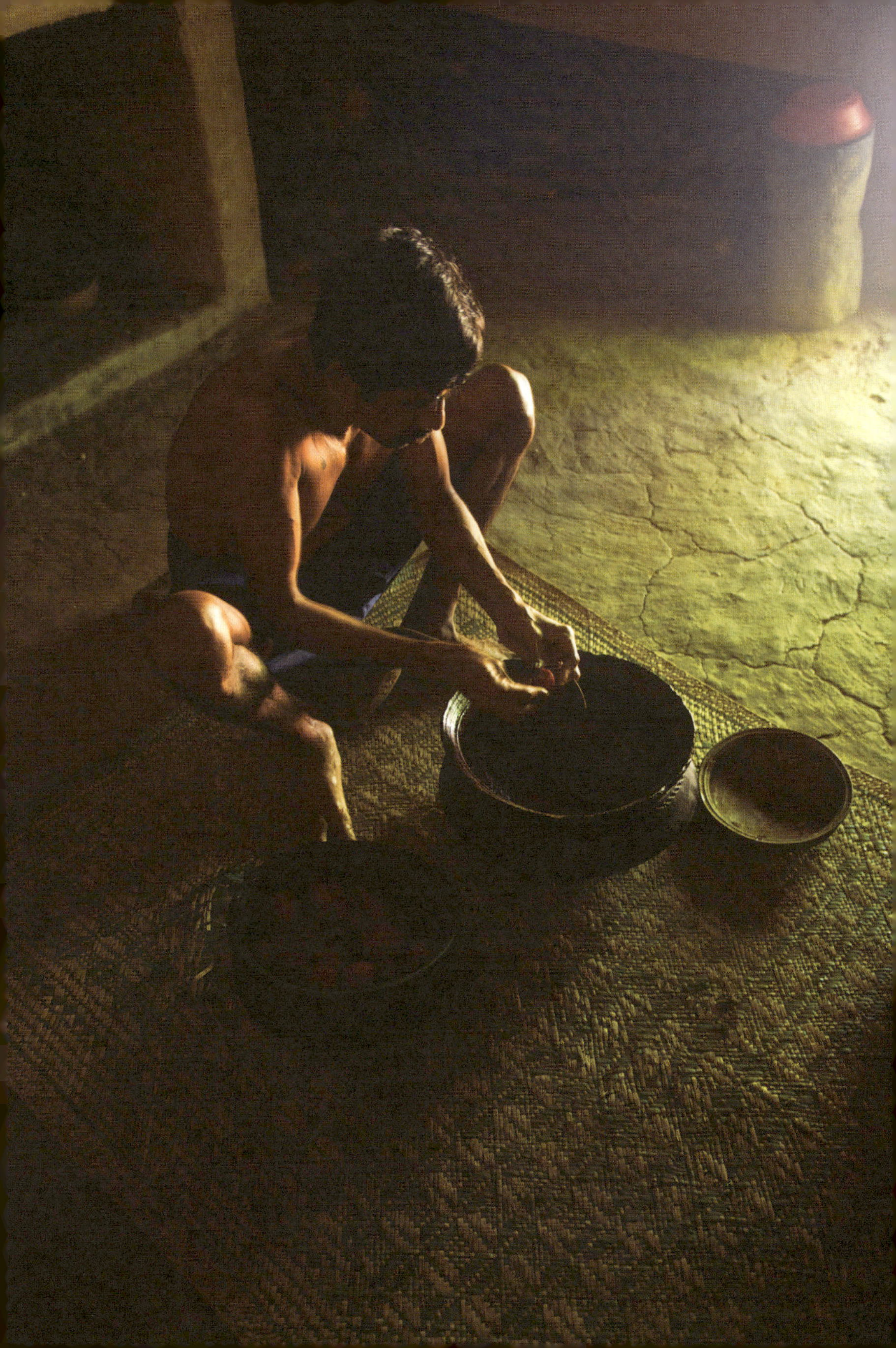

52 ULPOTHA - A KITCHEN IN PARADISE

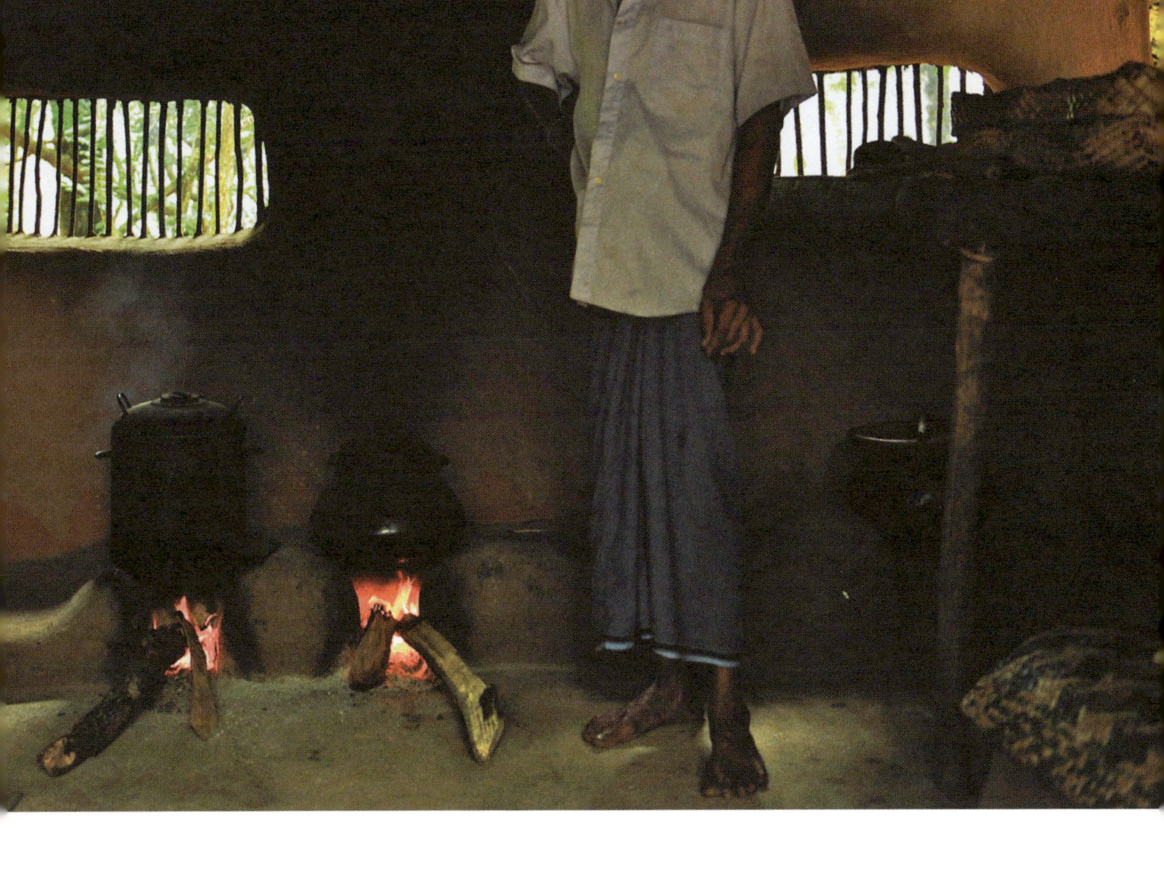

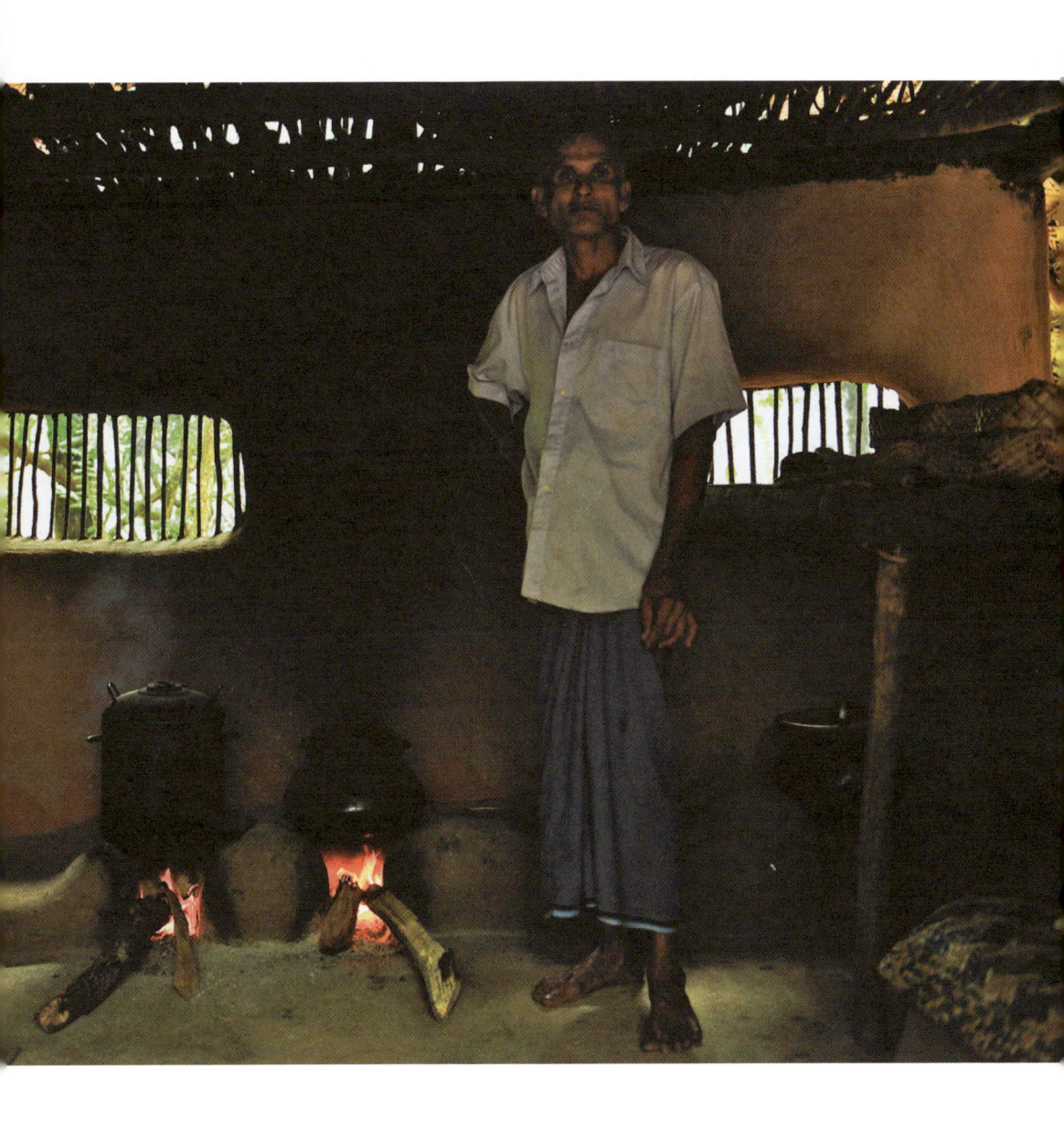

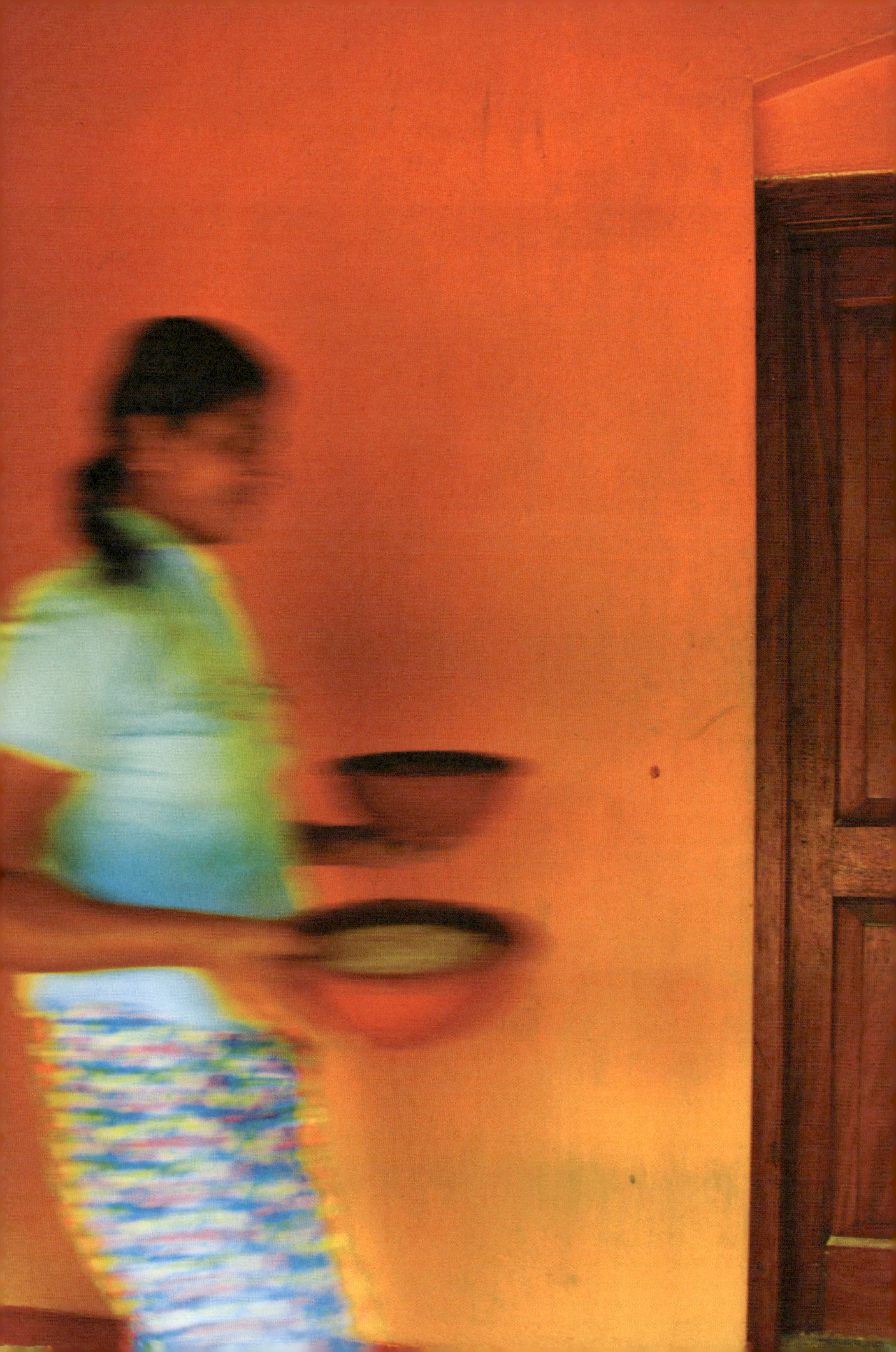

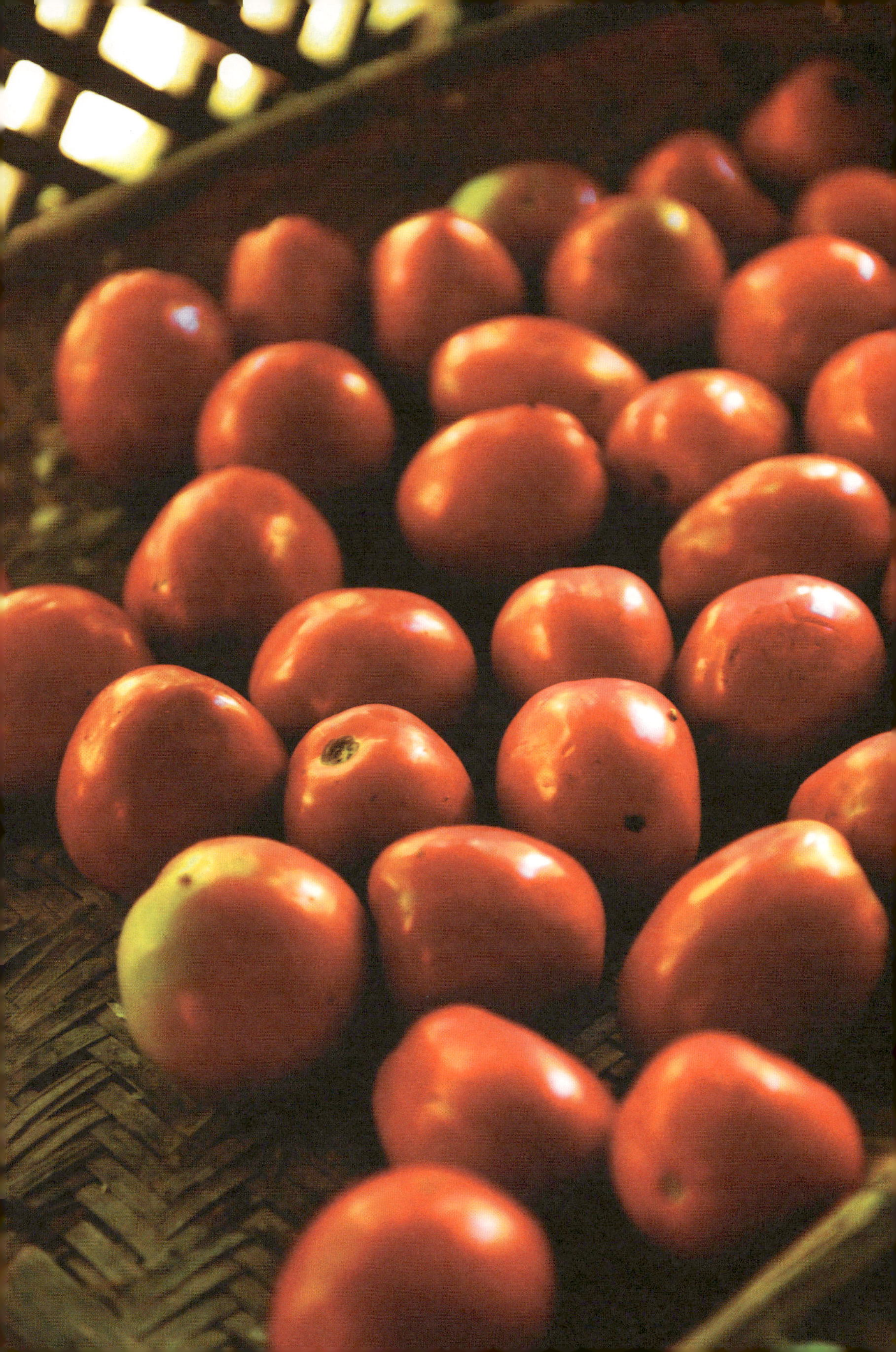

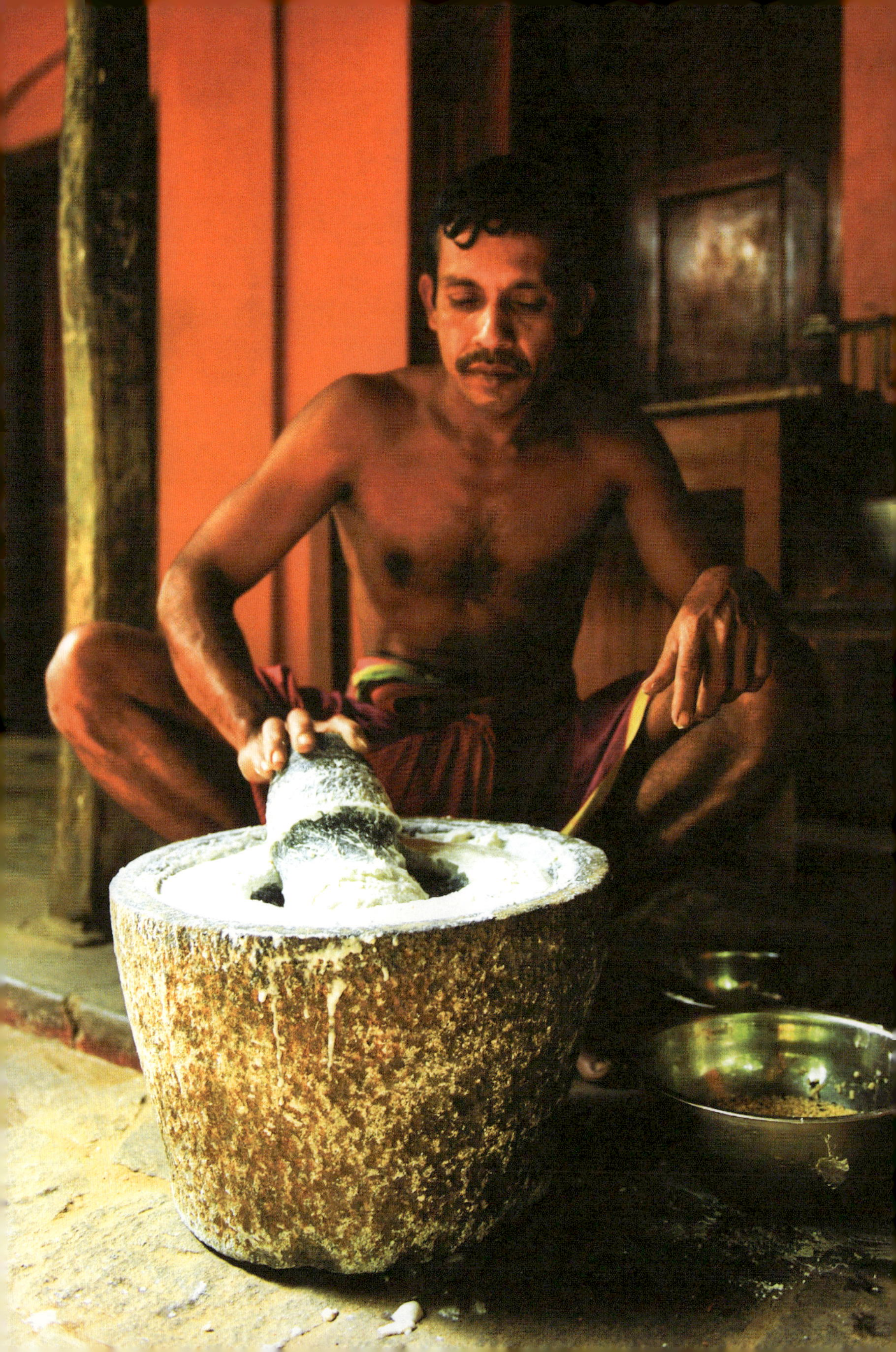

57　THE KITCHEN

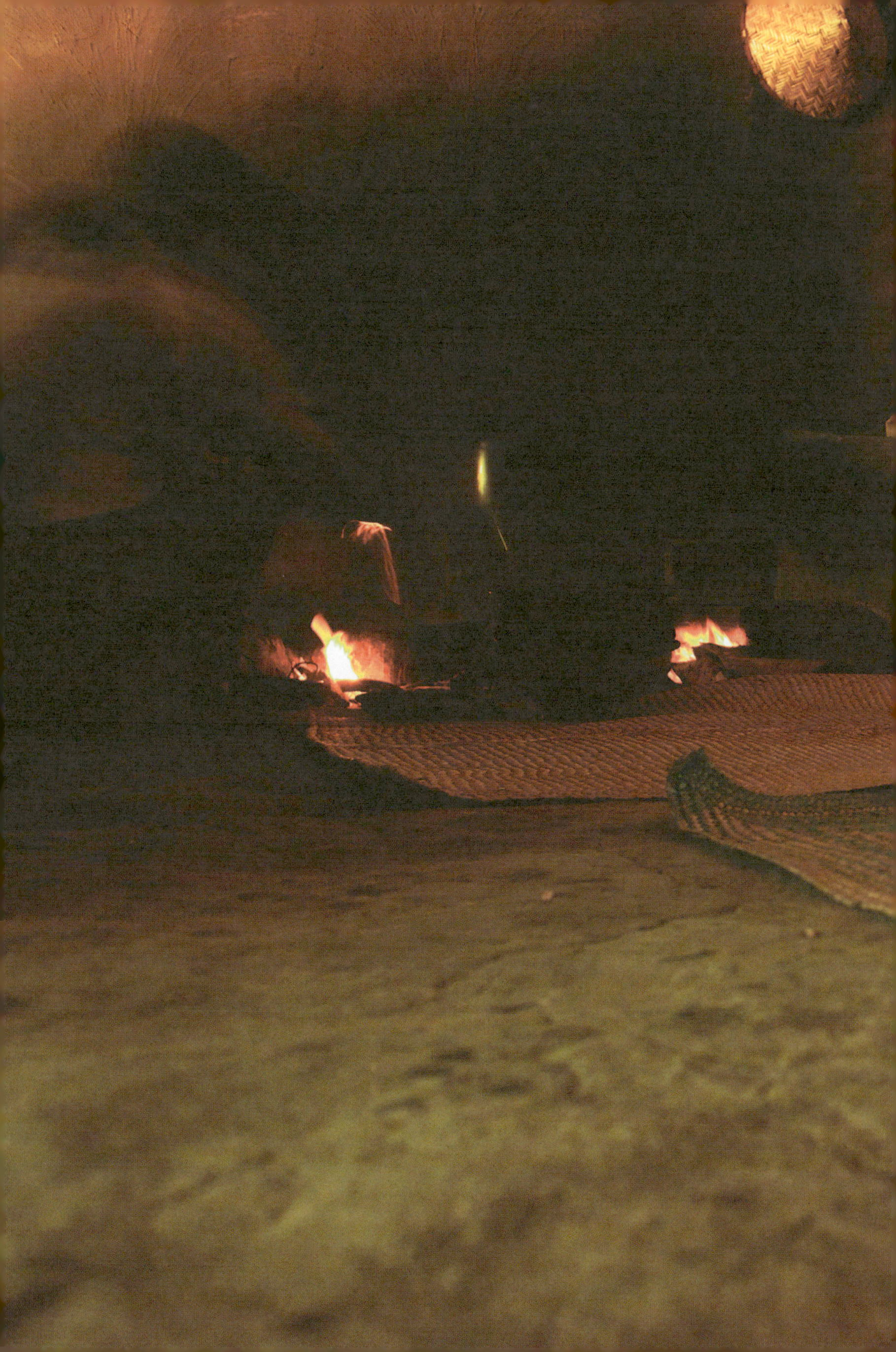

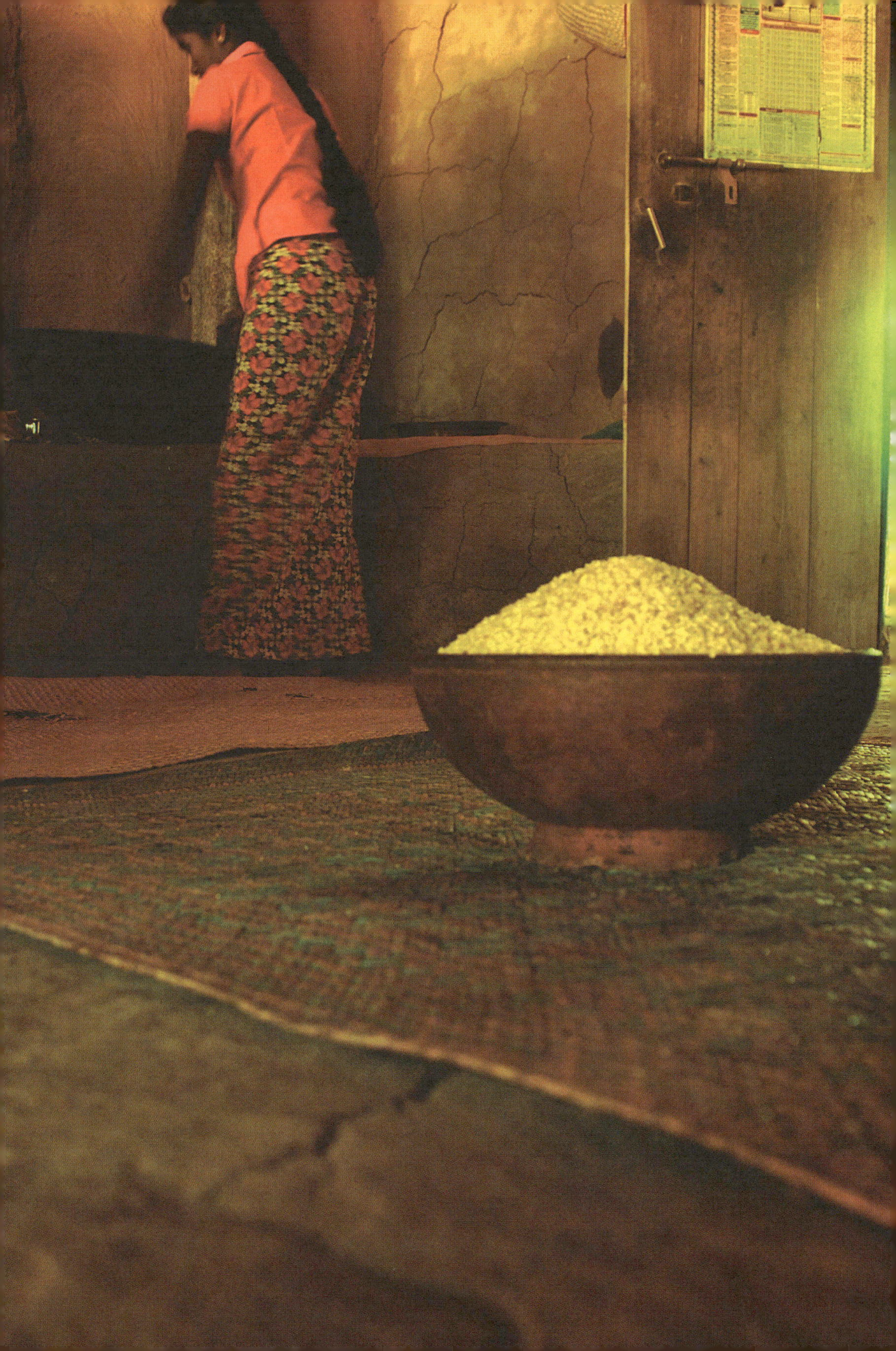

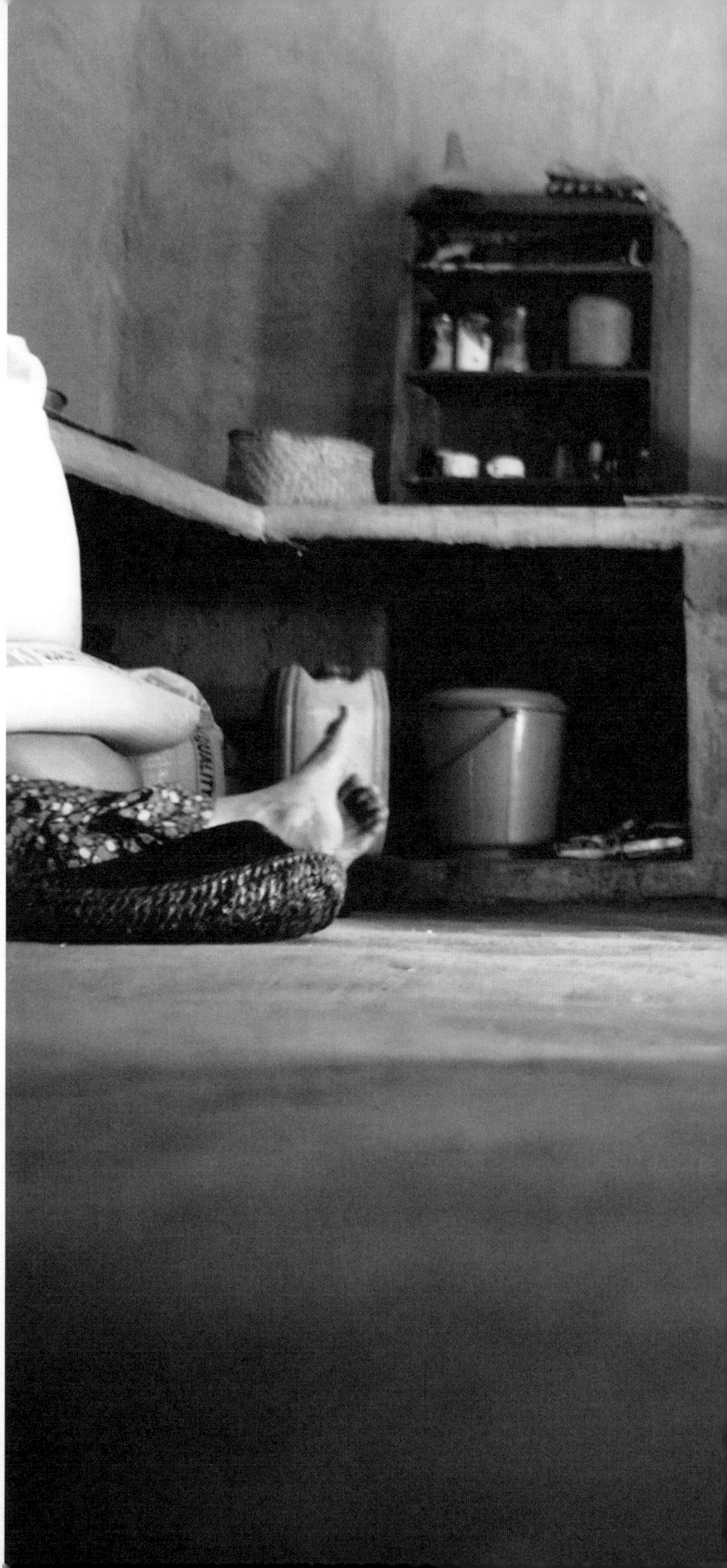

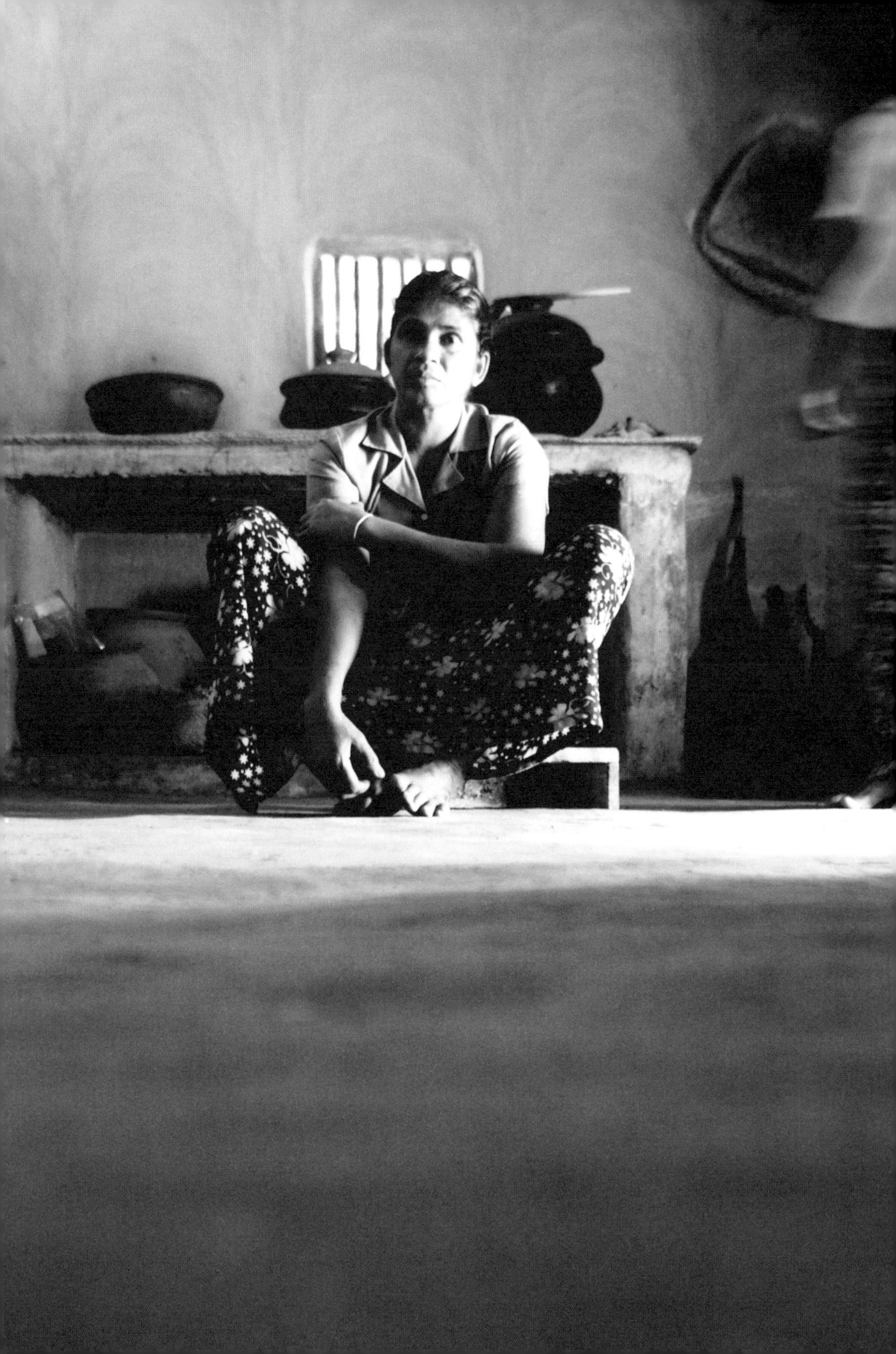

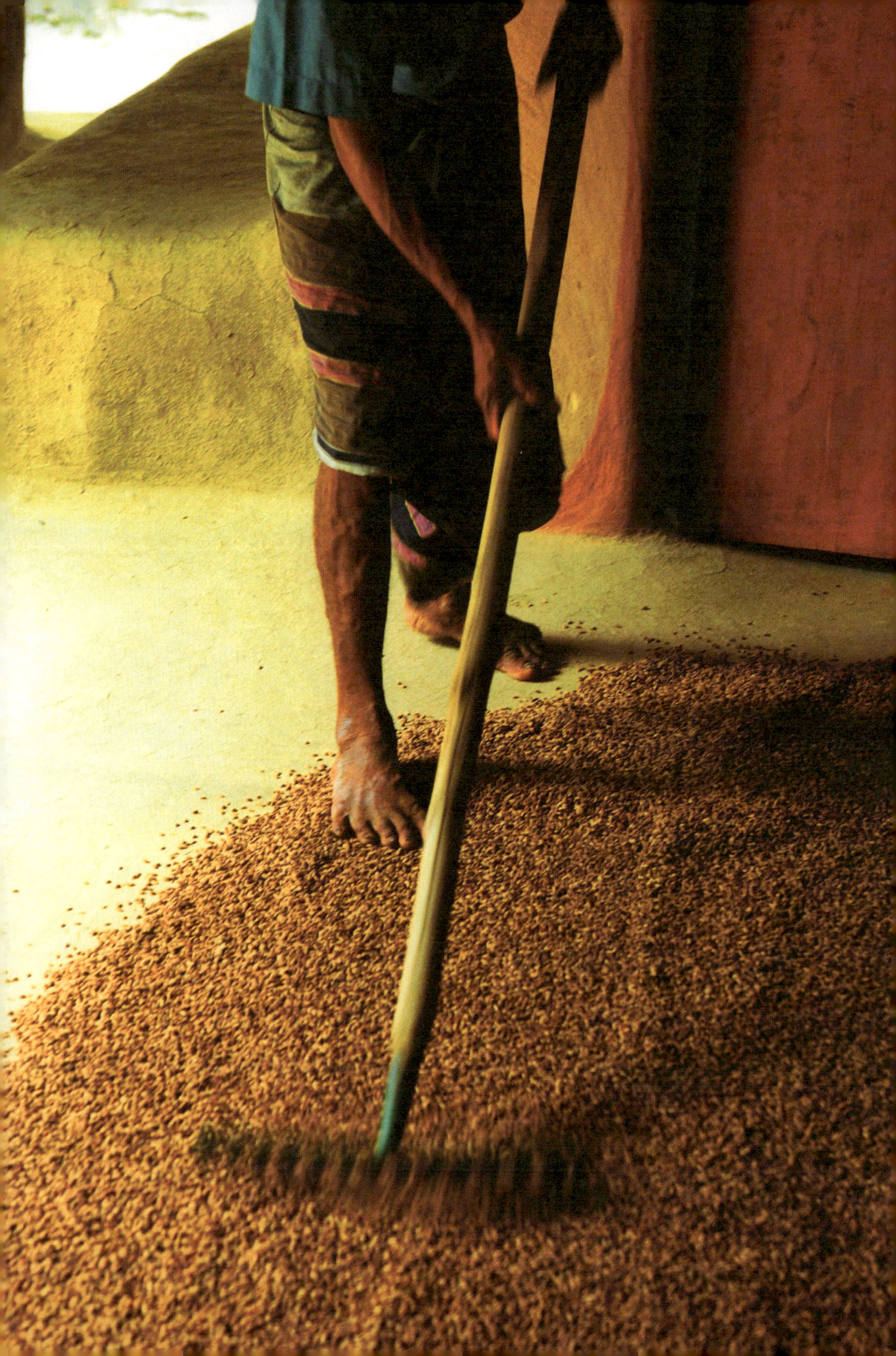

RICE

There were over 400 different varieties of rice grown in Sri Lanka before the introduction of fertilizer-dependent hybrids. Now only a handful of strains are grown – almost all hybrids.

When Ulpotha was established in 1996, rare indigenous rice seeds were collected from traditional farmers across the country and a seed bank was established. Sadly, heritage rice varieties remain difficult to come by and many of those listed below will be unfamiliar to most, names evocative of bucolic times long since passed. In nutritional content, texture, appearance, aroma and – most importantly – taste, they are unlike any other rice.

Dhikwee is a soft and wholesome red rice that is high in nutritional value.

Gonabaru is a very rare old variety of red rice that formed the staple diet of both peasants and kings.

Keluheenati (Ulpotha rice) literally means dark, fine grain and is highly nutritious red rice that is considered to have medicinal properties. It is particularly recommended for breastfeeding mothers.

Kuruwee literally translated means small rice and is a sweet and soft red rice.

Murungakayan is wholegrain red rice that is high in nutritional value.

Pachchaperumal is wholesome short grain red rice that when cooked takes on a deep rich burgundy color. Pachchaperumal means Buddha's colour and has been considered divine rice in traditional Singhalese culture. It has been used for centuries in 'Dhanés' (offerings to the monks during a thanksgiving or vows to the gods for rain, or protection of crops).

Samba is a soft and delicious white rice that has been the traditional rice of choice for festivities and alms giving.

Suwandel is a rare variety of white rice that is, as its translated name implies, fragrant.

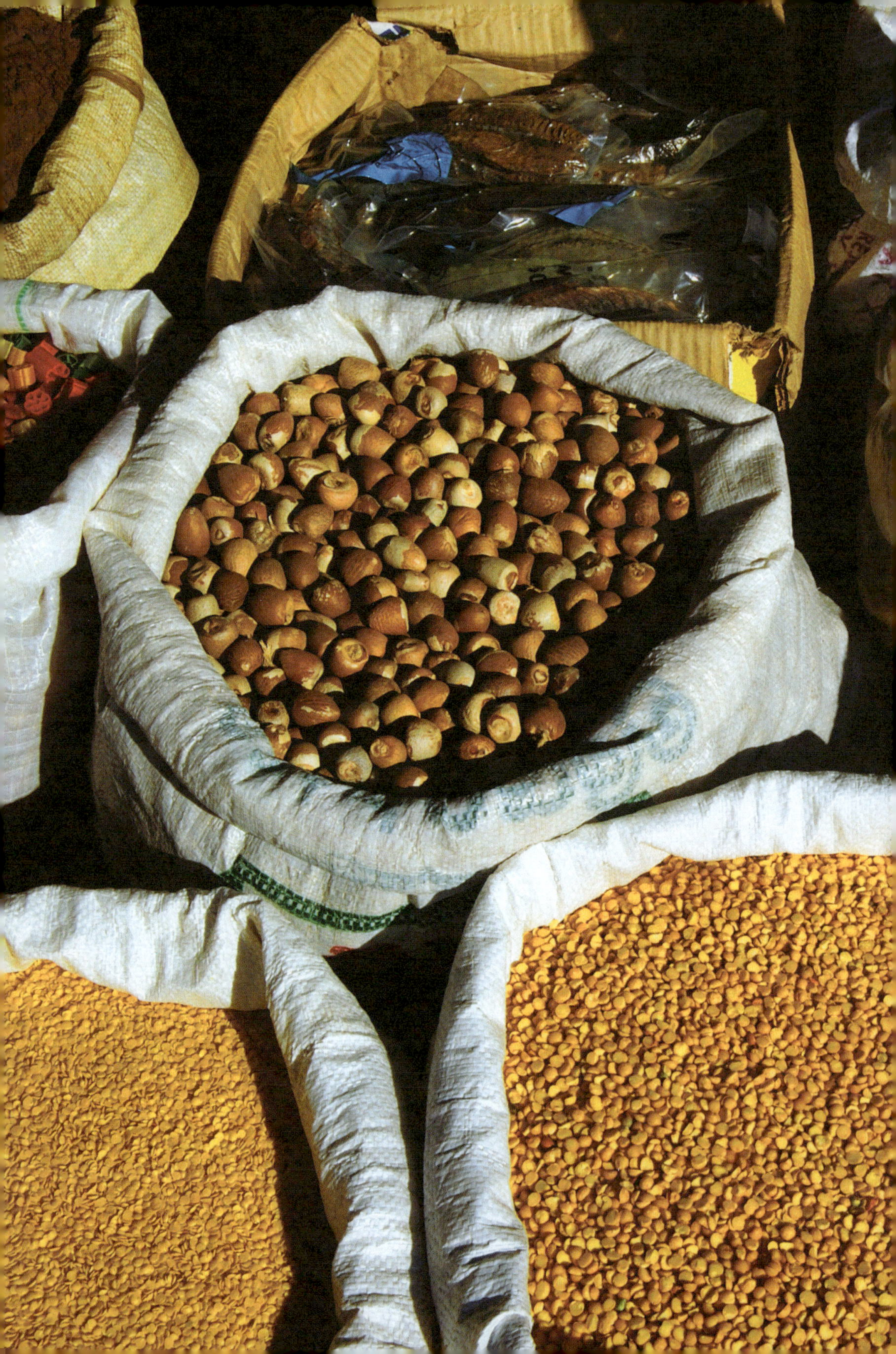

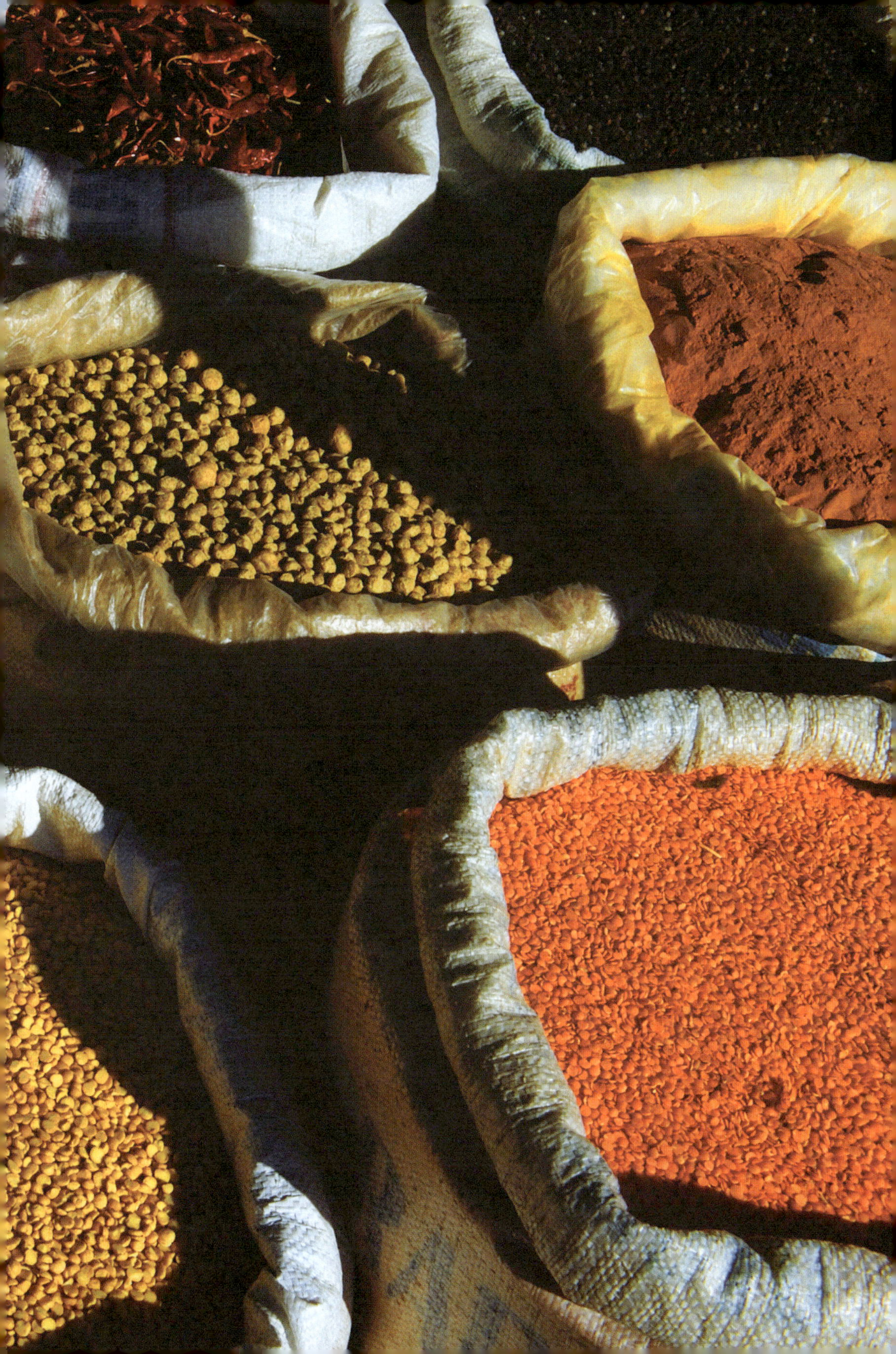

SPICES

CINNAMON
The best quality *cinnamon* in the world comes from Sri Lanka. Cinnamon is used as a remedy for diabetes, indigestion and colds and is often recommended for balancing Kapha.

CARDAMOM
Cardamom is effective in improving digestion and stomach cramps and also helps in cleansing the body as it has detoxifying properties and is beneficial for treating infections of the urinary tract. Cardamom is known to be helpful in balancing all three 'doshas' in the human body. Hence it is termed as 'tridoshic'.

MUSTARD SEEDS
Mustard seed benefits may include anti-cancer and anti-inflammatory properties. Being a great source of selenium and magnesium, mustard seeds can decrease inflammation and reduce the symptoms of such diseases as rheumatoid arthritis or asthma.

FENUGREEK
Fenugreek is used to treat arthritis, asthma and bronchitis, improve digestion and maintain a healthy metabolism.

GARLIC
Garlic helps to boost the body's metabolism rate to reduce weight easily; it regulates blood sugar and prevents blood clots from forming. It may also prevent cancer, especially of the digestive system and also to remove heavy metals such as lead and mercury from the body. It's a proven natural antibiotic and can still kill some strains of bacteria that have become immune or resistant to modern antibiotics.

PEPPER
Pepper, one of the oldest known spices, is rich in essential oils, which help digestion. In Ayurveda, pepper seeds are used in the form of medication for relief from sinusitis and nasal congestion. Sucking a few peppercorns provides instant relief from dry cough and throat irritation.

PAPRIKA
Paprika is a good source of Vitamin C and an excellent source of Vitamin A. It contains Vitamins E and K, which are vital for the health of the veins and capillaries in the body.

CHILLI POWDER
Chillies are an excellent source of Vitamin, A, B, C and E. Chilli contains seven times more vitamin C than an orange. Ever since its introduction to India in 1498, chillies have been included in Ayurvedic medicines and used for slimming as it helps burn calories. Chillies also stimulate the digestive system and clear the lungs.

CORIANDER SEEDS
Coriander is used for its anti-inflammatory properties and for lowering cholesterol as well as maintaining overall health.

CUMIN
Cumin is useful as an aid to digestion and absorption. It reduces abdominal gas and counters the effects of heavy foods, such as cheese, yogurt, beans, potatoes or overeating.

TURMERIC
Turmeric has been used for at least 1,000 years in Ayurvedic medicine especially for the spleen, stomach, and liver. It is used to stimulate and purify and as an antibiotic, antiviral and an analgesic.

NUTMEG
Nutmeg is used to cure insomnia, help with eczema, soothe diarrhoea, calm hiccups, rehydrate the body and as an aid to rheumatism.

MACE
Mace is the lacy covering of the nutmeg. It's used as a stimulant and to help the digestive system.

CURRY LEAVES
Curry leaves are a mild laxative yet also beneficial in the treatment of diarrhoea and dysentery as well as stimulating the appetite. The bark or root of the curry plant may be used to relieve kidney pain or prevent prematurely greying hair and treat eye disorders. Shamanic healers use curry leaves to treat insect bites, burns and bruises.

GINGER
Ginger is perhaps the best root for digestion. It helps break down proteins to rid the stomach and intestines of gas. It also aids in the digestion of fatty foods as well as alleviating high blood pressure. Ginger's warming quality improves and stimulates circulation and relaxes the muscles surrounding blood vessels, facilitating the flow of blood throughout the body.

COCONUT

The Coconut is considered to be the mother of all trees. It supplies fuel, fodder, fibre and food. and is thought of as a divine plant in the Vedic tradition with life-restoring properties. It's used for burning fat and lowering of cholesterol and helps detoxify and flush toxins out of the body, strengthens muscles and helps cleanse the urinary tract as well as rehydrate the body.

COCONUT OIL

Coconut oil does not change its composition when heated, so is excellent for cooking. It is rich in fibre, vitamins and minerals and may reduce the risk of cancer and other degenerative conditions. It helps prevent bacterial, viral and fungal infections, helps control diabetes and provides an immediate source of energy.

FRESH COCONUT MILK

Coconut milk is a key ingredient of many Sri Lankan curries and is used in two ways: full strength 'primary' coconut milk for finishing curries, and diluted (equally with water) 'secondary' coconut for bases. To extract coconut pierce the 'soft eyes' of the coconut with a skewer, drain and discard liquid. Place whole coconut in an oven heated to 180C and roast for twenty minutes to loosen flesh from shell. Crack with a hammer, then prise flesh with a knife. Peel brown skin, and finely chop flesh. Process with 500ml (2 cups) warm water for 2 minutes. Strain, squeezing solids to extract liquid.
Makes 500ml (2 cups).

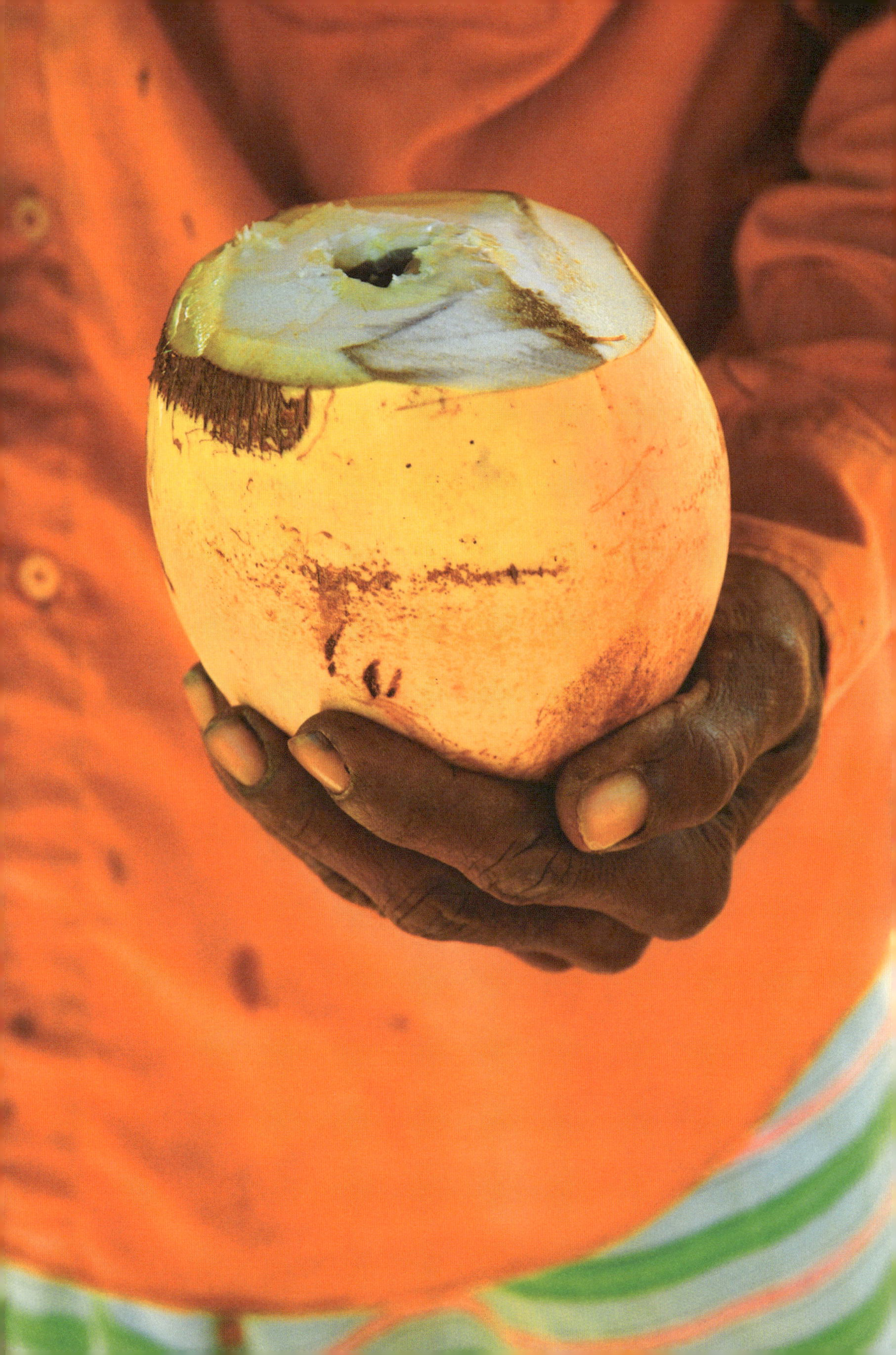

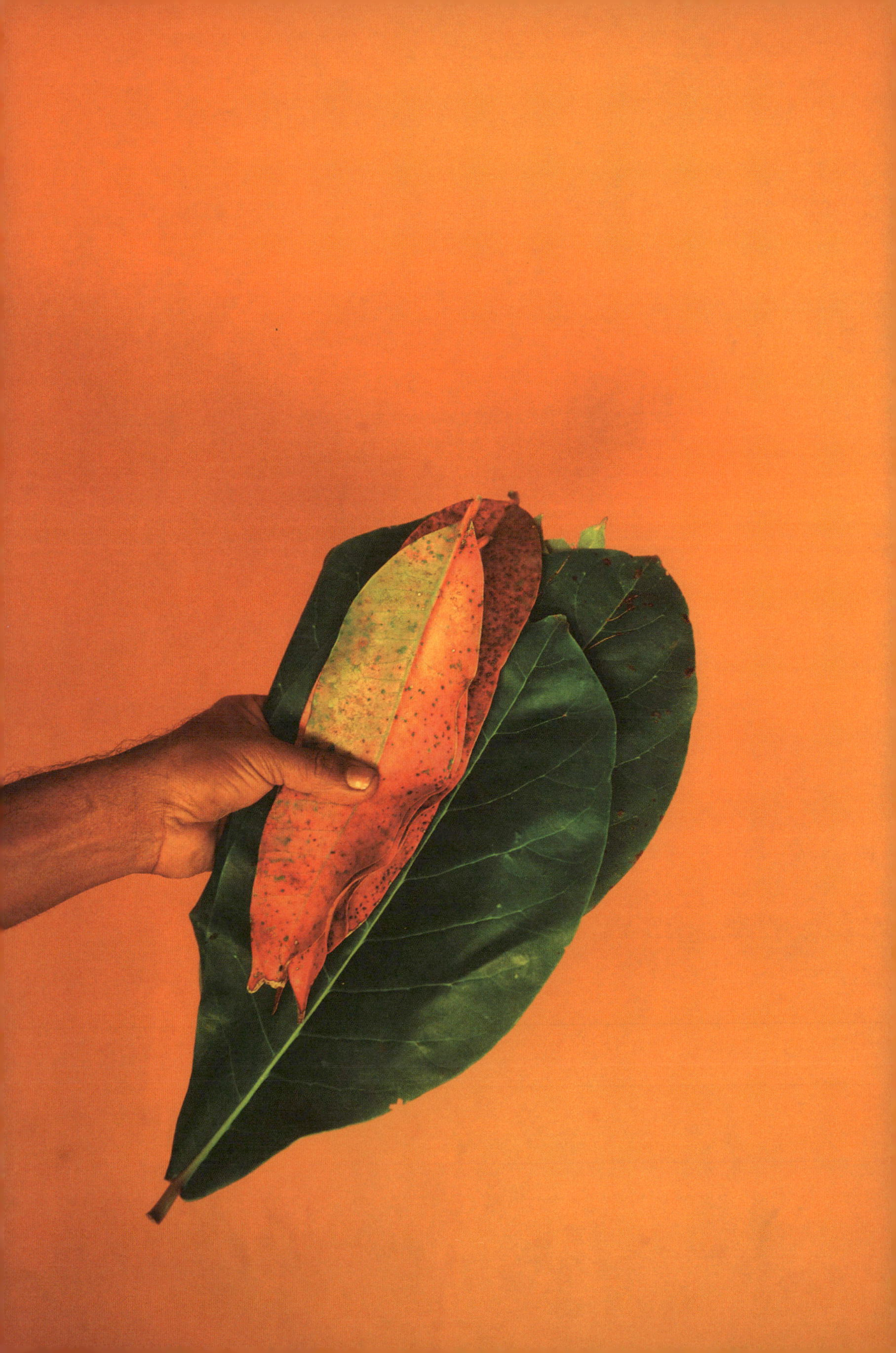

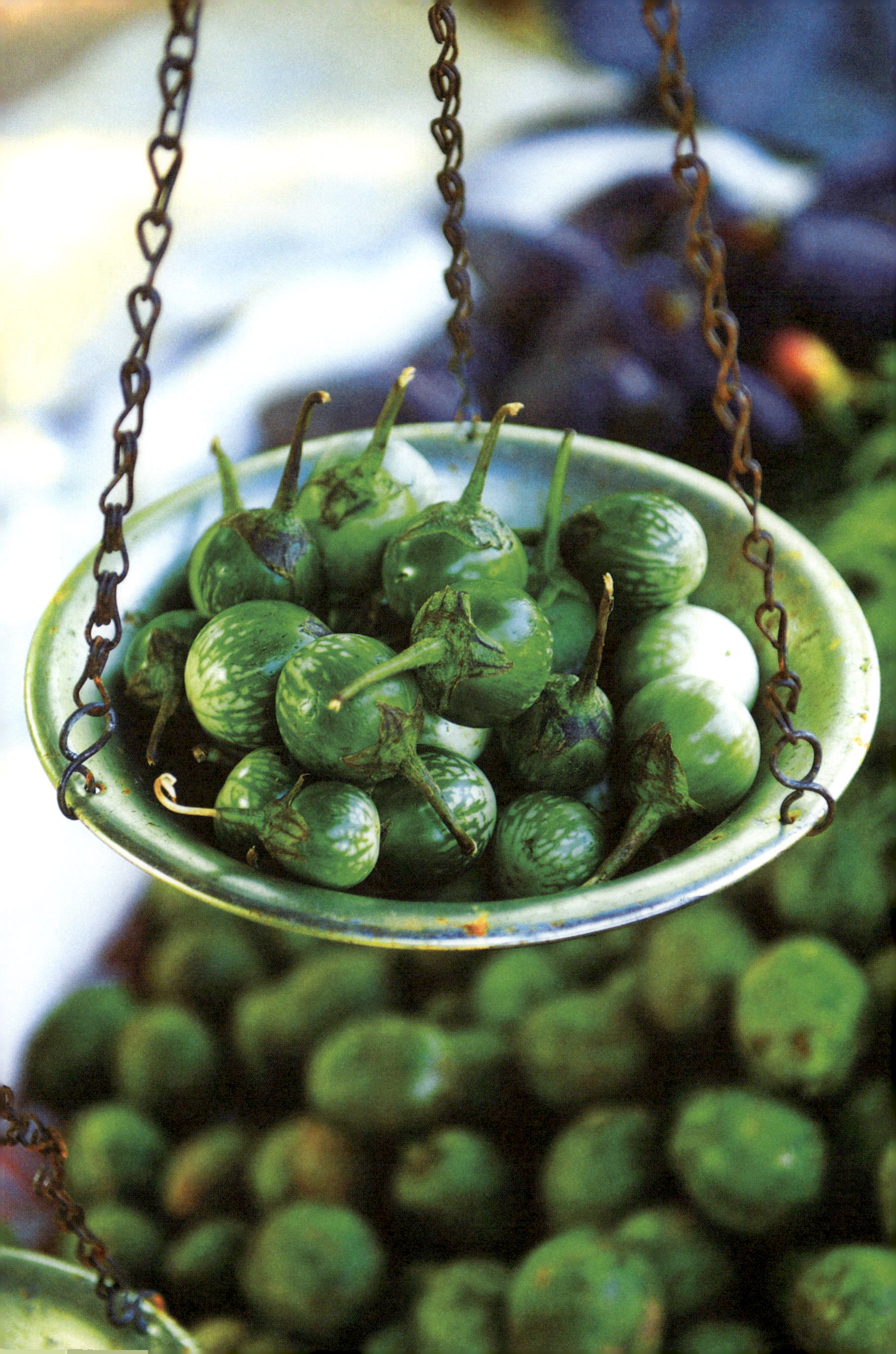

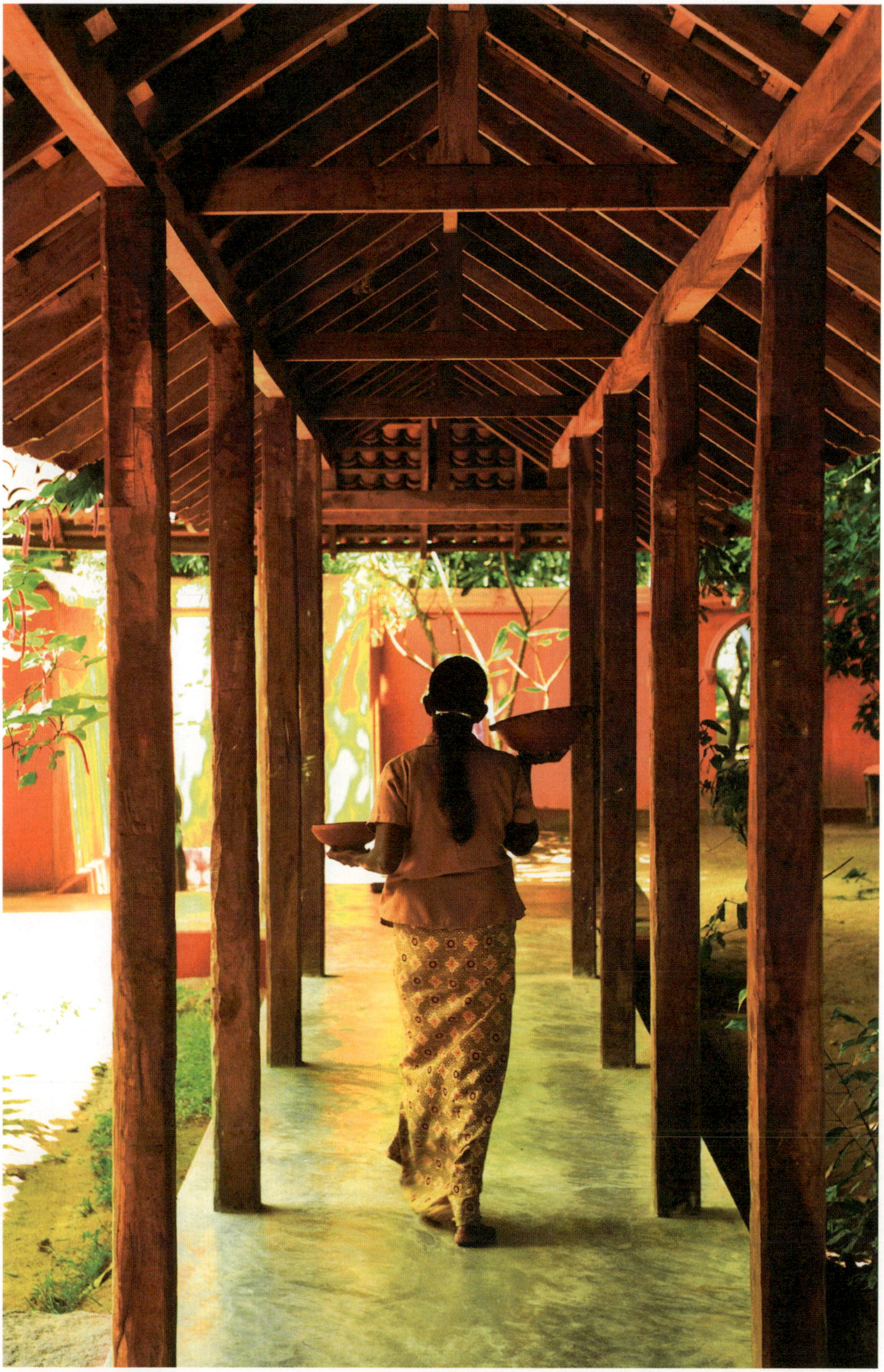

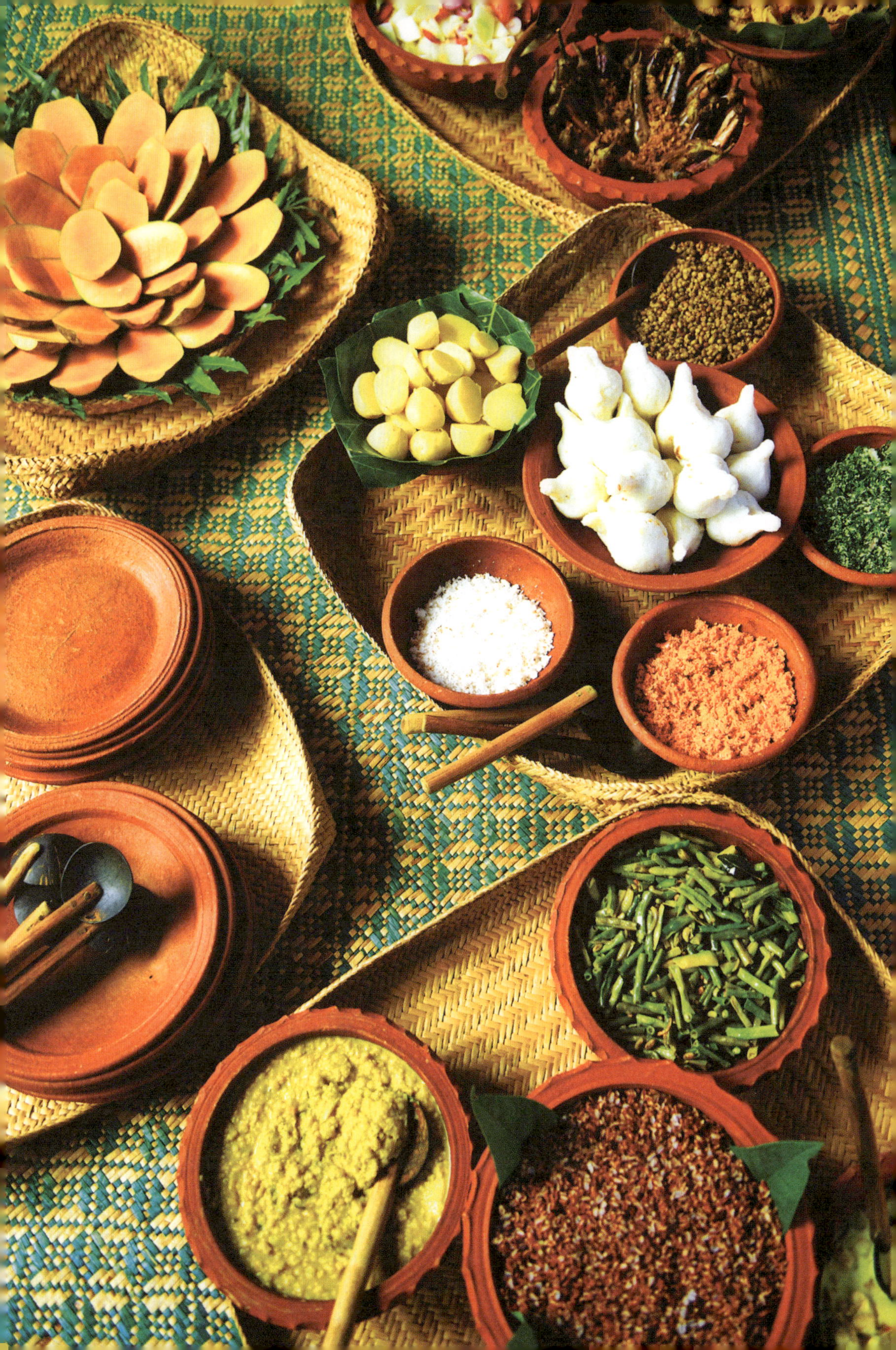

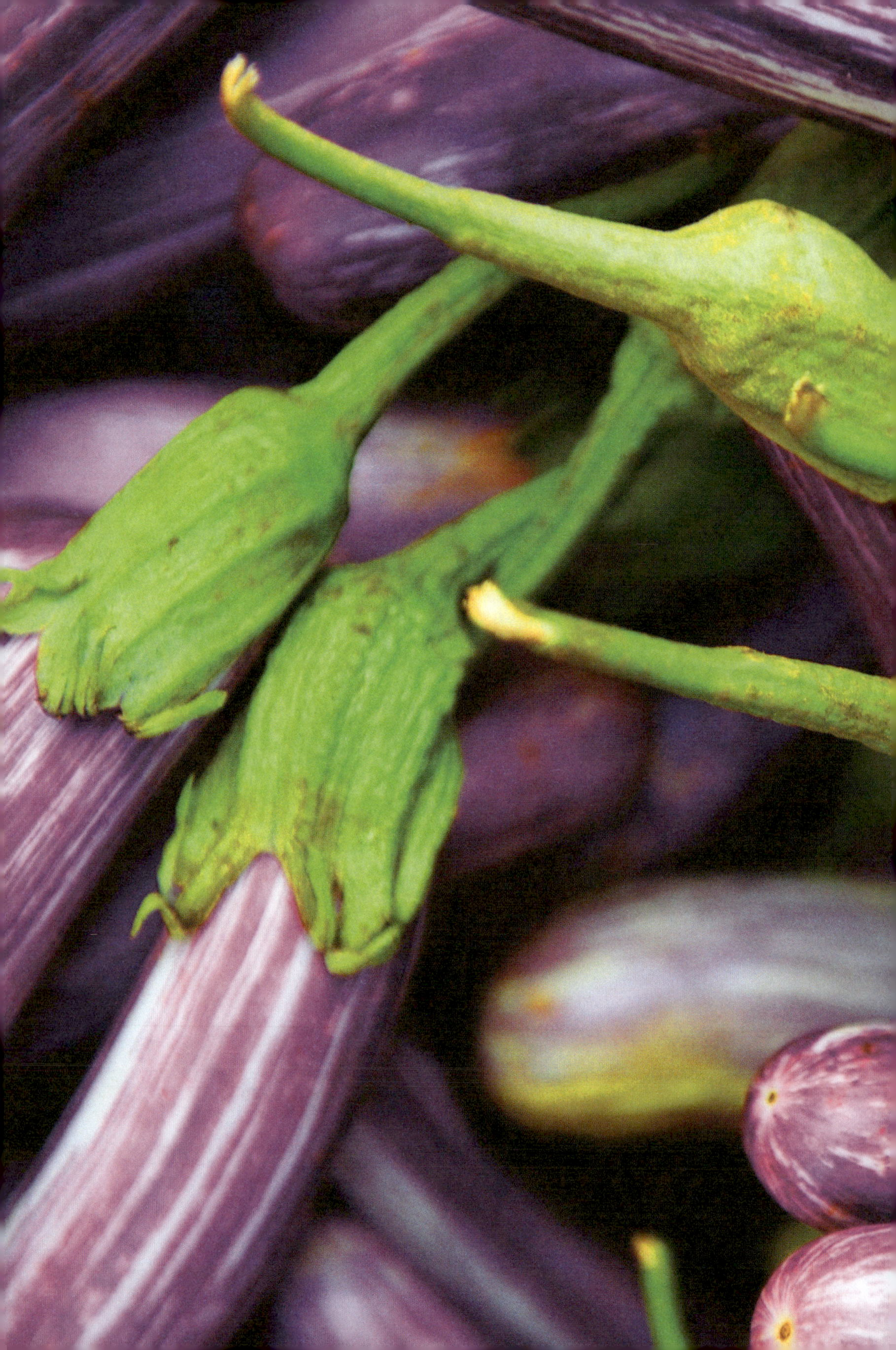

SALADS

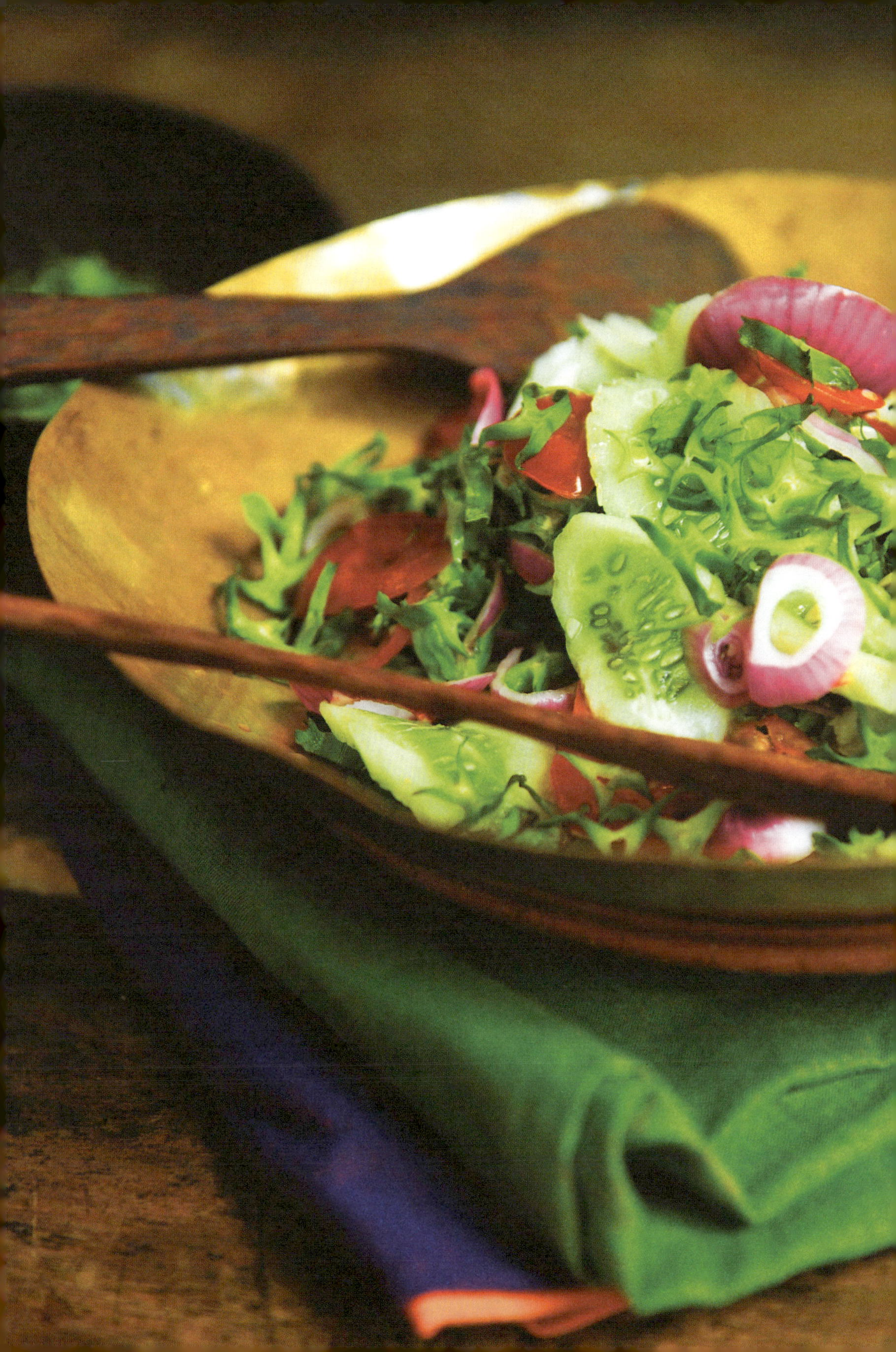

ROCKET, CUCUMBER & TOMATO SALAD WITH LIME, BASIL & SALT

Rory Spowers (author of 'A Year in Green Tea and Tuk Tuks') bought some rocket and basil seeds to Ulpotha and both have grown well in the kitchen garden there. The peppery leaves of the rocket are always great in a salad and work surprisingly well with lime.

SERVES ONE AS AN ACCOMPANIMENT

1 small cucumber peeled and diced

6 cherry plum tomatoes halved

1 handful of rocket

1 lime, juiced

1 small red onion cut into thin rings

A small handful of fresh basil leaves

1 large pinch of salt

Freshly ground black pepper

Place the ingredients in a salad bowl.

Mix the lime juice with salt in a glass. Pour over when ready to eat.

Toss; add another pinch of salt and a few turns of the pepper grinder.

Eat whilst fresh.

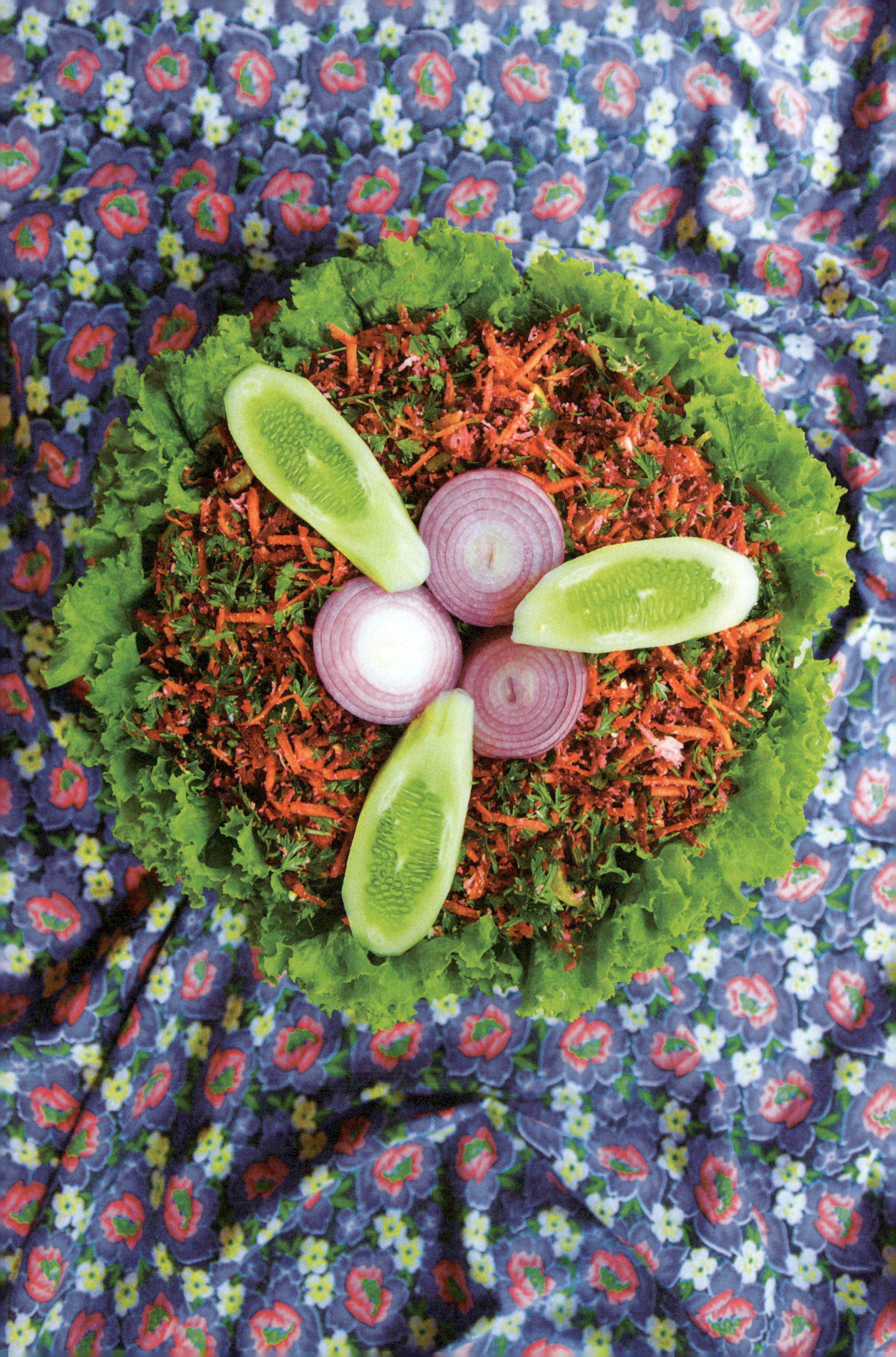

BEETROOT, RED ONION, CARROT & FLAT LEAF PARSLEY SALAD

This could be called a rainbow salad.
It's brimming and bursting with goodness.

SERVES FOUR AS AN ACCOMPANIMENT

2 medium raw beetroots
washed & grated

1 red onion
sliced into fine rings

2 medium sized carrots
washed and grated

A bunch of flat leaf parsley
finely chopped

1 lime, juiced

Sea salt flakes

Freshly ground pepper

Mix all the ingredients in a salad bowl.

Season to taste.

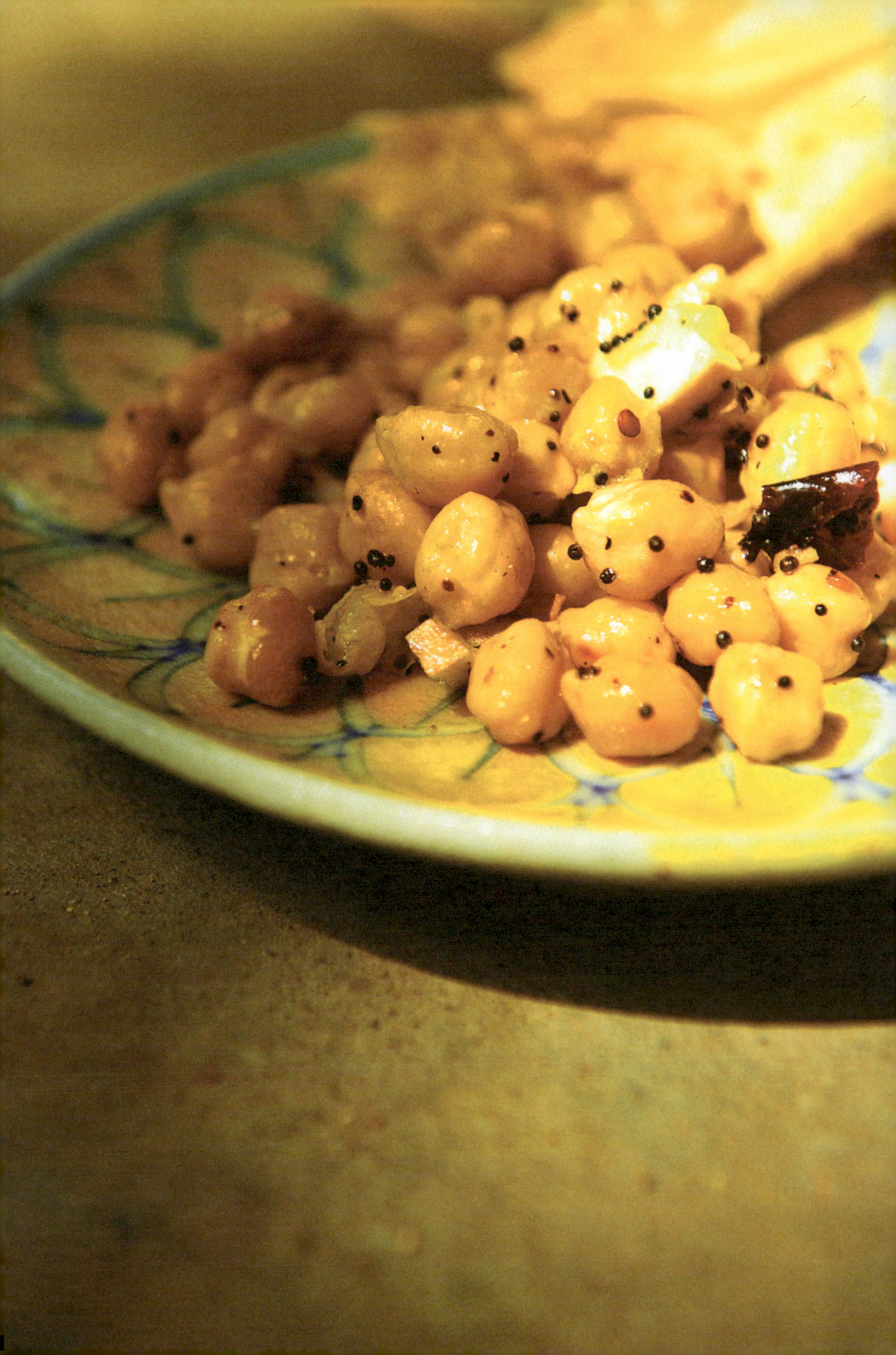

SALAD OF CHICKPEAS WITH SHALLOTS, COCONUT & MUSTARD SEEDS

Chickpeas are a long way from the finishing line when it comes to taste, but they are good for texture and supporting other flavours that cannot substantiate as a dish on their own. Essentially the shallots, coconut and mustard seed hitch a ride on the back of the chick peas.

SERVES FOUR AS AN ACCOMPANIMENT

200g dried chickpeas soaked overnight or tinned chickpeas

2 shallots, finely chopped

2 garlic cloves finely chopped

1 dessertspoon of coconut oil

1 dessertspoon of dessicated coconut

1 tsp of mustard seeds

1 handful of coriander leaves, finely chopped

Sea salt flakes

Boil the chickpeas in plenty of boiling salted water. Keep topping up with water and drain when tender.

Warm the coconut oil in a frying pan on a medium heat and sauté the onions and garlic until soft. Add the cooked chickpeas. Toss in the coconut and mustard seeds and season well.

Serve either warm or cold and decorate with the coriander leaves.

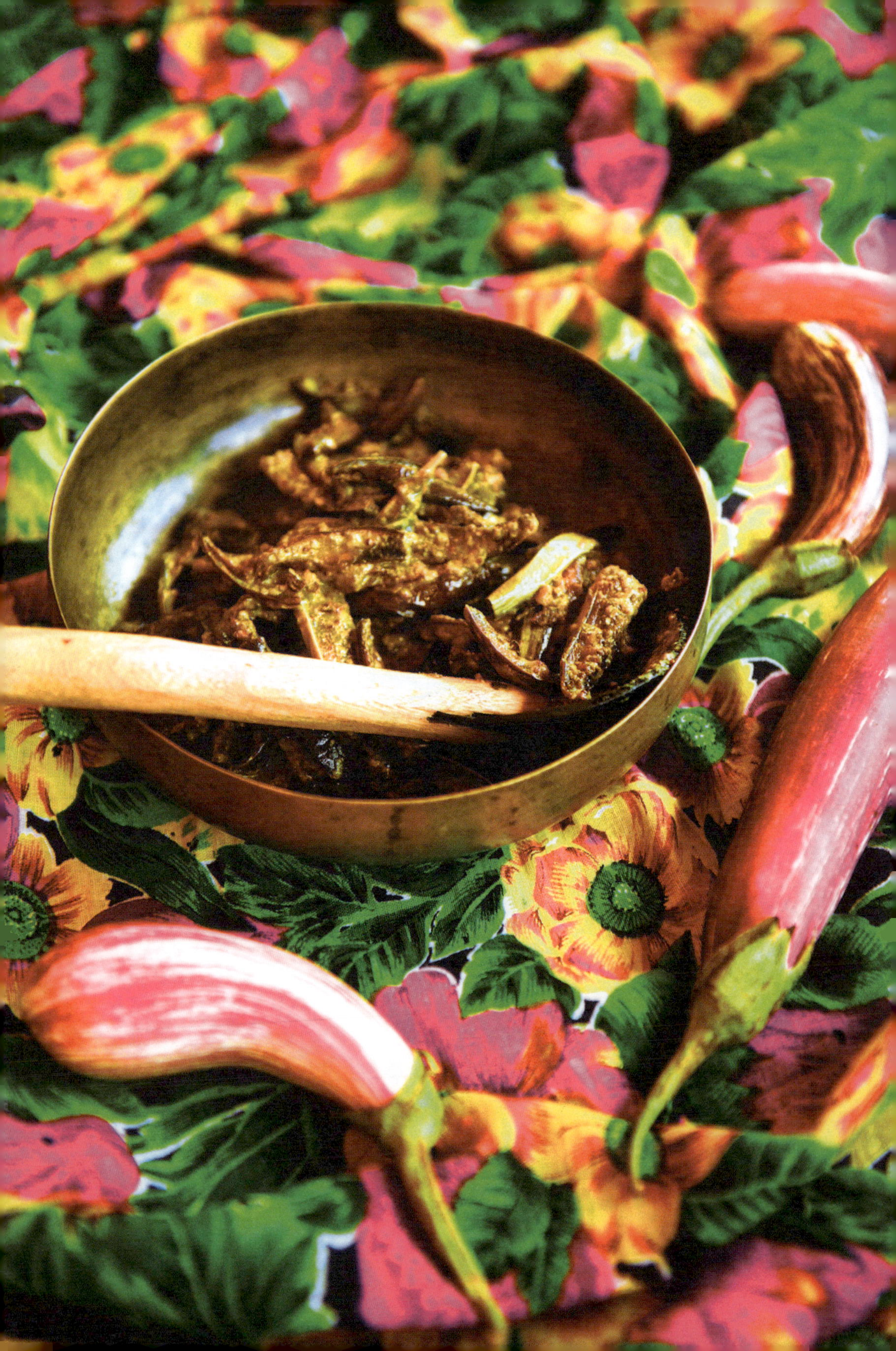

WARM AUBERGINE SALAD

This is a delicious salad and has the unusual ingredient of mustard.

SERVES FOUR AS AN ACCOMPANIMENT

1 large aubergine sliced into rough chunks

2 cloves garlic finely sliced

1 tomato thinly sliced into quarters

1 red onion thinly sliced

1 teaspoon of natural sugar

1 teaspoon of Dijon mustard

1 teaspoon of turmeric

Vegetable oil

Coconut oil

Sea salt flakes

In a frying pan warm a swirl of vegetable oil, fry the aubergine until cooked. Remove and dry on kitchen paper. Place them in a bowl add salt, sugar, mustard and turmeric and mix well.

Scantily cover the bottom of a heavy-based frying pan in a thin coating of coconut oil. When the oil starts to shimmer add the onion, tomato and garlic. When the ingredients are almost cooked, add the aubergine mixture, season well and serve warm.

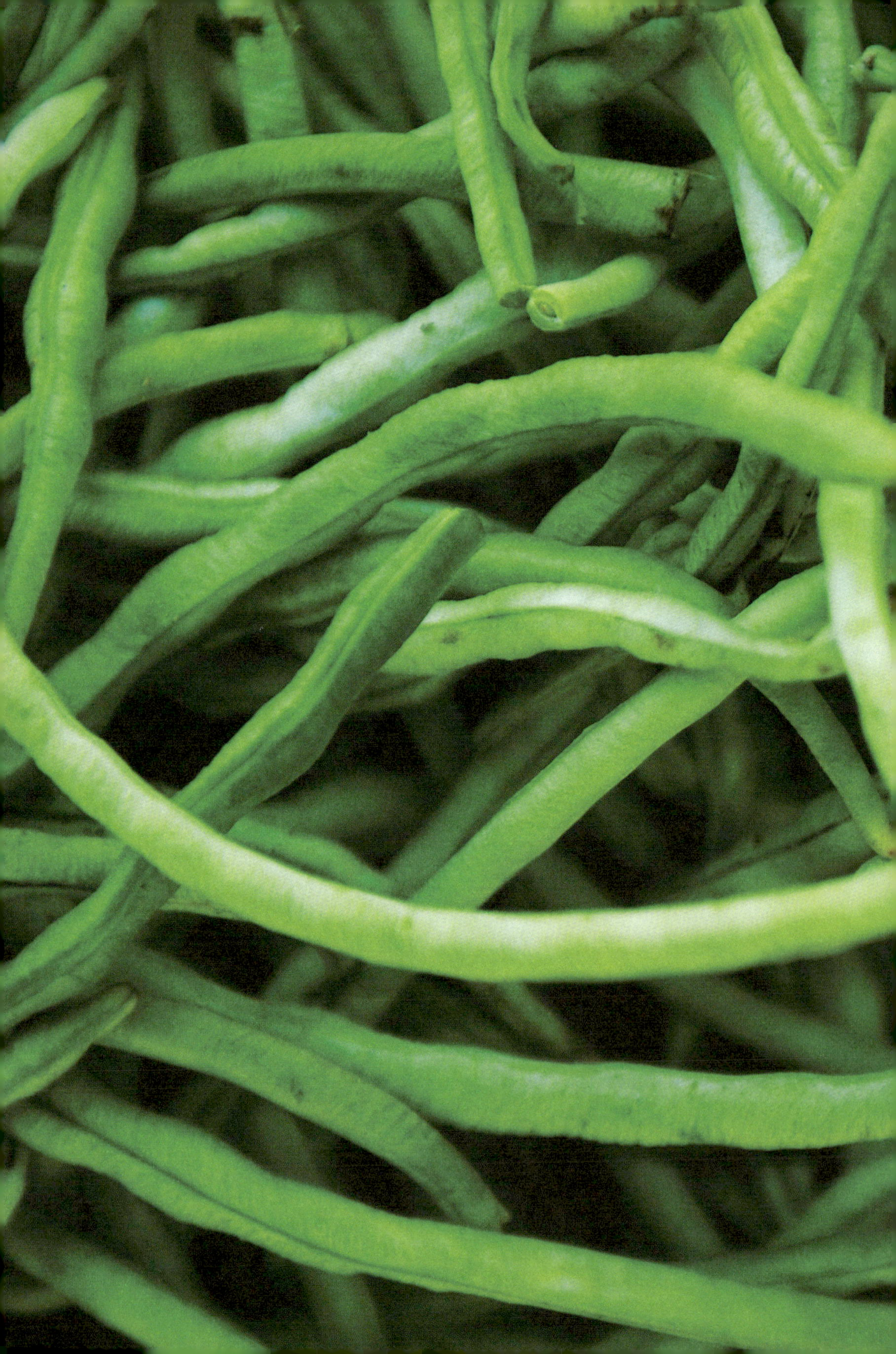

VEGETABLES

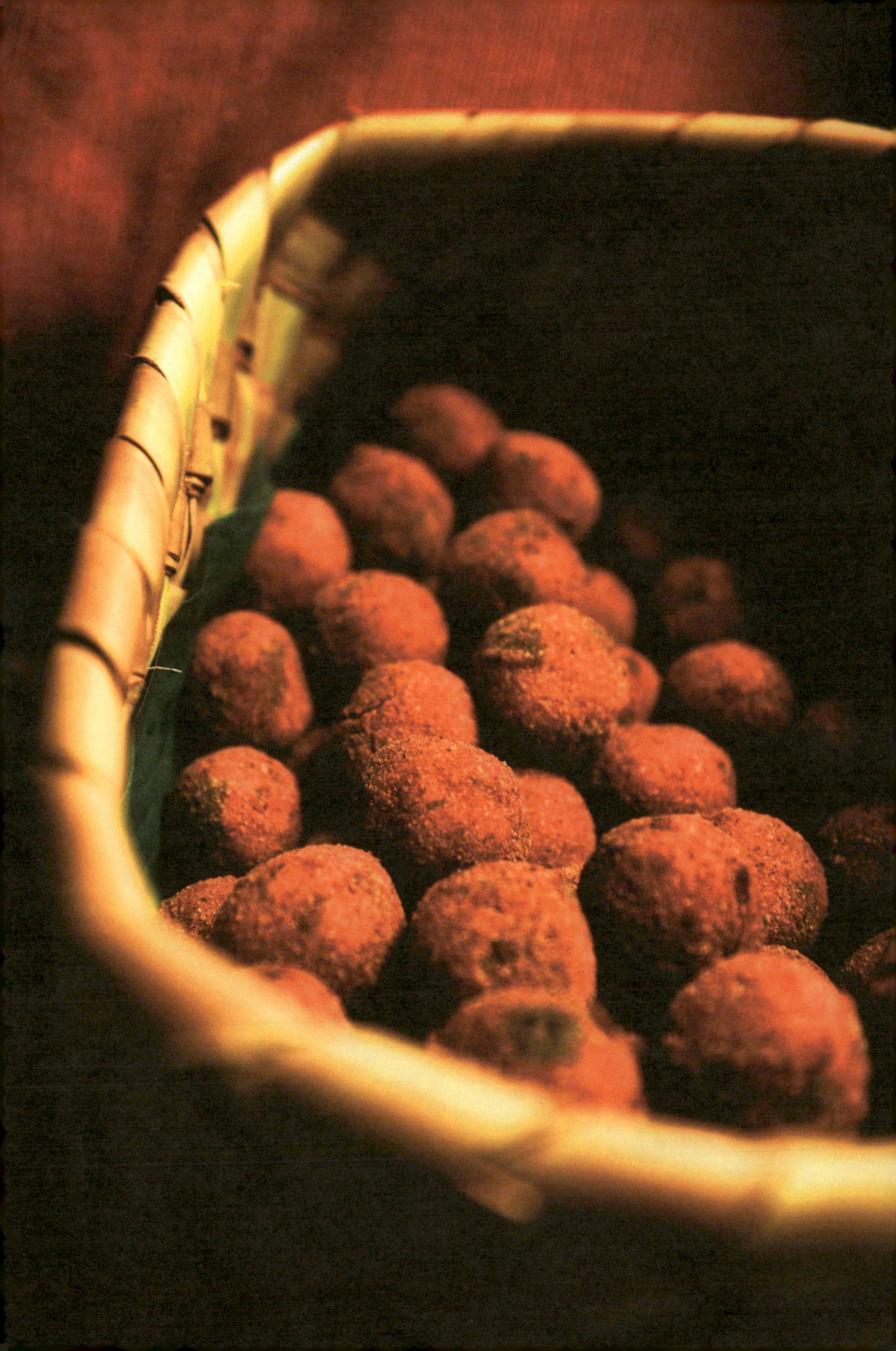

BREADED POTATO CUTLETS

These are rather like potato croquettes, and I wonder if the influence of the Brits being around in the past inspired this recipe.

SERVES FOUR TO SIX AS AN ACCOMPANIMENT

4 medium potatoes
peeled, boiled, mashed

2 carrots
peeled, finely chopped

2 leeks
finely chopped

2 shallots
finely chopped

5 green beans
finely chopped

1 handful of curry leaves

Vegetable oil

Rye breadcrumbs

Sea salt flakes

Parboil the carrots, leeks, shallots, and green beans for 5 minutes or until al dente. Drain well.

Add the ingredients to the mashed potato. Double the mashed potatoes to the vegetables. Season and mix together well.

Combine the ingredients to form small balls, about the size of golf balls. Roll in the breadcrumbs.

Heat the oil in a deep enough pan or wok. Gently place in the cutlets and fry until brown and crispy. Remove to kitchen paper to absorb any excess oil.

Serve straight away.

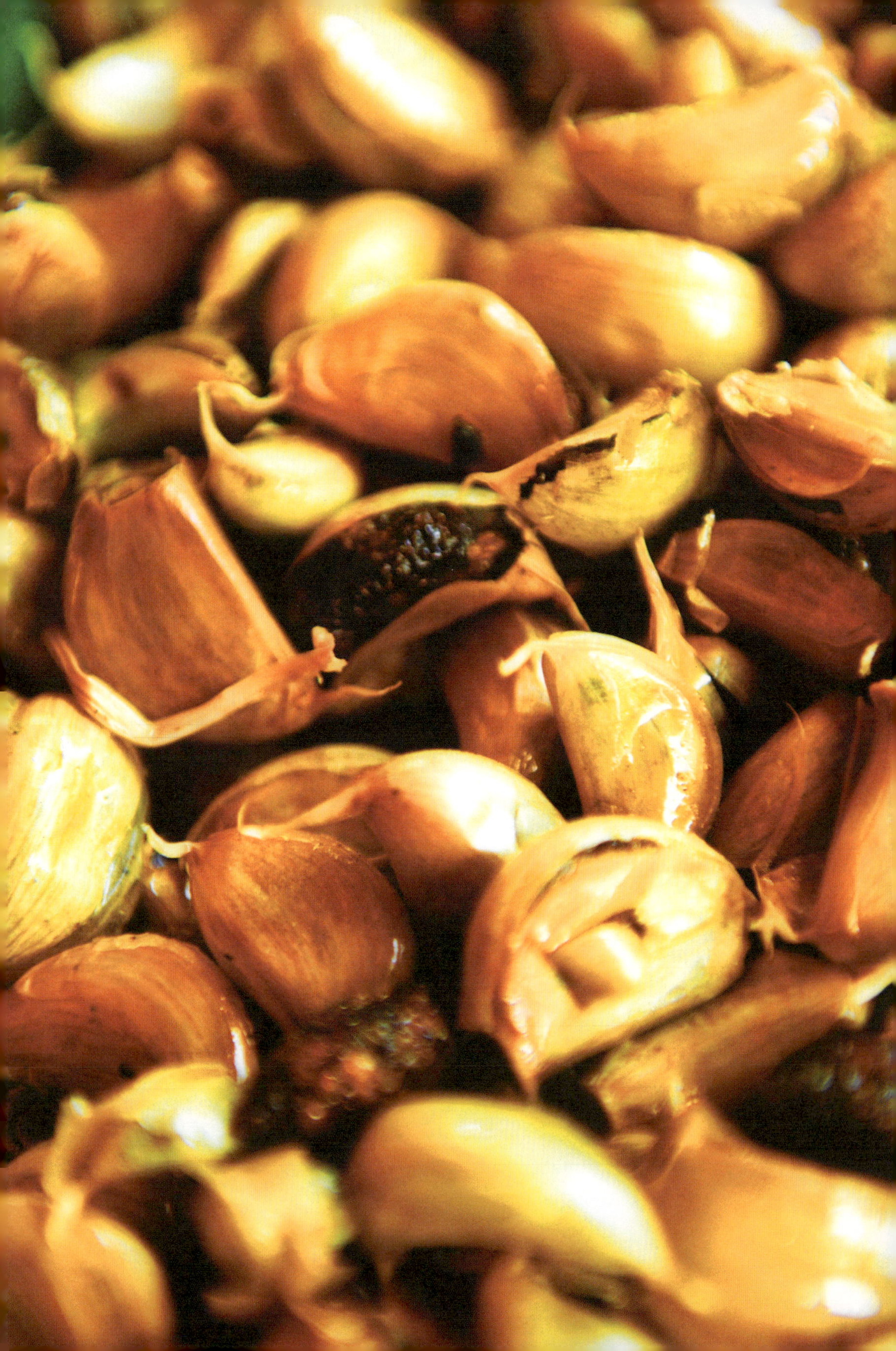

ROAST GARLIC IN THEIR SKINS

If you are partial to garlic, you'll be piling these on your plate. At Ulpotha they deep-fry them, but I don't have a deep fryer and I like shutting the oven door and leaving them to do their thing.

SERVES FOUR TO SIX AS AN ACCOMPANIMENT

4 whole bulbs of garlic that break down into approximately twenty cloves, separated and kept in their skins

1 dessertspoon coconut oil

Heat the oven to 200°C.

Place all the ingredients in a terracotta or ceramic dish on the middle shelf of the oven for approximately 25 minutes or until the garlic is soft and slightly caramelised.

Serve in their skins warm with any Ulpotha dish.

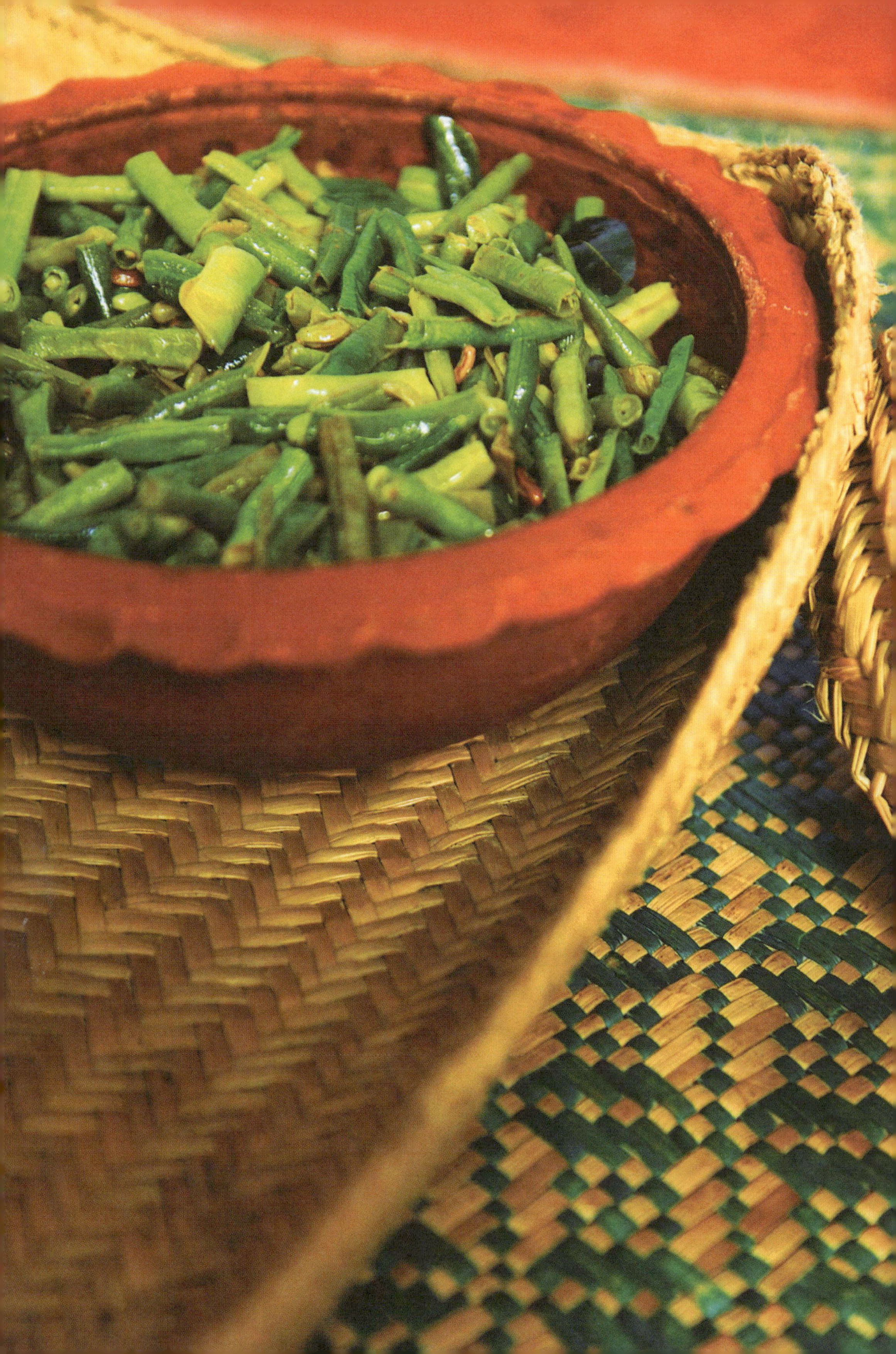

TEMPERED GREEN BEANS WITH WILTED ONIONS, GRATED COCONUT & CINNAMON

Tempered, means to "fry and season". The startlingly fresh green beans mixed with small flashes of purple from the onion and the scent of cinnamon is quite divine. It's important for the beans to be steamed until crunchy and not overcooked so they retain their brightness.

SERVES FOUR AS AN ACCOMPANIMENT

1 handful of tailed green beans, steamed until crunchy

1 tablespoon of coconut oil

1 red onion roughly chopped

1 dessertspoon of desiccated coconut

1/2 teaspoon ground cinnamon

Sea salt flakes

Heat the coconut oil in a frying pan. Sauté the onions until they turn brown around the edges. Add the coconut and cinnamon and a good pinch of salt.

Place the green beans in a serving dish. Add all the ingredients from the frying pan over the beans and toss well.

Serve warm.

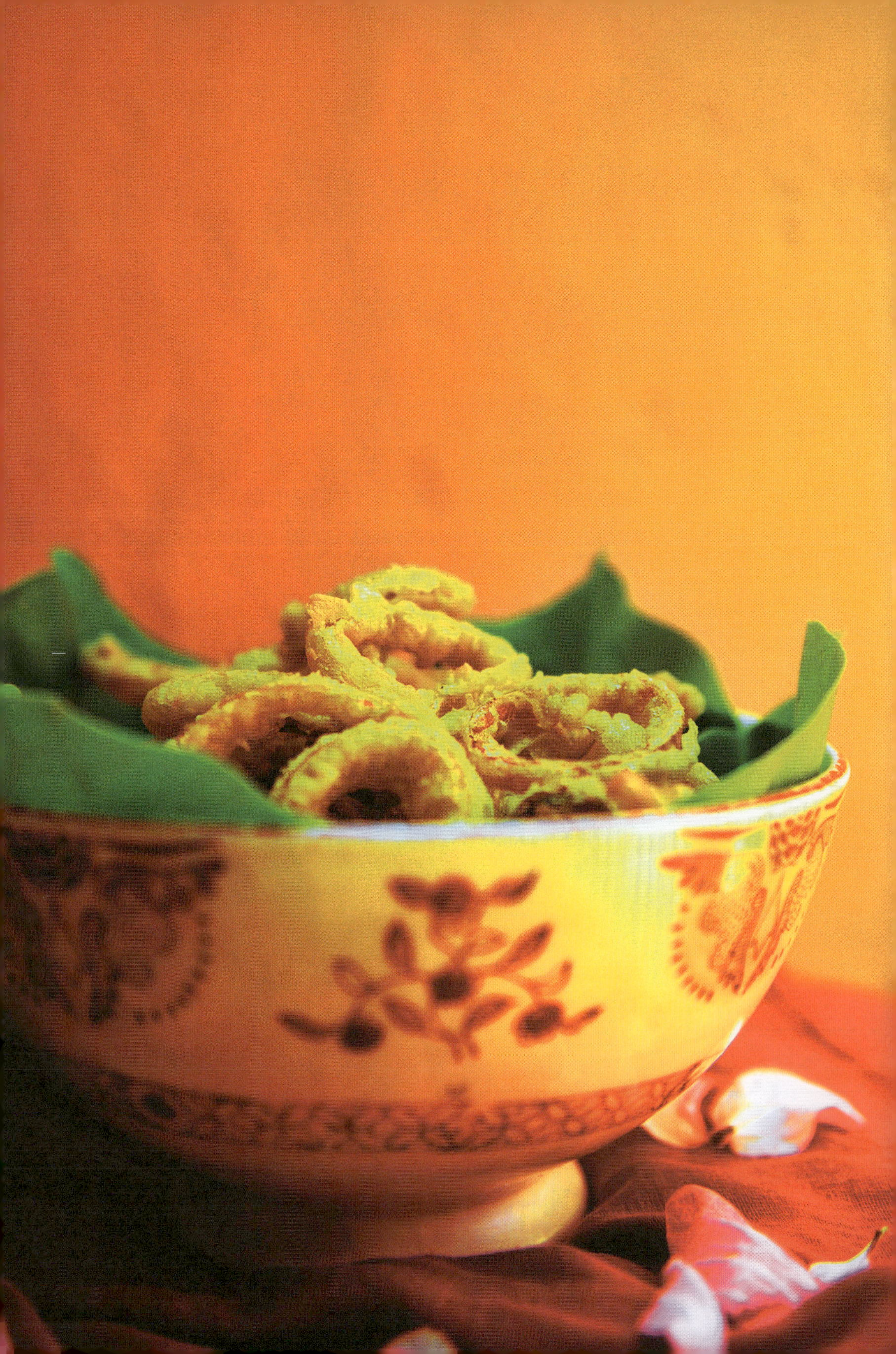

FRIED ONION RINGS WITH MUSTARD SEED, TURMERIC & NUTMEG

I was always amazed when onion rings were produced in the Ambalama (meeting place) as they didn't fit with my image of healthy food. But when cooked lightly with a few spices added, they are really quite a delicate dish and depending on the sweetness of the onion truly gorgeous, as in gorging. When my daughter tasted these when I cooked them in Devon, she said they bought back memories of being in the Kadé Hut at teatime.

SERVES FOUR TO SIX AS AN ACCOMPANIMENT

175g rice flour

1/2 teaspoon baking powder

Pinch of ground turmeric

1 pinch of black mustard seed

250ml of fresh or canned coconut milk

1 egg

1 pinch of ground nutmeg

Coconut oil for frying

3 Spanish onions sliced into 1cm-thick rings separated

Sea salt, fine

Whisk together 75g rice flour, baking powder, turmeric, coconut milk, egg, nutmeg, mustard seeds and a pinch of crushed sea salt in a bowl until smooth.

Fill a wok or deep frying pan with approximately 5cm of coconut oil. Heat over a medium heat to the point when the oil shimmers or when a drop of batter browns in 20 seconds.

Dust onion rings in remaining flour, shaking off the excess. Working in 3 batches, add onion rings to batter and using tongs remove rings from batter, allowing excess batter to drain off. Lower onion rings into the oil and fry for three minutes, turning halfway or until golden.

Drain on paper towel and serve immediately.

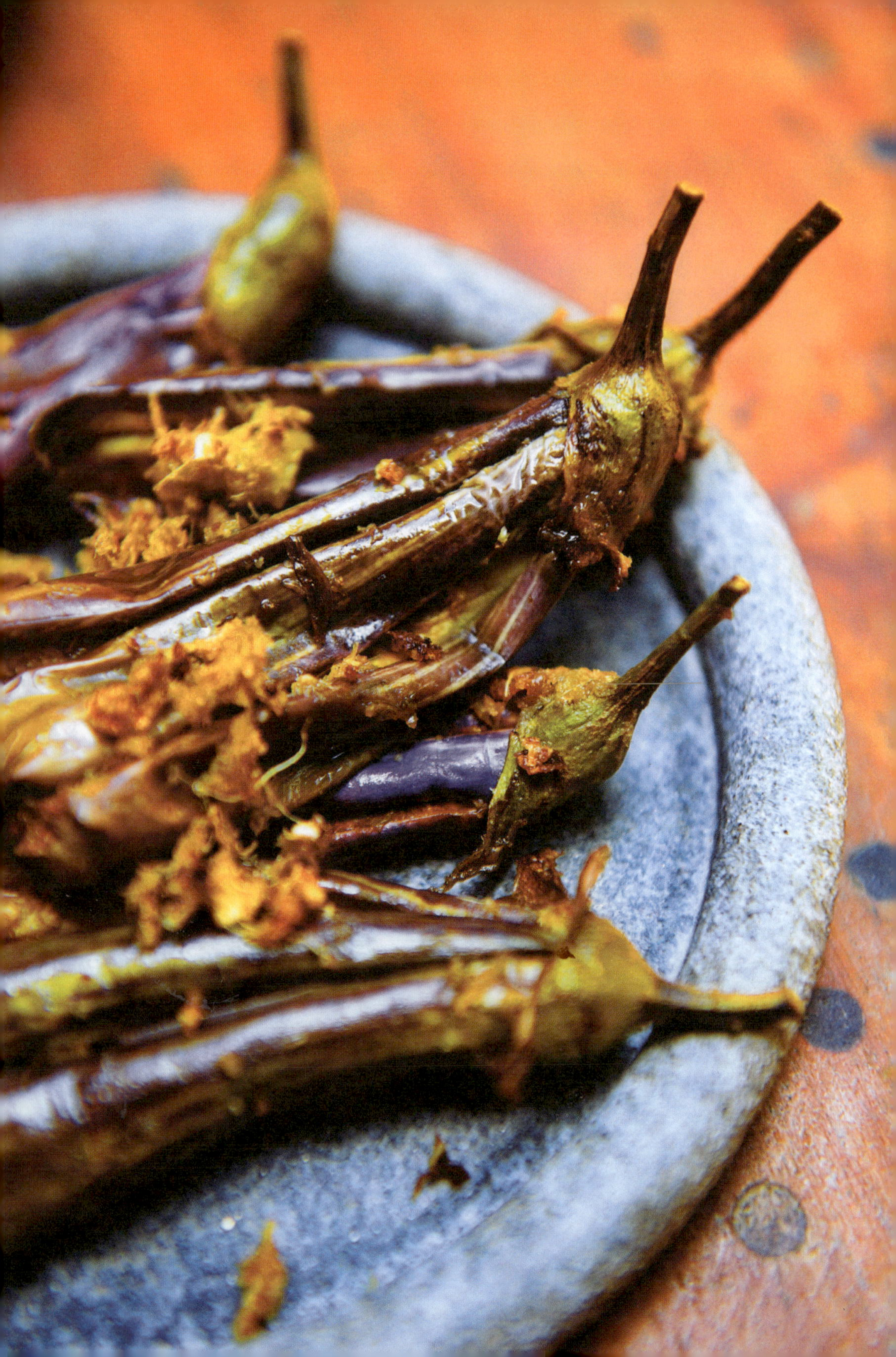

ROAST AUBERGINE WITH GRATED GINGER & CINNAMON

They don't roast food at Ulpotha as they don't have an oven, but I've found this dish works better roasted as the aubergines become more crispy.

SERVES FOUR TO SIX AS AN ACCOMPANIMENT

1 tablespoon of coconut oil

1 large aubergine diced and salted

2 cloves garlic, crushed

1 dessertspoon of grated ginger

1 pinch cinnamon powder

Sea salt flakes

A few fresh coriander leaves

Preheat the oven to 160°C.

In an oven proof dish add the coconut oil. Spread out the diced aubergine evenly. When the aubergine starts to brown, add the grated ginger, garlic and a generous pinch of ground cinnamon. Mix well and cook until crispy and golden.

Add a splash of colour with the coriander leaves.

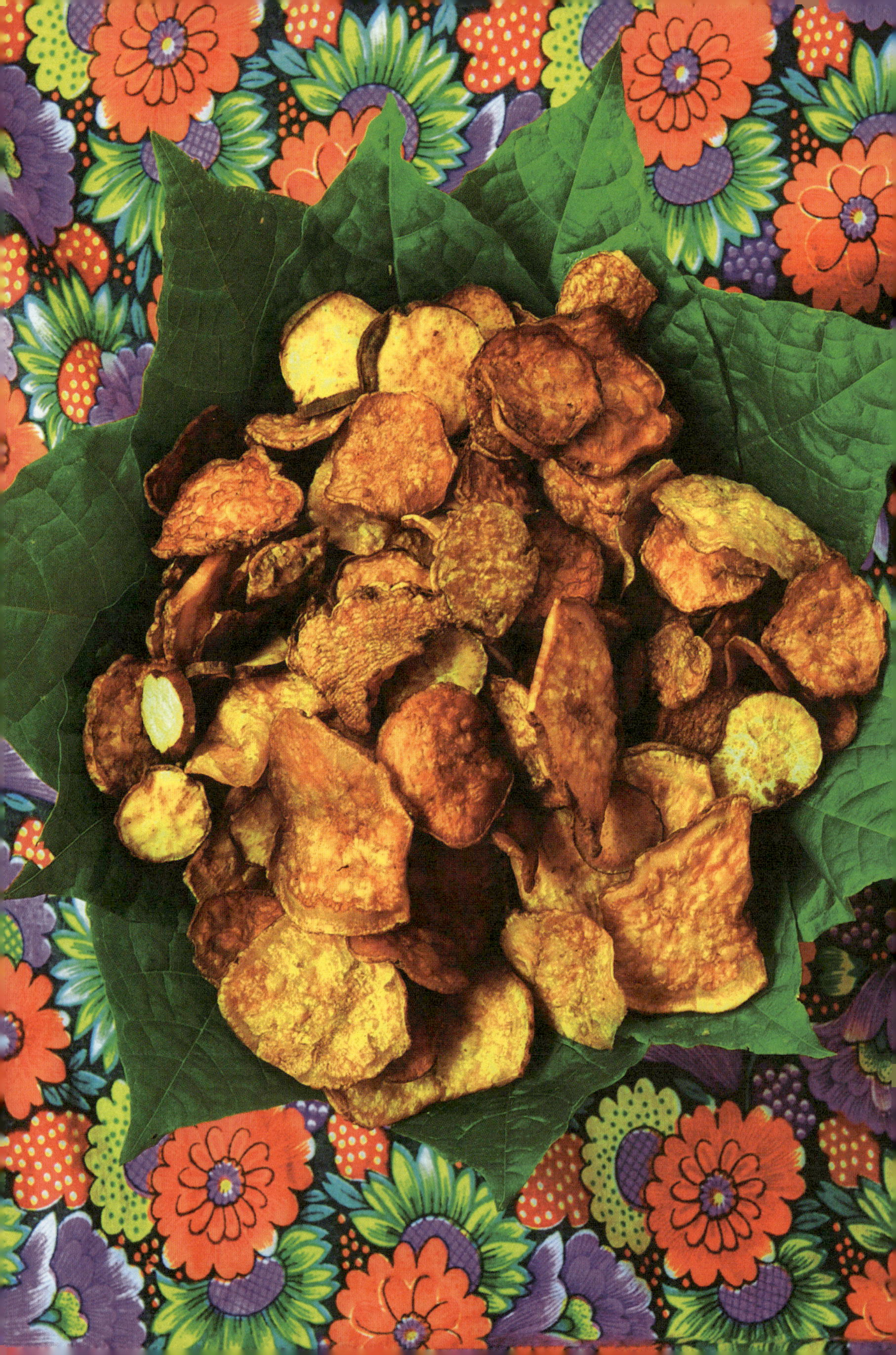

FRIED POTATO CRISPS WITH PAPRIKA

Who can't resist crispy potatoes. The paprika adds a certain 'Je ne sais quoi' Sri Lankan style. Use potatoes good for frying.

SERVES FOUR TO SIX AS AN ACCOMPANIMENT

1 kilo Maris Piper potatoes peeled and sliced thinly

Sunflower oil

Paprika

Seas salt flakes

Using a large, deep, heavy based saucepan, pour in about two inches of oil. Heat gently on a low heat. When the oil starts to shimmer and gently bubble, place in some of the sliced potatoes with a slotted spoon or netted spoon. Don't crowd them. Let them fry until brown and crispy. Remove to a plate with kitchen paper to absorb any excess oil.

Place the cooked potatoes in a 150°C warm oven and keep cooking the rest in batches. Place on a serving dish.

Mix the paprika and salt together and lightly sprinkle over the crispy potatoes.

Serve immediately.

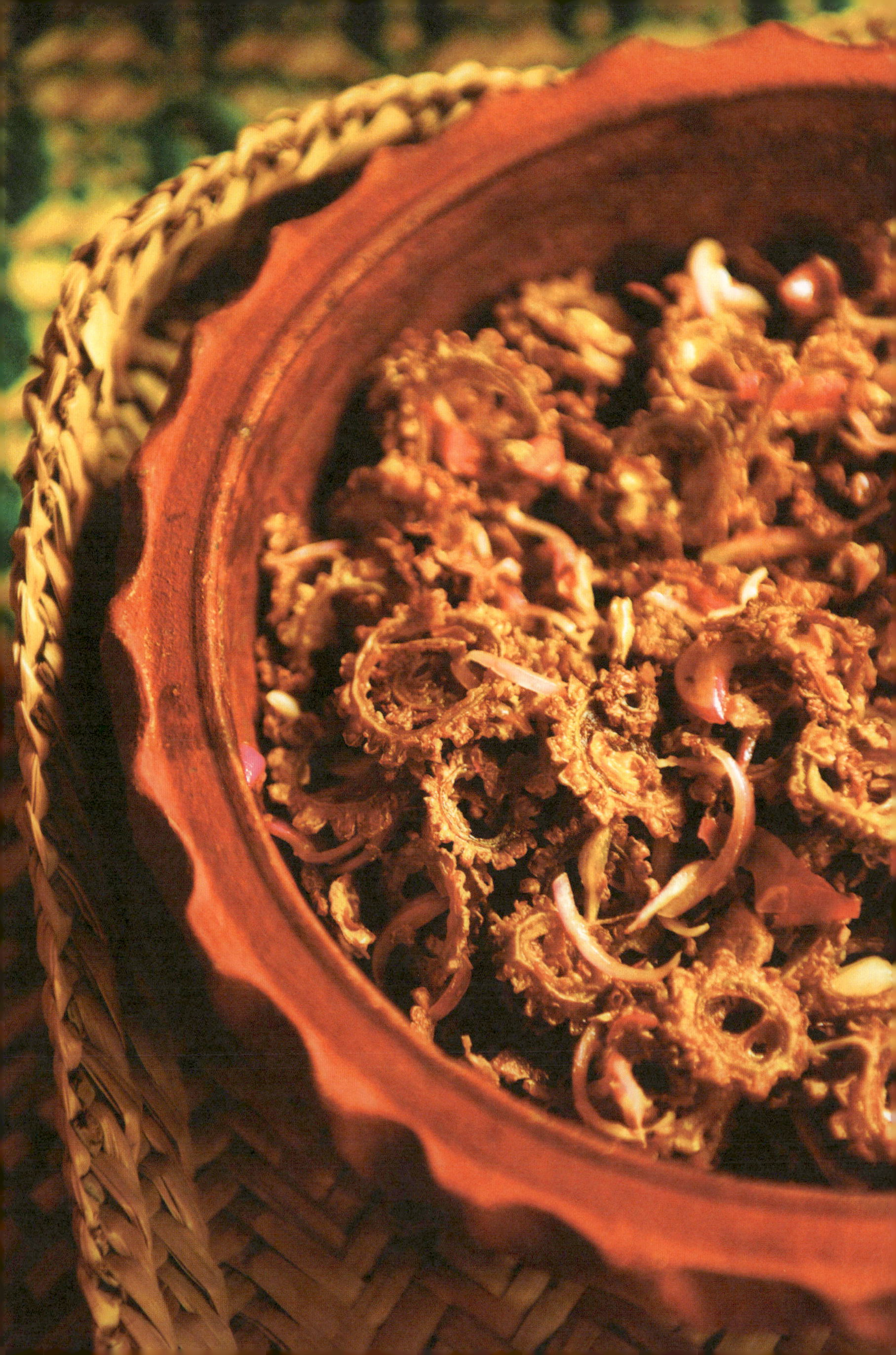

FRIED BITTER GOURD

This is a food I crave and I find deeply more-ish. The only way you'll be able to source this is by going to an Asian supermarket. It's well worth the effort.

SERVES FOUR AS AN ACCOMPANIMENT

2 bitter gourds
sliced into thin disks

2 tomatoes
thinly sliced

Vegetable oil

1 red onion
thinly sliced

Freshly ground
black pepper

Sea salt flakes

In a heavy-based frying pan cover the bottom with a swirl of vegetable oil. Heat until the oil starts to shimmer. Add the bitter gourd and fry until they start to turn crispy and brown. Remove to a plate with kitchen paper to remove any excess oil.

Place in a serving dish and add the raw tomato and onions. Season well with salt and pepper and serve.

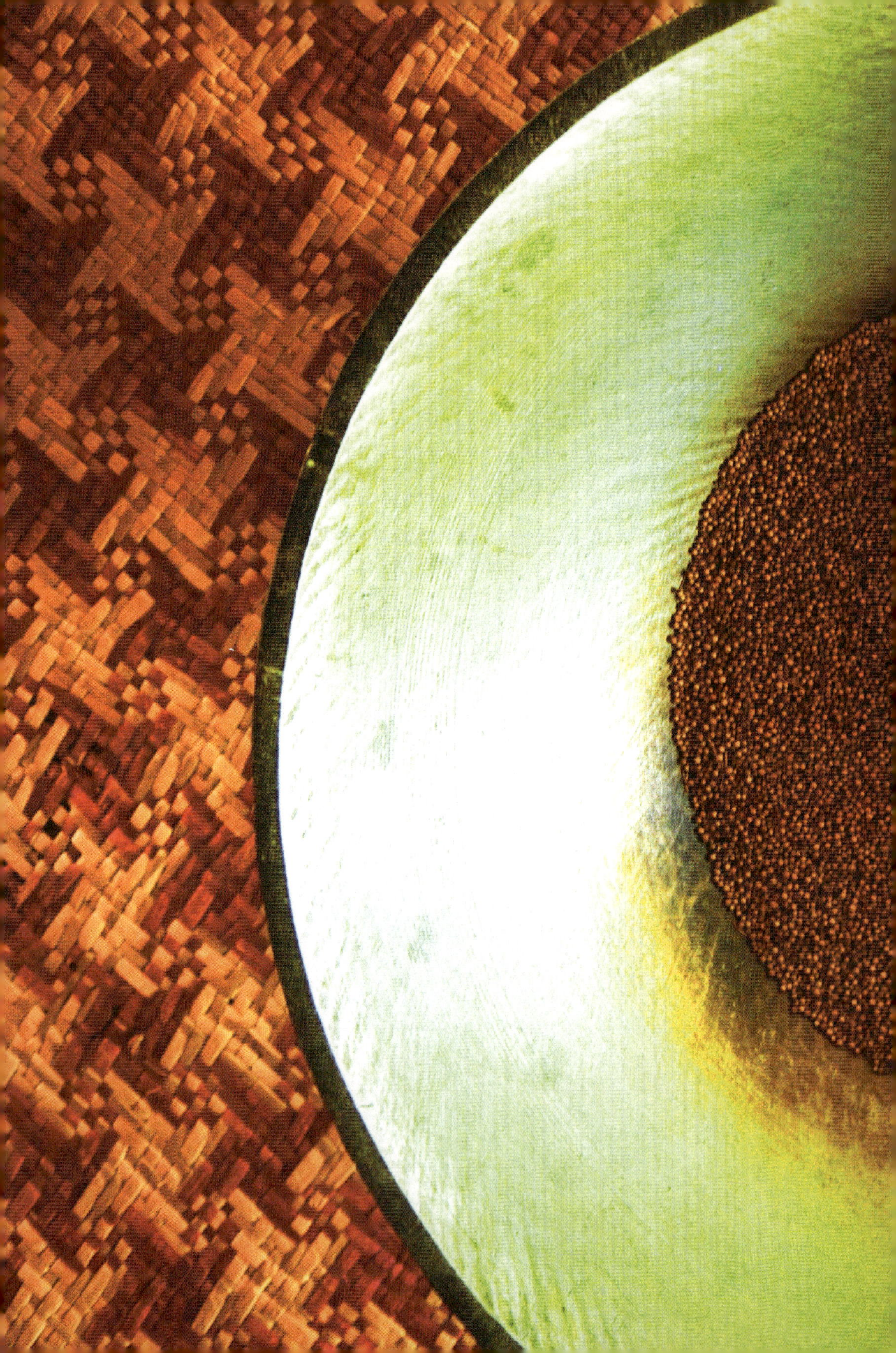

RICE LENTILS PULSES & GRAINS

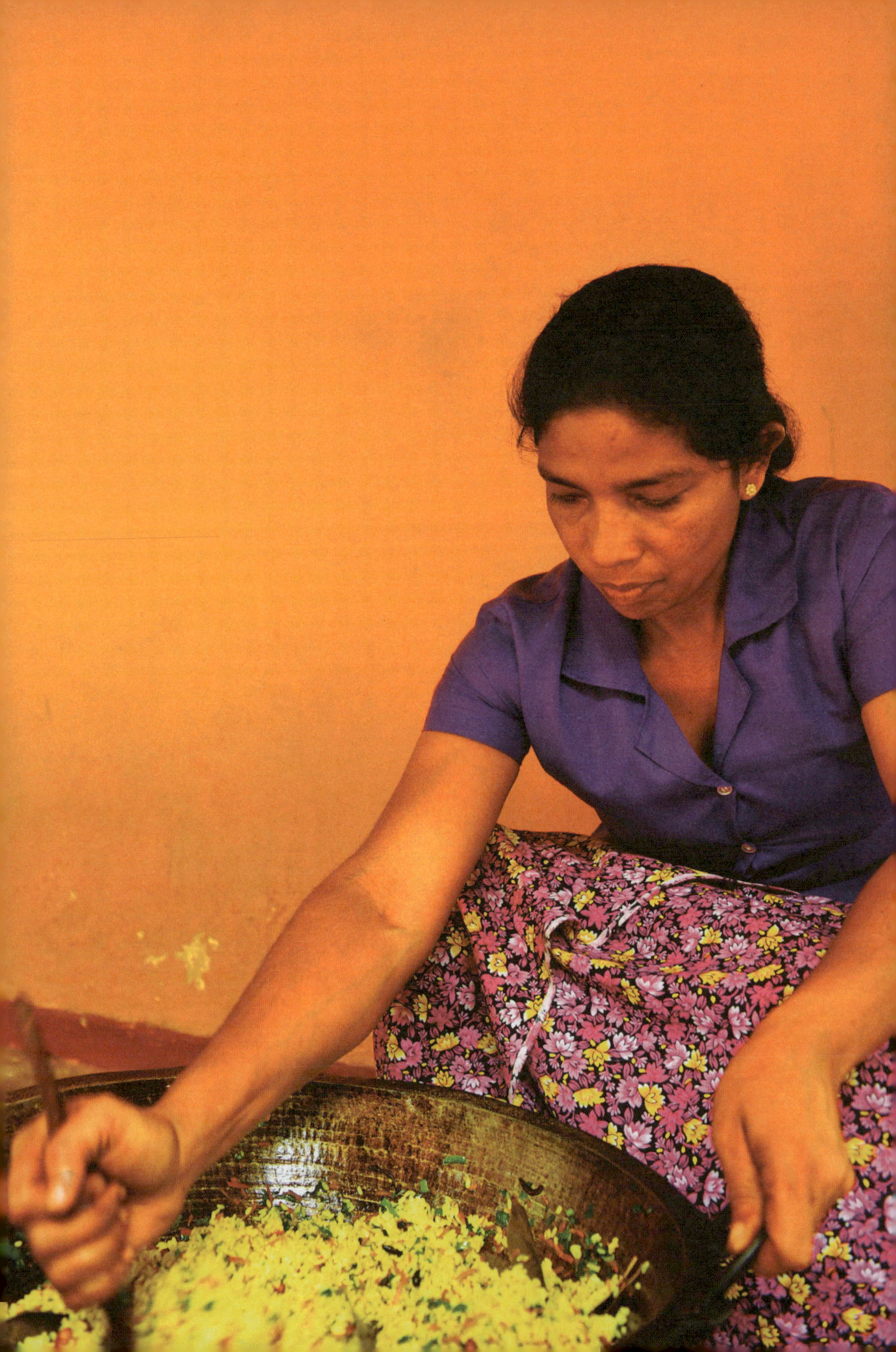

VEGETABLE RICE PILAF

This is a meal in one pot.

SERVES FOUR TO SIX

400g (2 cups) long grain rice

1 cinnamon stick

1 teaspoon ground turmeric

1 1/2 tablespoons vegetable oil

1 large red onion finely chopped

2 leeks trimmed and julienned

2 carrots, julienned

10 fresh curry leaves

50g peanuts, roasted

1 teaspoon ground cinnamon

1 handful of raisins

Sea salt

Rinse rice in a sieve until water runs clear. Drain, then place in a large saucepan with a hearty pinch of sea salt, cinnamon stick, turmeric and 750ml water and stir well. Bring to the boil over a medium heat, cover with a lid, reduce heat to low and cook for 12-15 minutes or until the liquid has been absorbed. Remove from the heat and stand covered for 10 minutes until the rice is tender.

Meanwhile heat the vegetable oil in a large heavy-based frying pan and cook onions until starting to soften. Add leeks, carrots and curry leaves, and cook for a further 8 minutes until all the vegetables are soft.

Stir vegetable mixture into rice and then stir in peanuts, ground cinnamon and raisins until well combined. Season well with sea salt and serve.

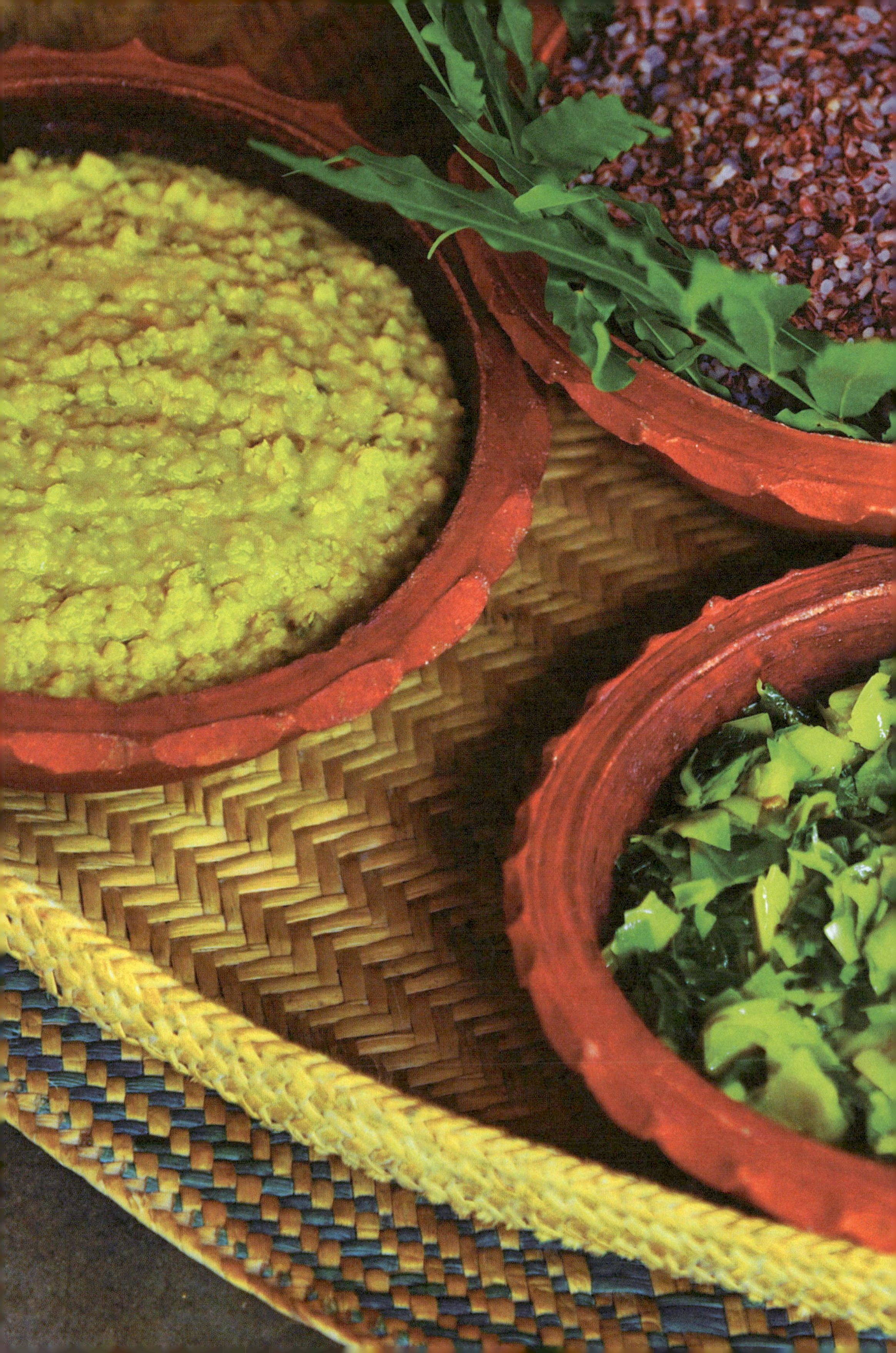

PARIPPU *DHAL*

This is such a delicious dish. On an autumn night it can be warming and nourishing. When I last made it, we were all rubbing our tummies afterwards.

SERVES FOUR TO SIX

1 cup of red split lentils

1 small onion
finely chopped

2 cloves garlic
finely chopped

1/2 teaspoon of turmeric

1 handful of fresh chives
finely chopped

5-10 curry leaves
I had dried although I wish I had fresh

400ml coconut milk

One generous pinch
sea salt flakes

Place all the ingredients except the chives in a heavy based saucepan or clay pot with a lid on a low heat. Bring to simmering point and cook until the lentils are mushy and have absorbed all the liquid.

Serve with the sprinkled chives on top.

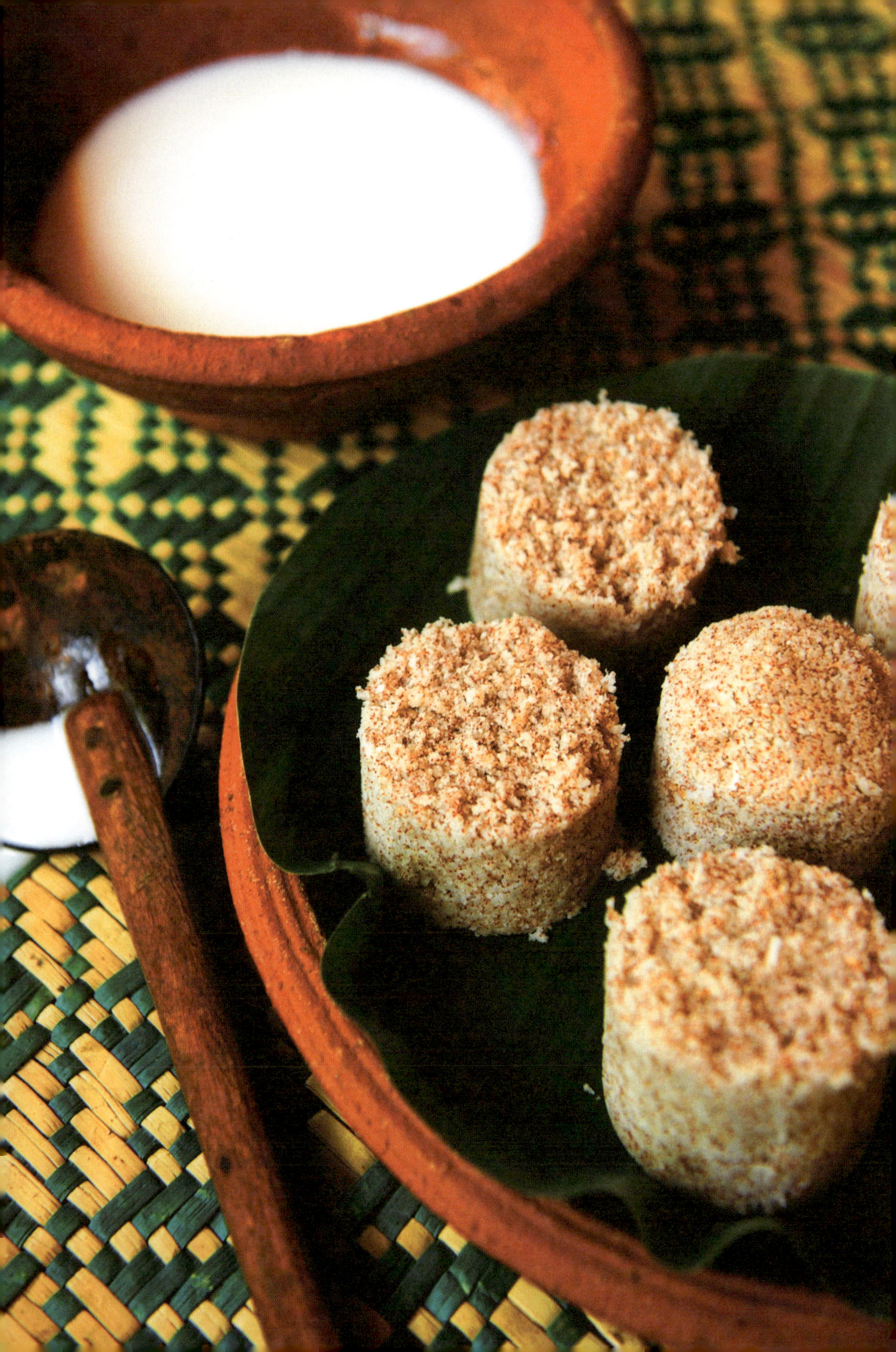

PITTU

This is a dish that is often served for breakfast in Sri Lanka. They have a special utensil for steaming, which I've never seen in the west, so I've used a bamboo steam basket instead, lined with a thin tea towel.

SERVES FOUR

2 cups of rice flour

2 cups of desiccated coconut

1 cup of coconut milk

Fine sea salt

In a mixing bowl mix together the rice flour and desiccated coconut. Slowly stir in the coconut milk and a pinch of salt. Integrate all the ingredients well.

Place the steamer over a boiling saucepan of hot water, lay the tea towel inside the steamer. Spoon in the rice mixture, cover and steam for ten minutes. Remove and mould the rice in to a cup cake shape or log. You now have pittu. Serve warm with buffalo kurd or yogurt.

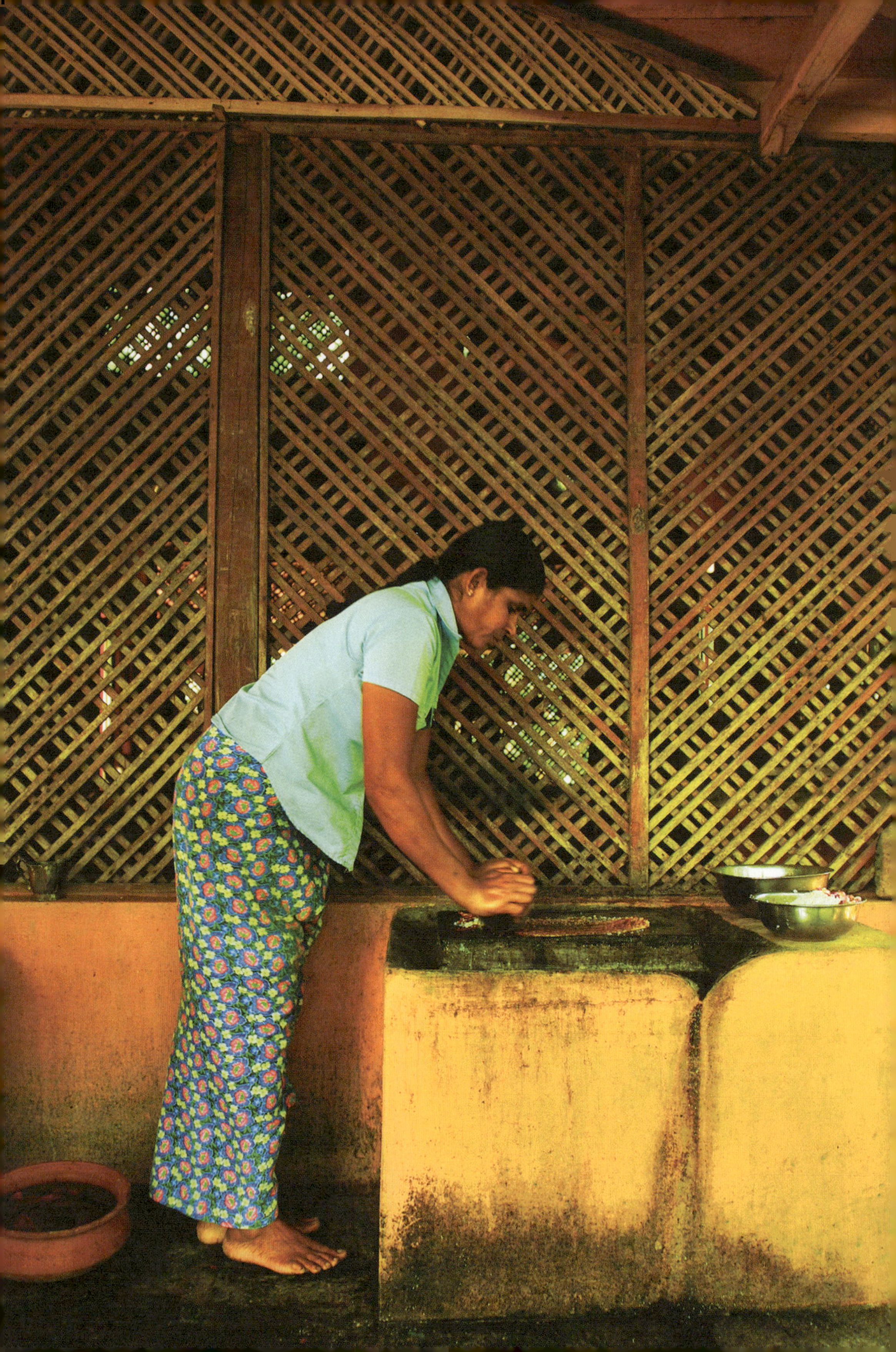

COCONUT ROTI

Similar to the Indian flat breads, this Sri Lankan version contains fresh grated coconut or in its absence, desiccated coconut. It is a popular breakfast in Sri Lanka and is often served with curries and sambols.

SERVES FOUR TO SIX

2 cups of rice flour

1/2 cup dessicated fresh coconut

1 teaspoon salt

1 cup of water

Ghee or oil

Mix flour, coconut and salt in a mixing bowl. Add enough water to form a soft dough.

Knead the dough until it forms a ball and does not stick to sides of the bowl. Leave the dough to rest for approximately 30 minutes then shape into golf ball size balls.

Pat each one out into a circle the size of a saucer.

Cook on a hot griddle or in a heavy frying pan very lightly greased with ghee or oil. Serve hot.

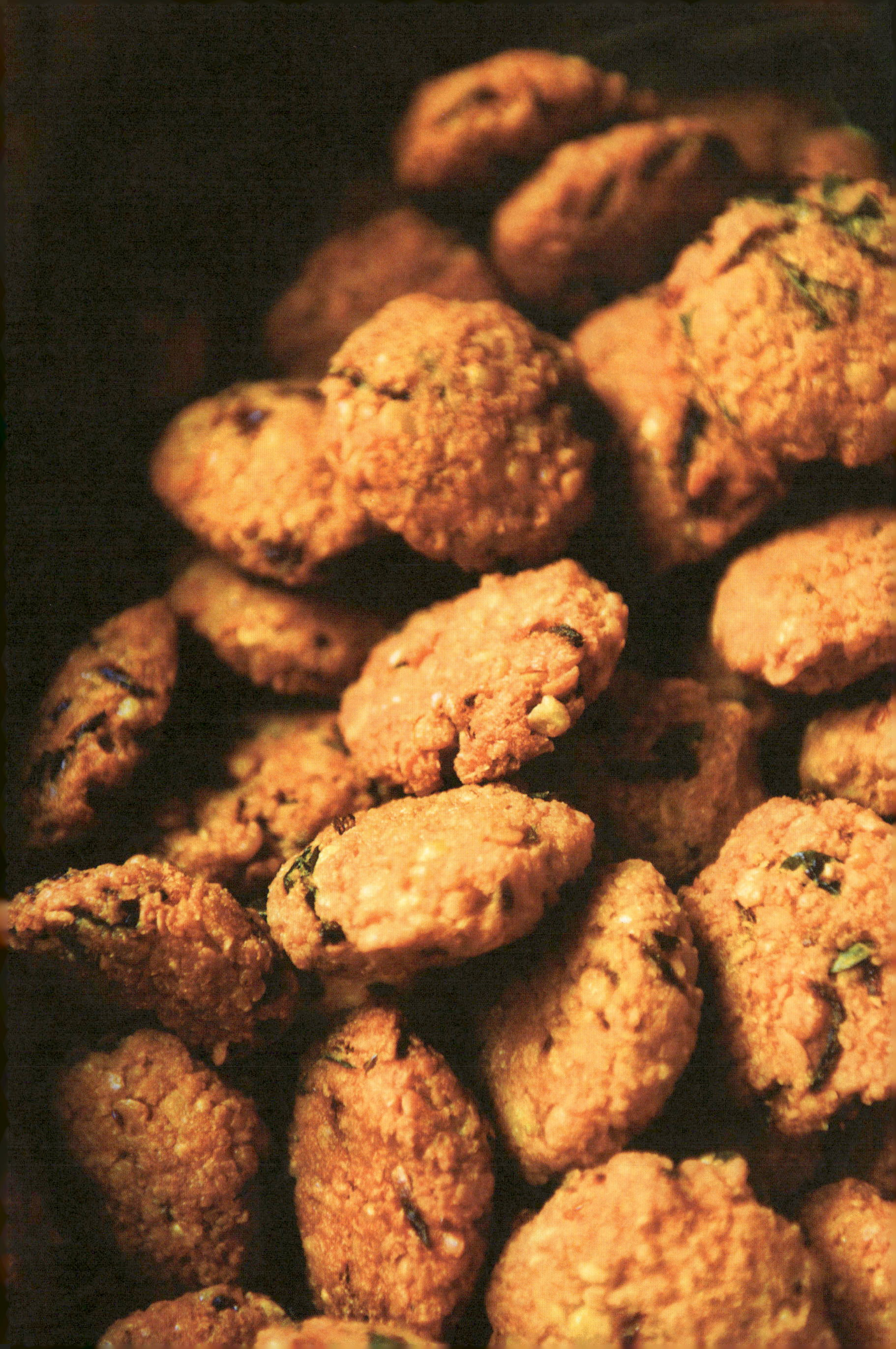

WADÉ

Pronounced waday, these are delicious crunchy vegetarian fritters. In Ulpotha they are served in the afternoon as a snack in the Kadé Hut. I added ginger and chilli flakes to punch up the flavour a little.

SERVES FOUR TO SIX

400g canned chickpeas drained

1 large red onion finely chopped

2 gloves garlic, crushed

1 handful of curry leaves fresh if possible

1 hearty pinch of turmeric

1 slice of ginger, optional

A few chilli flakes, optional

Sea salt flakes

Vegetable oil for frying

In a mortar grind all the ingredients until crushed well.

In a frying pan heat the oil until it starts to shimmer.

Make a ball in your hand with the ingredients and flatten. Place in the oil and cook on both sides until dark brown and crispy. Remove each batch to kitchen paper to soak up any excess oil. Serve warm.

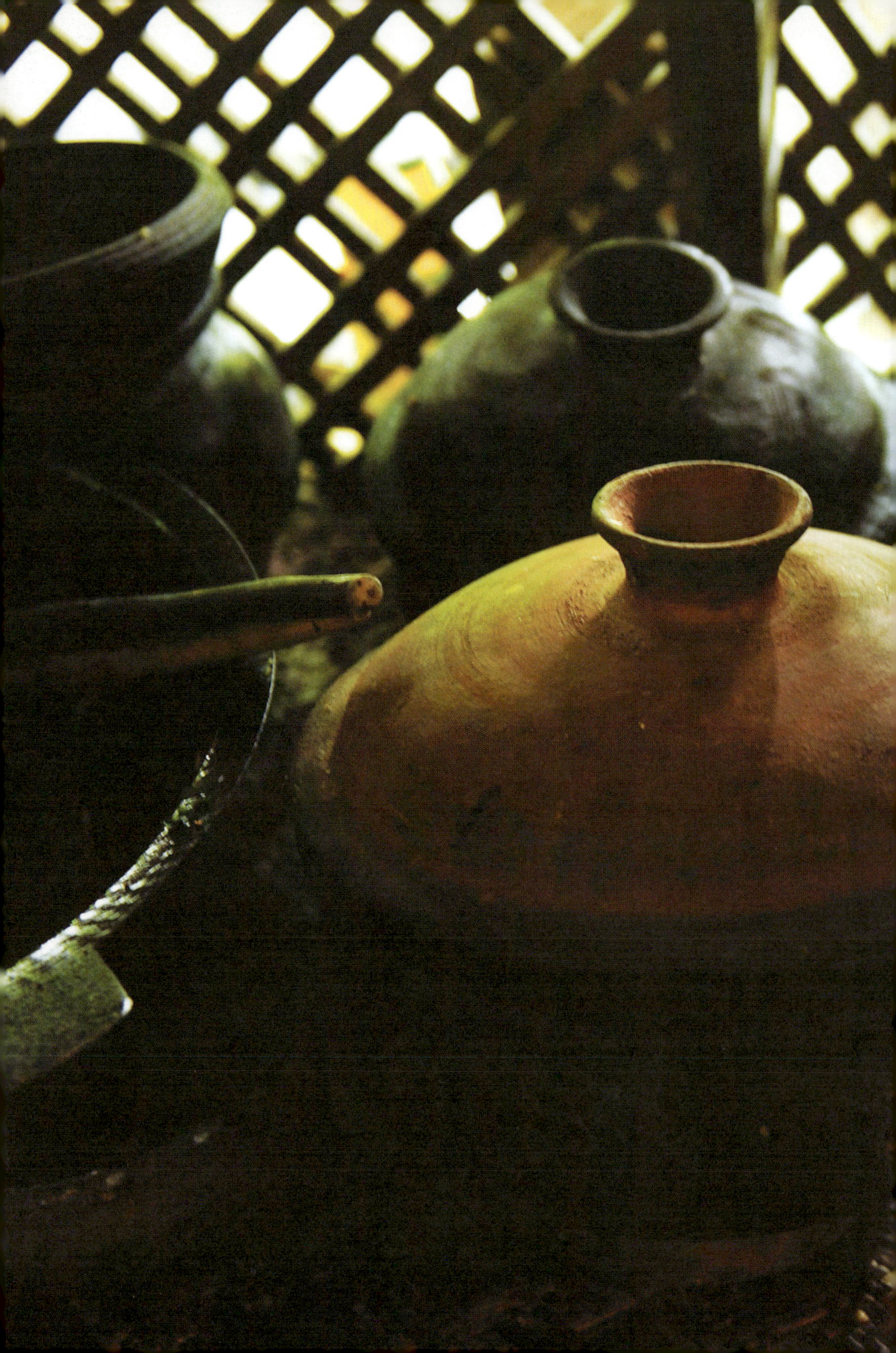

CURRY

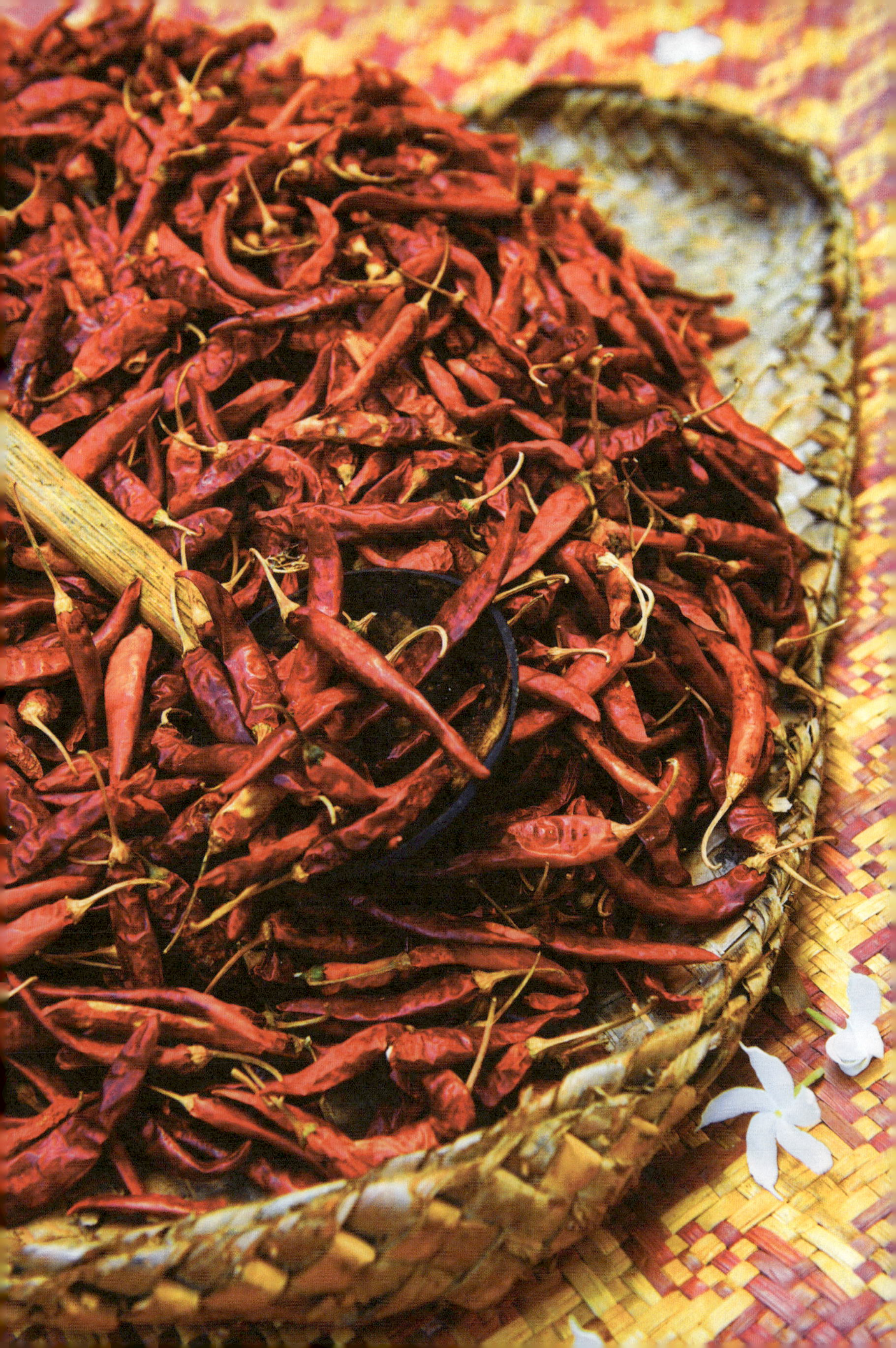

FRAGRANT CURRY POWDER

I like to make a fresh batch every time I need to use curry powder. It might seem like a lot of work, it's not; it's just a lot of spices thrown together. The grinding takes a bit of time, but use it as a meditation and the smell is very uplifting too.

SUFFICIENT FOR ONE CURRY

1 teaspoon coriander seeds

1 teaspoon cumin seeds

1 teaspoon fennel seeds

5 cardamom seeds

1 cinnamon stick

A pinch of turmeric

1/2 teaspoon of cinnamon powder, optional

Place the coriander seeds in a heavy-based frying pan on a low heat. Toss around the pan for a moment or two, then add the other spices. Move the pan constantly for a couple more minutes. As the spices become darker brown, remove from the heat. Do not let the spices burn.

When cool, place in a mortar and grind until the spices are fine.

For a little extra flavor add half a teaspoon of cinnamon powder.

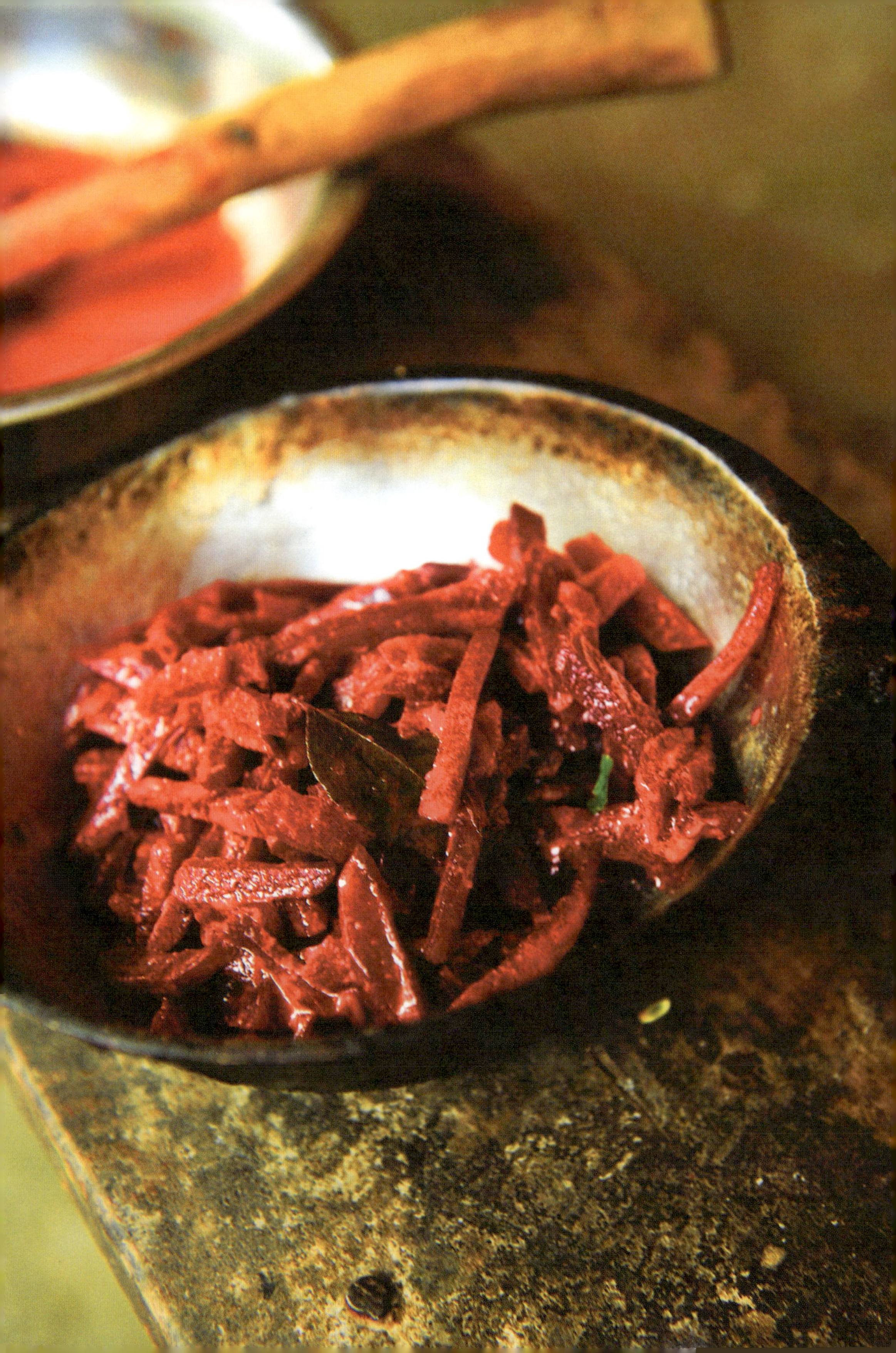

BEETROOT CURRY

This is a rich velvety jewel coloured dish. I cook this in an ovenproof earthenware pot (or casserole dish) and reheat the leftovers the next day. It is even better when all the ingredients have found their voice.

SERVES FOUR TO SIX

2 dessertspoons of coconut oil

1 large red onion roughly chopped

2 garlic cloves finely chopped

2 large beetroot cut into strips

1/4 green chilli, deseeded and finely chopped

1 cinnamon stick

4 cardamom pods, crushed

A handful of curry leaves

400ml coconut milk

2 tablespoons of fragrant curry powder

1 handful of desiccated coconut, keep a little for decoration

Sea salt flakes

A handful of fresh basil

1 lime

Put the coconut oil in a large earthenware pot or casserole dish over a low heat. Add the onions and garlic and sauté.

When the onions start to soften, add the cinnamon stick, curry leaves, curry powder, chilli and desiccated coconut. Stir together well. Add the beetroot and stir well and sauté for a few more minutes.

Pour over the coconut milk and add the crushed cardamom. Cover and simmer gently until the beetroot is tender but still crunchy, stirring occasionally.

Season well with salt.

Decorate with the fresh basil and sprinkle with a little bit of desiccated coconut and a squeeze of lime.

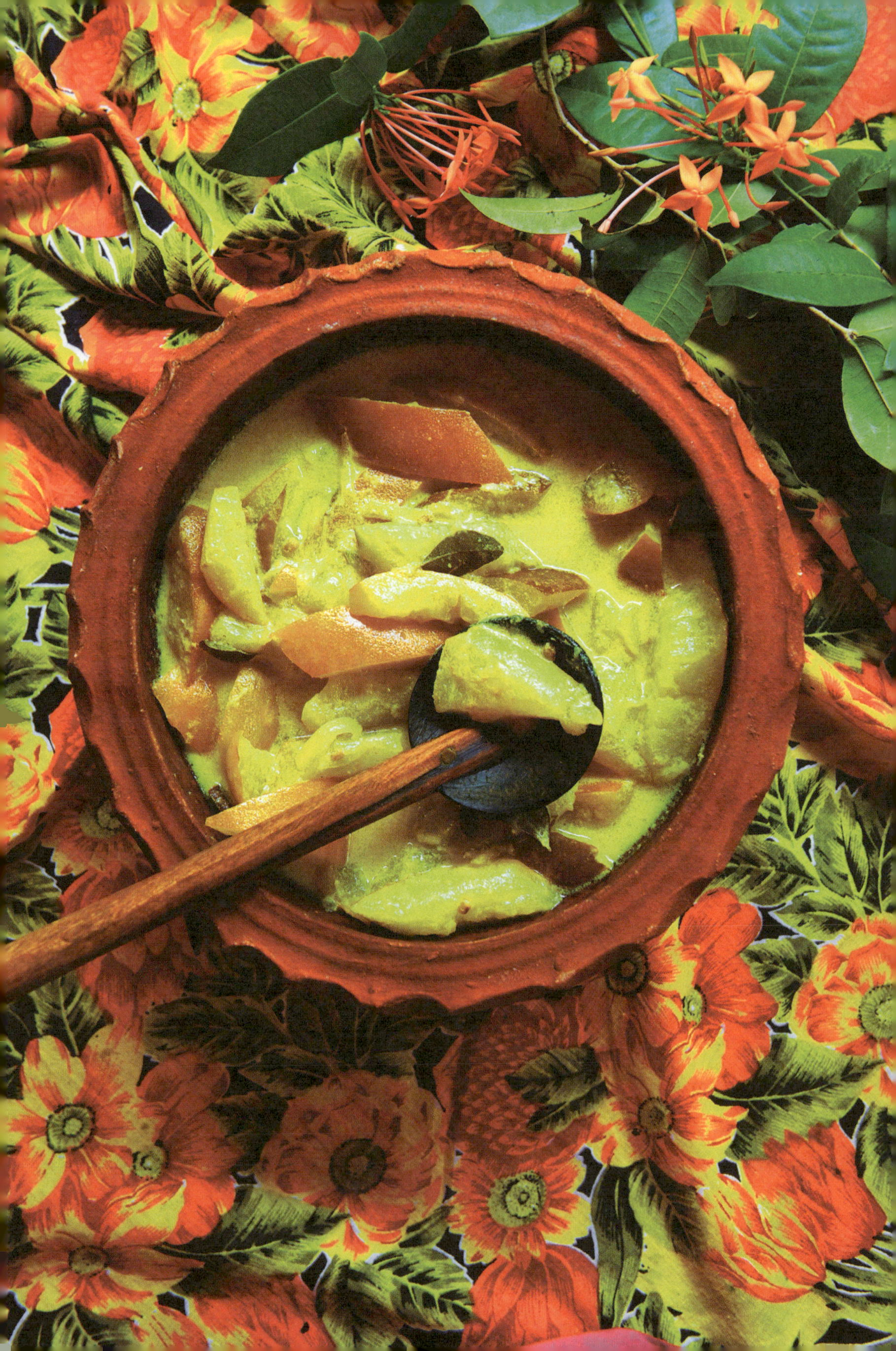

CUCUMBER CURRY

This is a perfect summertime curry and is very light and subtle in flavour.

SERVES FOUR

1 cucumber or two Lebanese cucumbers, peeled and cut into generous chunks

2 dessertspoons of coconut oil

1 large white onion finely chopped

2 tablespoons of desiccated coconut

10 fresh curry leaves

4 cardamom pods, crushed

1 stick cinnamon

1 teaspoon of mustard seeds

1 teaspoon of turmeric powder

1/4 green chilli, deseeded and finely chopped

1 handful of fresh chives, finely chopped

400ml of coconut milk

Sea salt flakes

In a mortar, crush the cardamom, mustard seeds, desiccated coconut and curry leaves with a large pinch of salt.

In a heavy-based pan add the coconut oil, sauté the onions and cinnamon stick. Add the spice mixture, followed by the cucumbers, stir-fry for a minute or two.

Pour in the coconut milk. Bring to simmering. Cook for a few minutes until cucumbers are soft, but still crunchy.

Season to taste and sprinkle with chopped chives. Serve immediately.

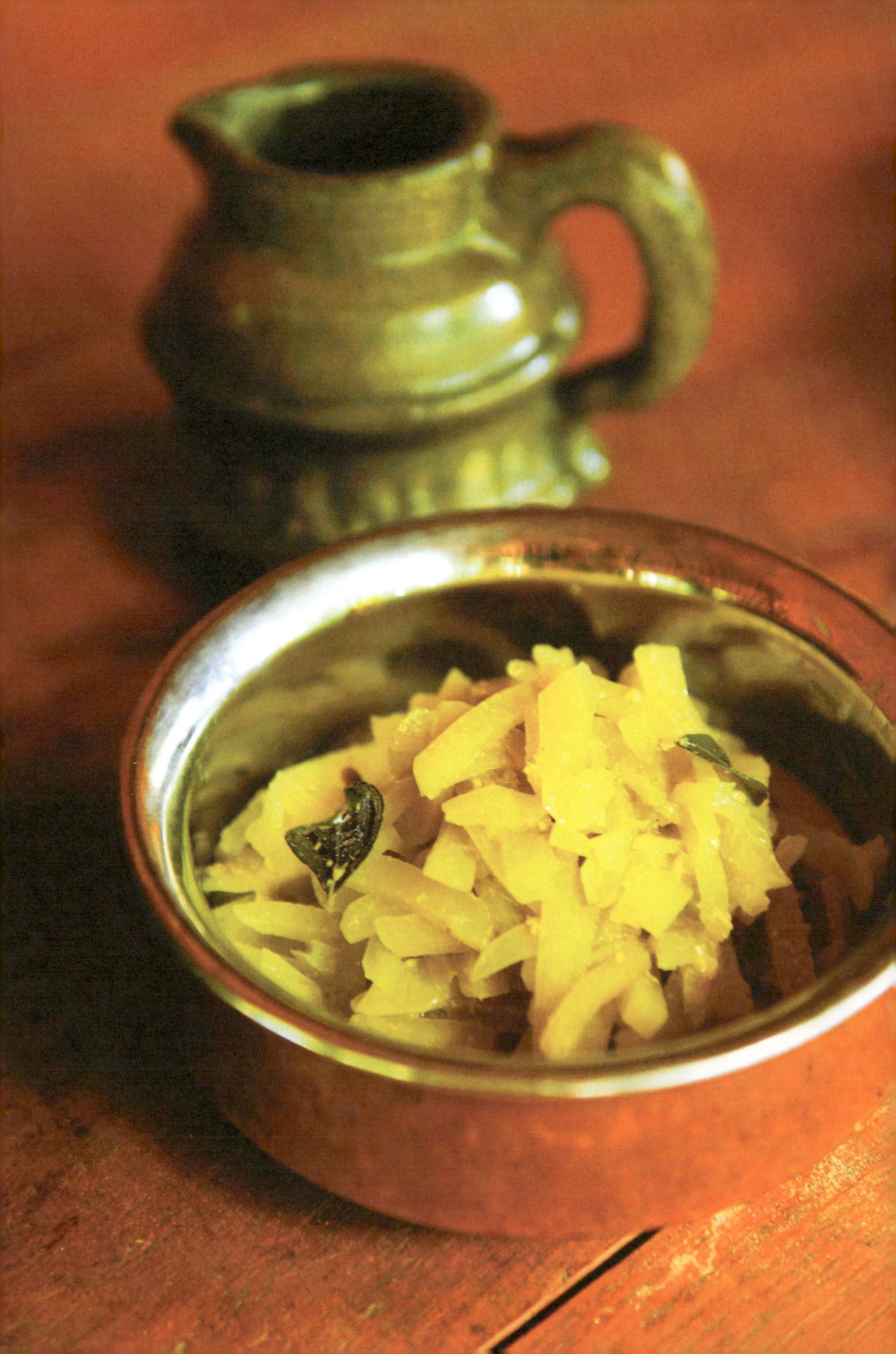

JACKFRUIT CURRY

I was able to use fresh jackfruit If you cannot source one, go to an Asian grocery store and buy tinned jackfruit and drain the liquid. Jackfruit has a meaty texture and a mild taste.

SERVES FOUR

1 tin of jackfruit or fresh jackfruit, peeled and shredded

400ml of coconut milk

2 dessertspoons of coconut oil

1 large white onion peeled and thinly sliced

4 cloves of garlic peeled and crushed

2 teaspoons of black mustard seeds

A handful of curry leaves

Sea salt flakes

Place the jackfruit in a saucepan and cover with the coconut milk. Bring to the boil and simmer for twenty minutes or until the jackfruit is soft.

In a frying pan add the coconut oil, sauté the onions and garlic and add the mustard seeds.

When the jackfruit is soft add the rest of the ingredients, mix together and season well with salt.

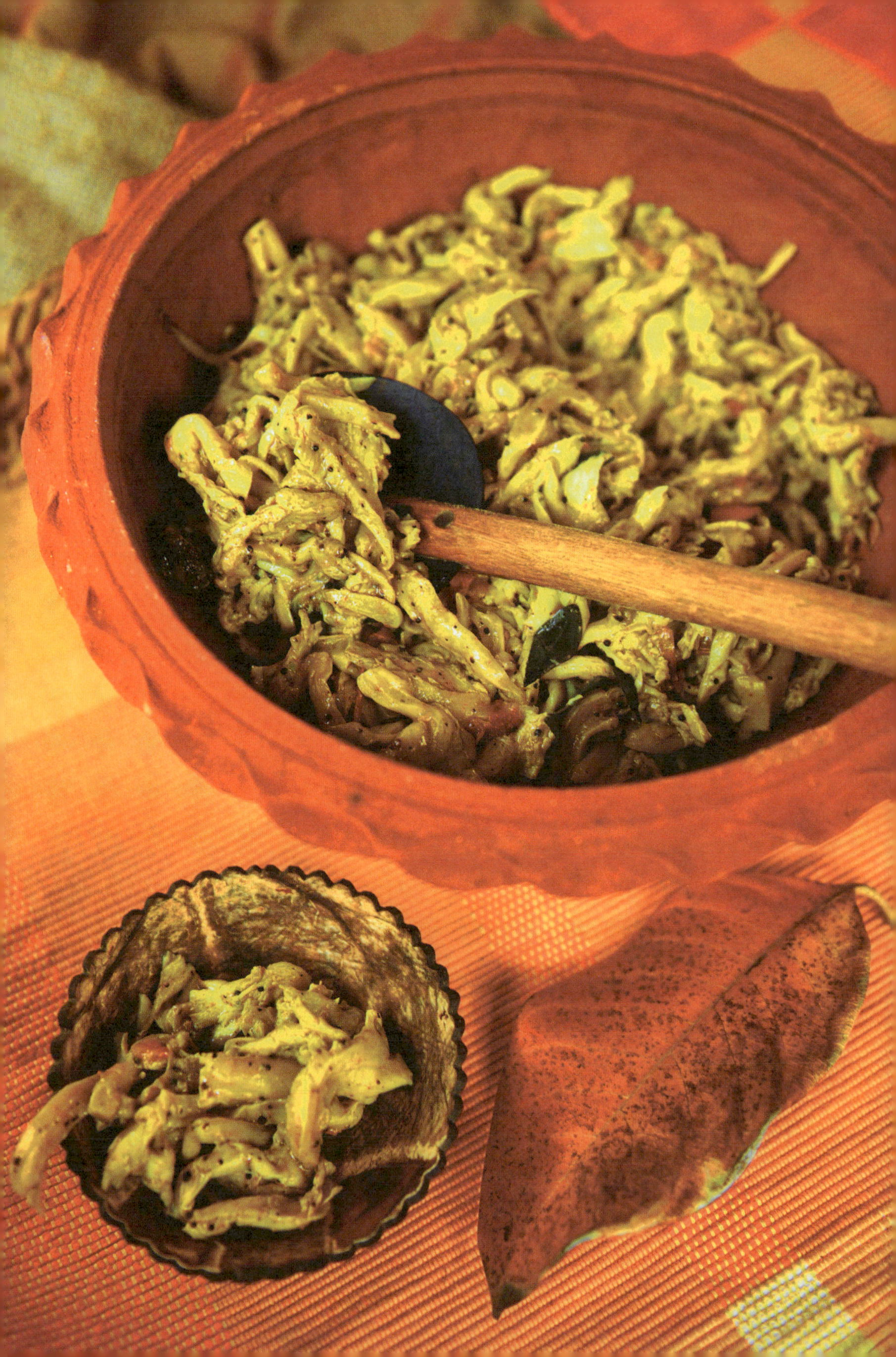

MUSHROOM CURRY

Use girole mushrooms if you can find them, or a medley of different varieties. In this recipe I've used Portobello mushrooms and instead of curry leaves fresh bay leaves.

SERVES FOUR TO SIX

1/2 teaspoon fennel seeds

1/2 teaspoon fenugreek seeds

1/2 teaspoon ground nutmeg

1/2 teaspoon cumin seeds

1/2 teaspoon of ground cumin

3 dessertspoons of coconut oil

500g mushrooms sliced

1 red chilli, deseeded and finely chopped

4 shallots, finely chopped

2 fresh bay leaves

Sea salt flakes

Heat the spices in a heavy-based frying pan, tossing them around until they become a couple of hues darker in colour. Remove from the heat and grind in a pestle and mortar until the spices are fine.

In a heavy-based frying pan add the coconut oil. Sauté the shallots followed by the mushrooms with the chilli, bay leaves and ground spices. Mix well and cook on a low heat until the mushrooms are cooked and have absorbed the spicy flavours.

Season well with salt and serve warm.

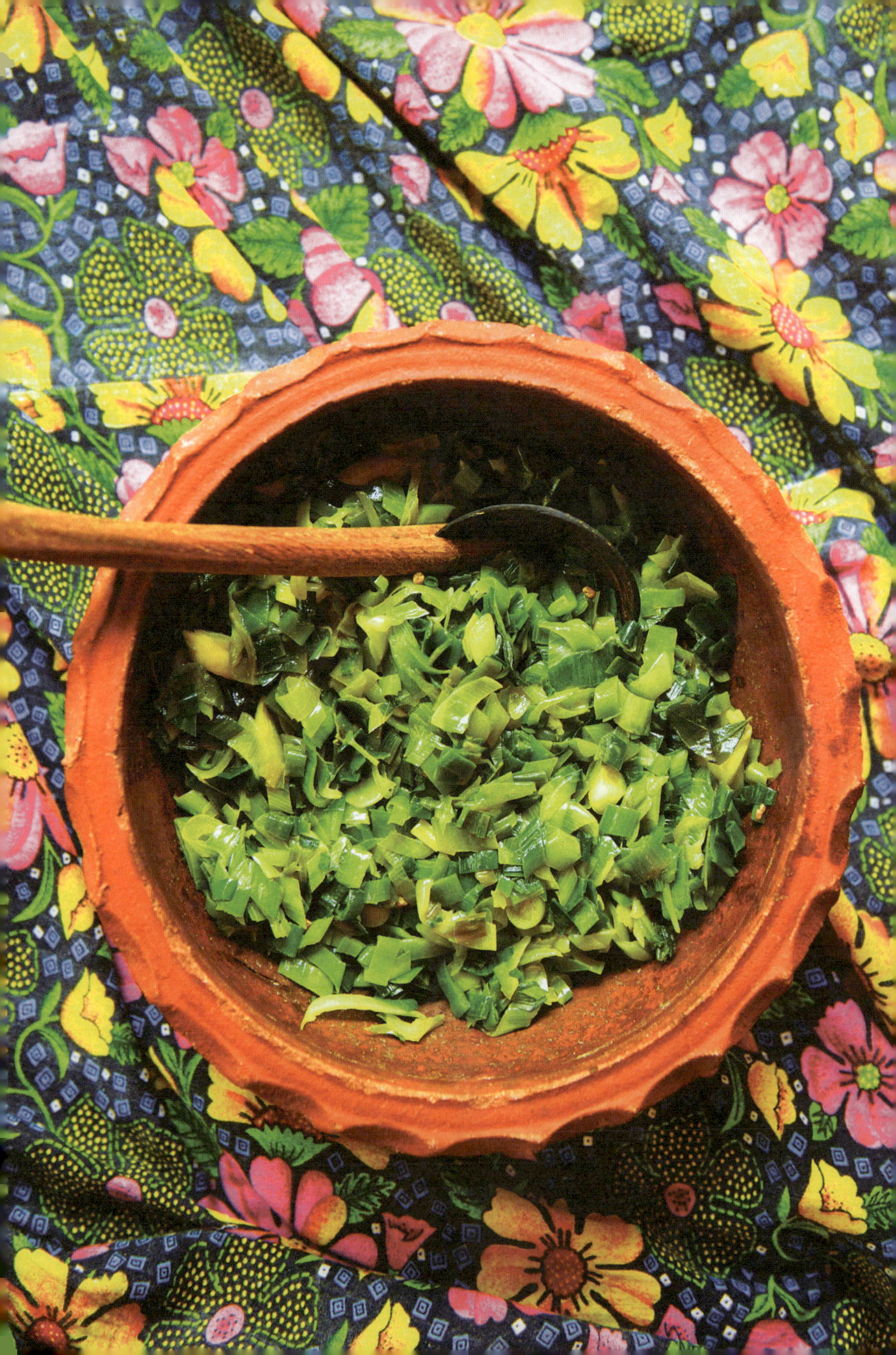

LEEK CURRY

Leeks display such a variety of greens and are delicious in all their guises. A flash of red from the tomatoes makes this such a tempting dish. The colour of food is like the paint on an artist's palette, ready to lure you in while giving anticipation to your taste buds.

SERVES FOUR TO SIX

4 leeks, sliced or diced

1 large tomato
finely chopped

3 dessertspoons of coconut oil

400ml coconut milk

1 teaspoon of turmeric

1 pinch fenugreek seed

Sea salt flakes

Freshly ground black peppercorns

In a saucepan, melt the coconut oil.

Sauté the leeks, then the tomato and add the fenugreek seed.

When the ingredients seem quite dry and have absorbed the oil, add the coconut milk, turmeric and cook for a further five minutes.

Season well with salt and pepper.

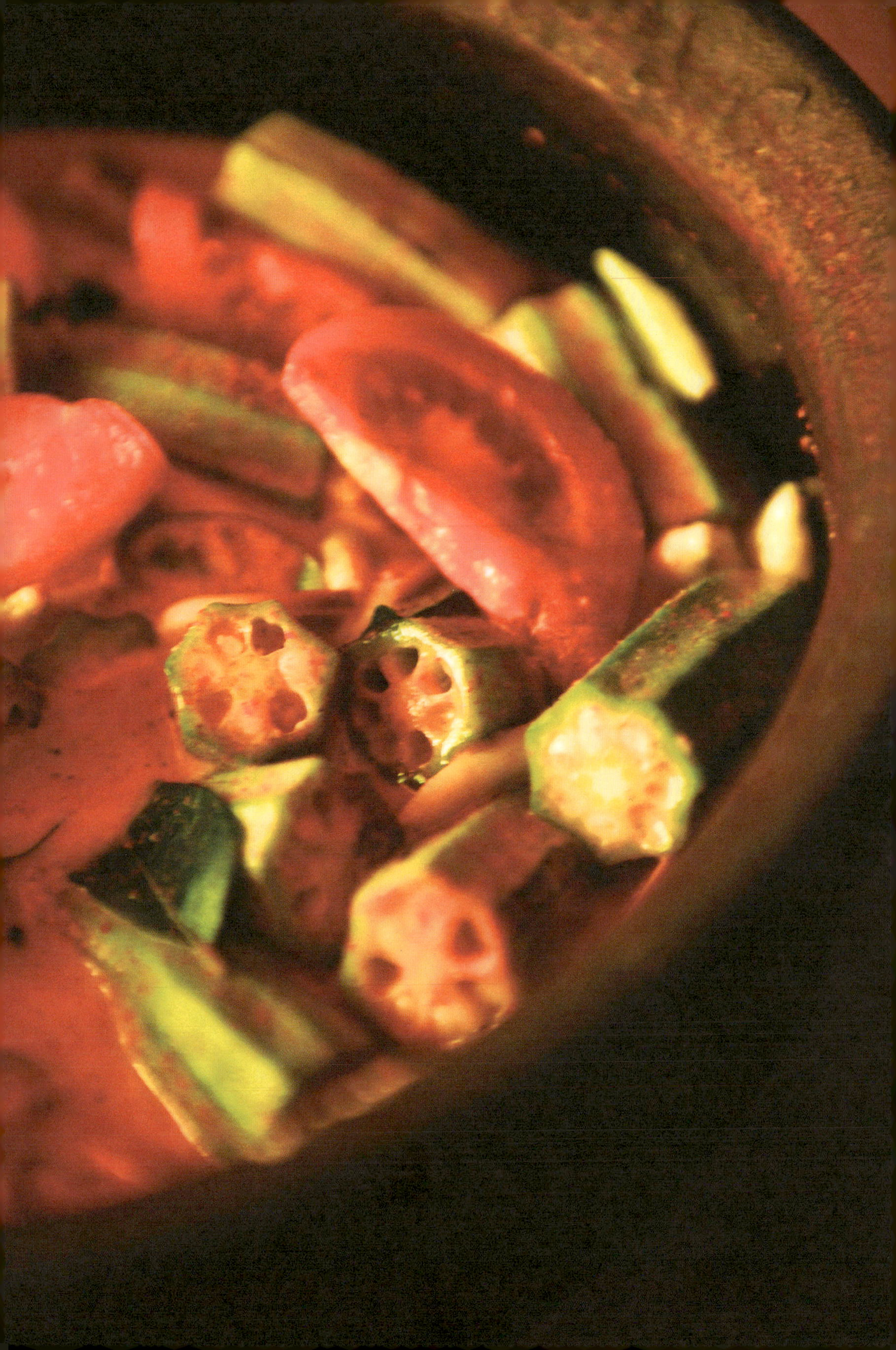

OKRA CURRY

I find Okra a hard vegetable to get right but somehow Sri Lankans manage to make a delicious curry of it.

SERVES FOUR TO SIX

2 dessertspoons of coconut oil

500g okra, roughly sliced

6 shallots, finely chopped

3 tomatoes, finely chopped

1 teaspoon of mustard seed

1 teaspoon turmeric

Sea salt flakes

In a heavy-based frying pan add the coconut oil, sauté the okra until soft. Remove from the oil and place in a serving dish.

In a clean frying pan, add the coconut oil. Sauté the shallots and garlic until soft, then add the tomato, turmeric and mustard seed.

Cook for a further few minutes, season to taste, then add to the okra in the serving dish.

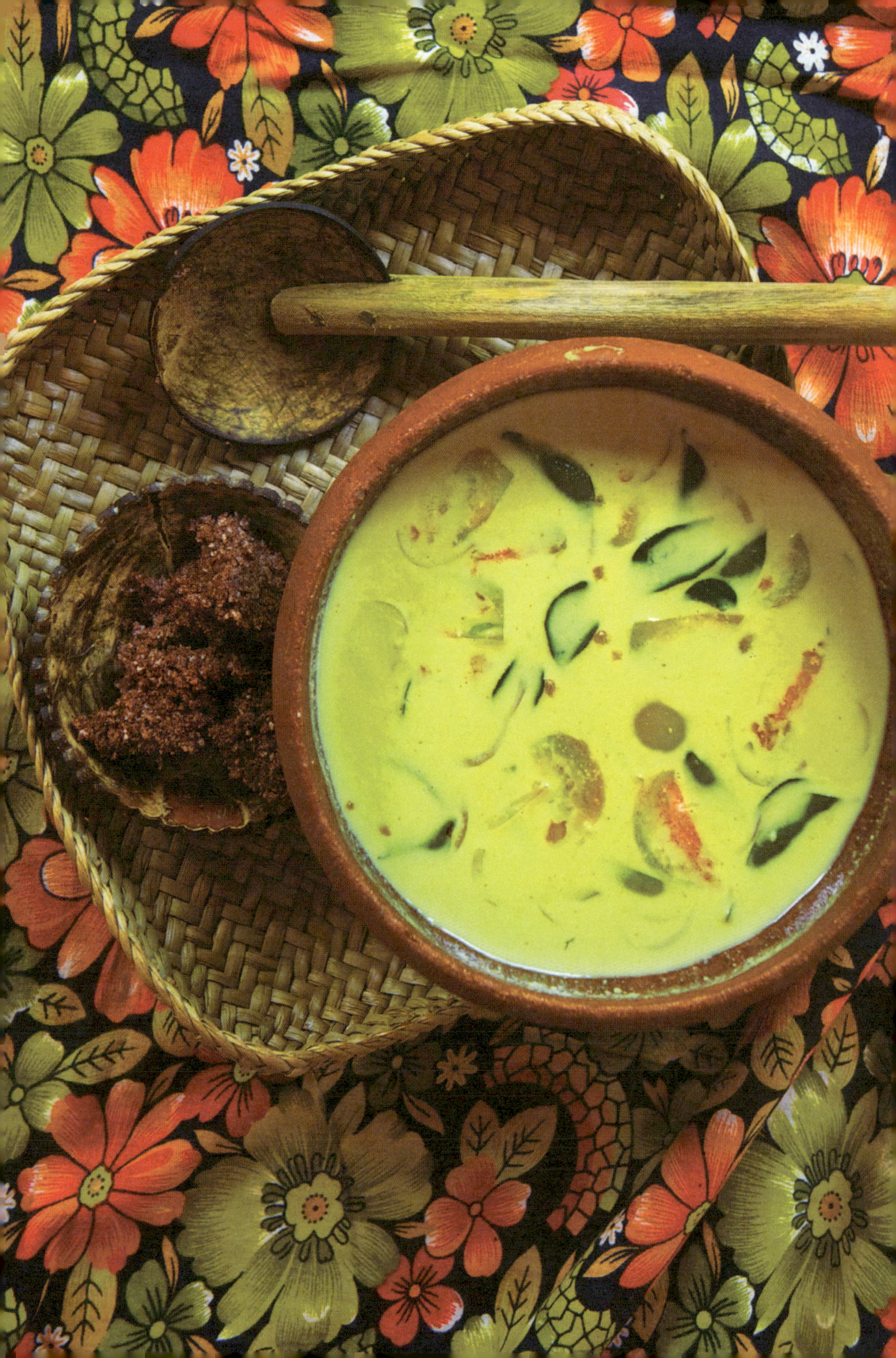

THAKKALI
TOMATO CURRY

Hunt down delicious sweet tomatoes. It doesn't matter if they are plum, cherry, or vine ripened, just make sure they are the best you can get your hands on.

SERVES FOUR TO SIX

2 dessertspoons coconut oil

2 cloves garlic, crushed

2 onions cut in half moons

6 ripe tomatoes roughly chopped

1 small red pepper, cut into slivers

1 heaped teaspoon of turmeric

10 fresh curry leaves

Fragrant curry powder (see recipe on page 115)

400ml coconut milk

Sea salt flakes

1 dessertspoon of coconut cream

1 handful of desiccated coconut

A handful of fresh basil leaves

In a large heavy-based saucepan, add the coconut oil, heat and sauté the onions and garlic, add the turmeric and curry leaves. Sauté a little longer, all the ingredients should be well coated.

Add the tomatoes and peppers, followed by the curry powder. Mix together well.

Add the coconut milk, stir and cover. Bring up to simmering; cook until the tomatoes are soft.

Season generously with salt, add the coconut cream and desiccated coconut. Integrate well.

Remove from heat, serve decorated with fresh basil.

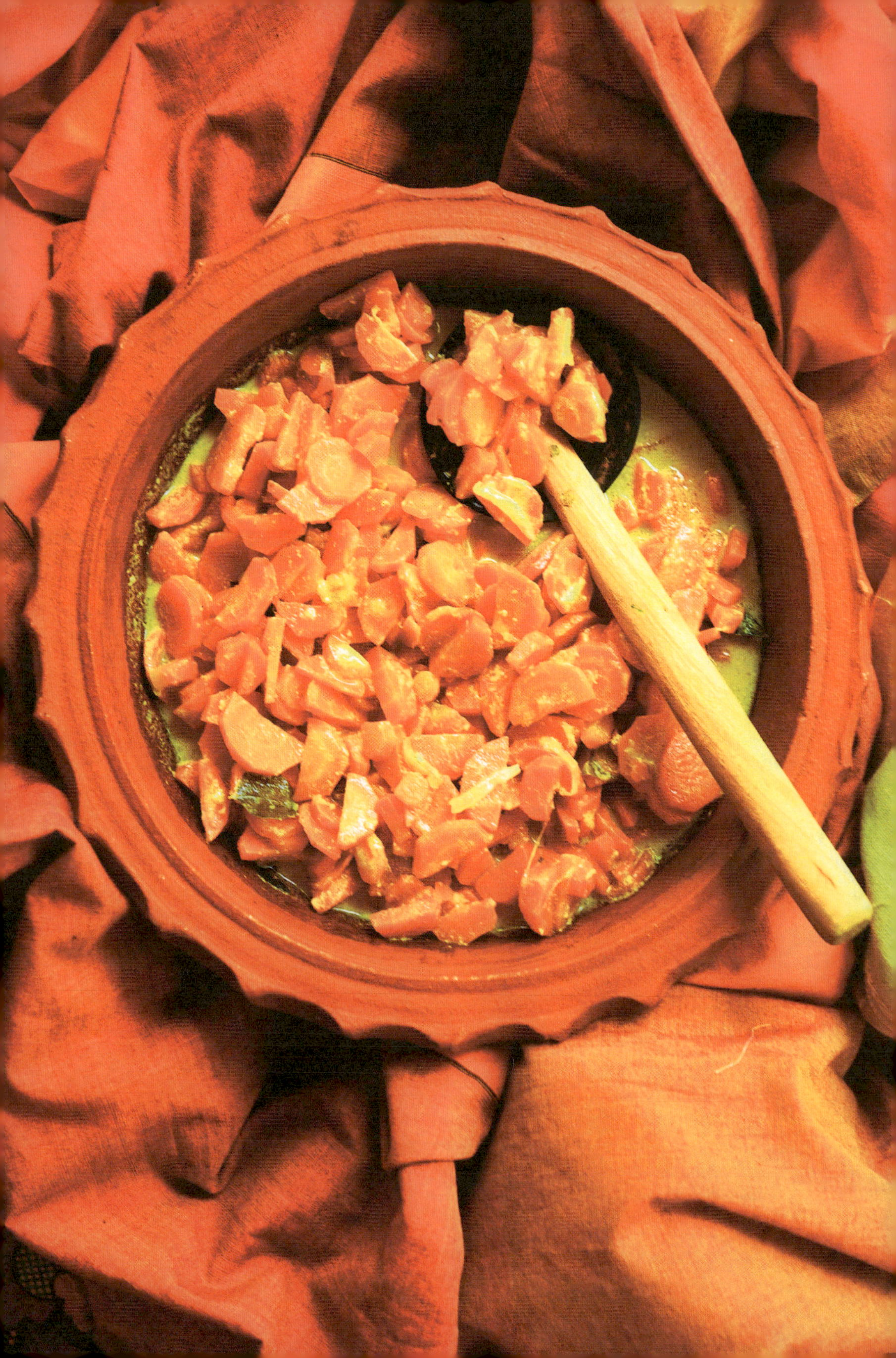

CARROT CURRY

This is a beautiful looking dish with the carrots a vibrant orange against the saffron-coloured sauce. If you want more of a kick, add some chopped chilli, but I rather like the gentle flavour of the cinnamon and onions.

SERVES FOUR TO SIX

5 carrots thinly sliced

2 white onions cut into fine half moons

1/2 teaspoon of fenugreek seeds

1 cinnamon stick

2 garlic cloves finely crushed

1 small handful of curry leaves, about 10 or 12, fresh if possible

1/4 teaspoon of turmeric

400ml coconut milk

A large pinch of sea salt flakes

1 handful of fresh coriander leaves

In a medium heavy-based saucepan, or ceramic fireproof dish, add all the ingredients except the salt and coriander.

Mix well and on a low heat bring gently to simmer. After a few minutes when the carrots and onions are a little al dente, season with salt and take off the heat.

Place in a serving dish and sprinkle with coriander leaves.

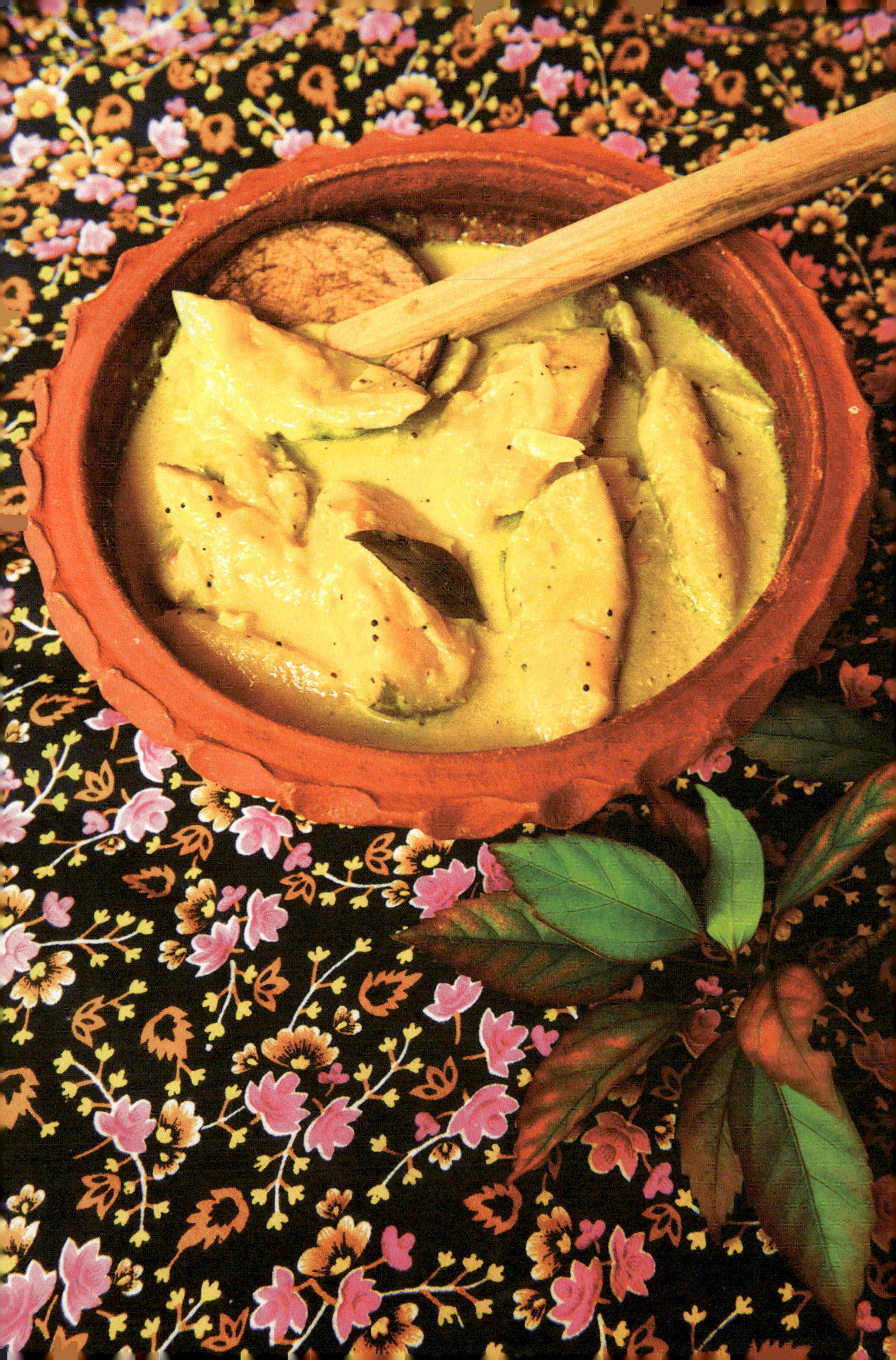

MANGO CURRY

Mangoes have to be in the top ten of my favourite fruit. Cooked, they go into another dimension, losing their tanginess but gaining a lovely slightly sweet and sour flavour. Use the stone as this holds all the flavour as well.

SERVES FOUR TO SIX

2 mangoes, peeled and cut into chunks

1 red onion, cut into rings

1 garlic clove, crushed

1 pinch of cumin powder

1 handful of curry leaves

1 pinch of turmeric

1/2 red chilli, deseeded, finely chopped (optional)

1 teaspoons of jaggery/ muscovado brown sugar

1 cinnamon stick

1 teaspoon of black mustard seeds

2 dessertspoons of coconut oil

400ml coconut milk

In a heavy-based frying pan, add the coconut oil, onion, garlic, cumin, curry leaves, turmeric, chilli and mustard seeds. Sauté until onion is soft.

In a saucepan place the mangoes and stones, cover with coconut milk, add the cinnamon stick and sugar. Stir in the onion mixture.

Simmer for 15 minutes or so until the mango is tender.

Season with salt and remove stones.

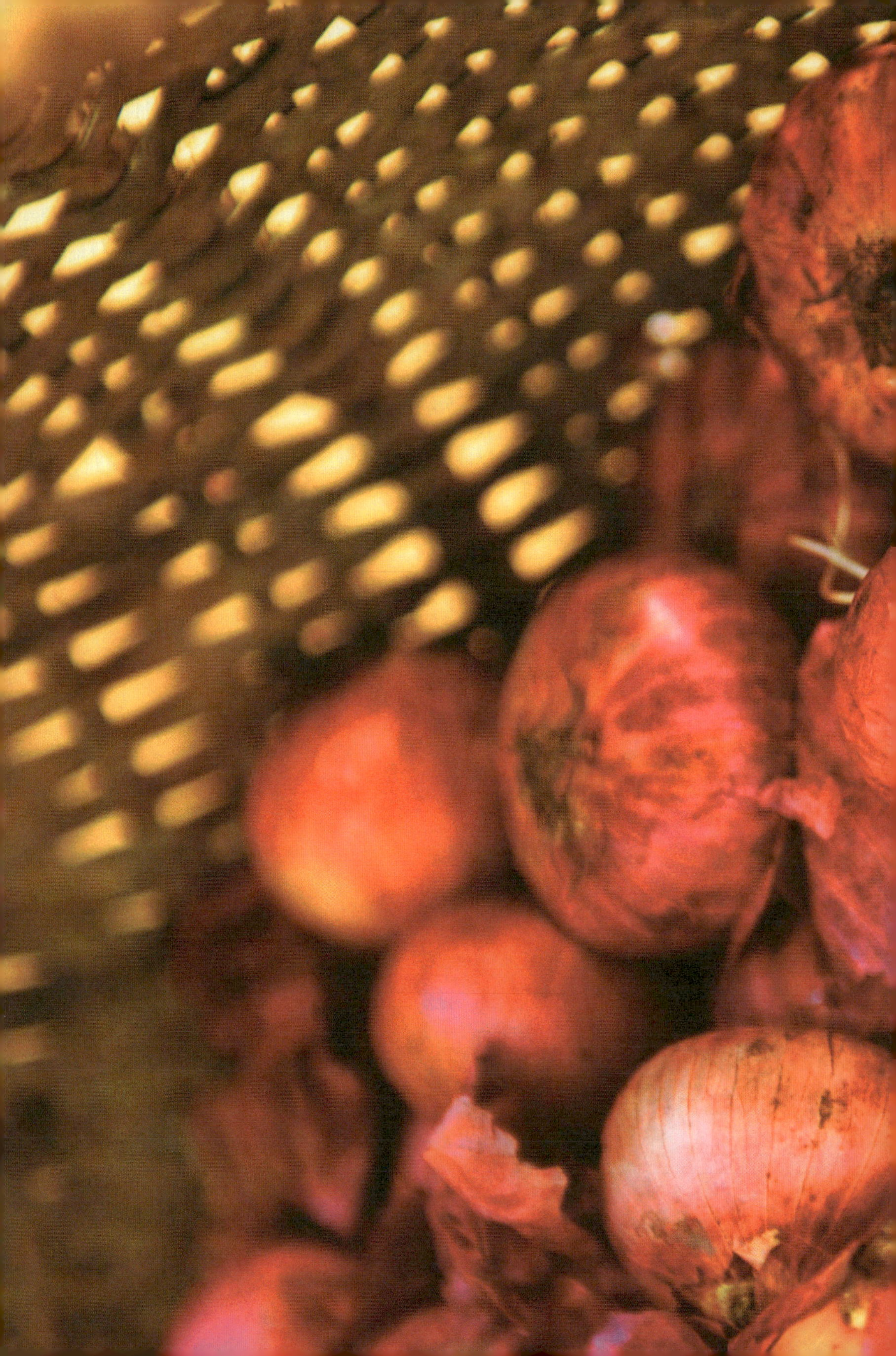

SAMBOLS & CHUTNEYS

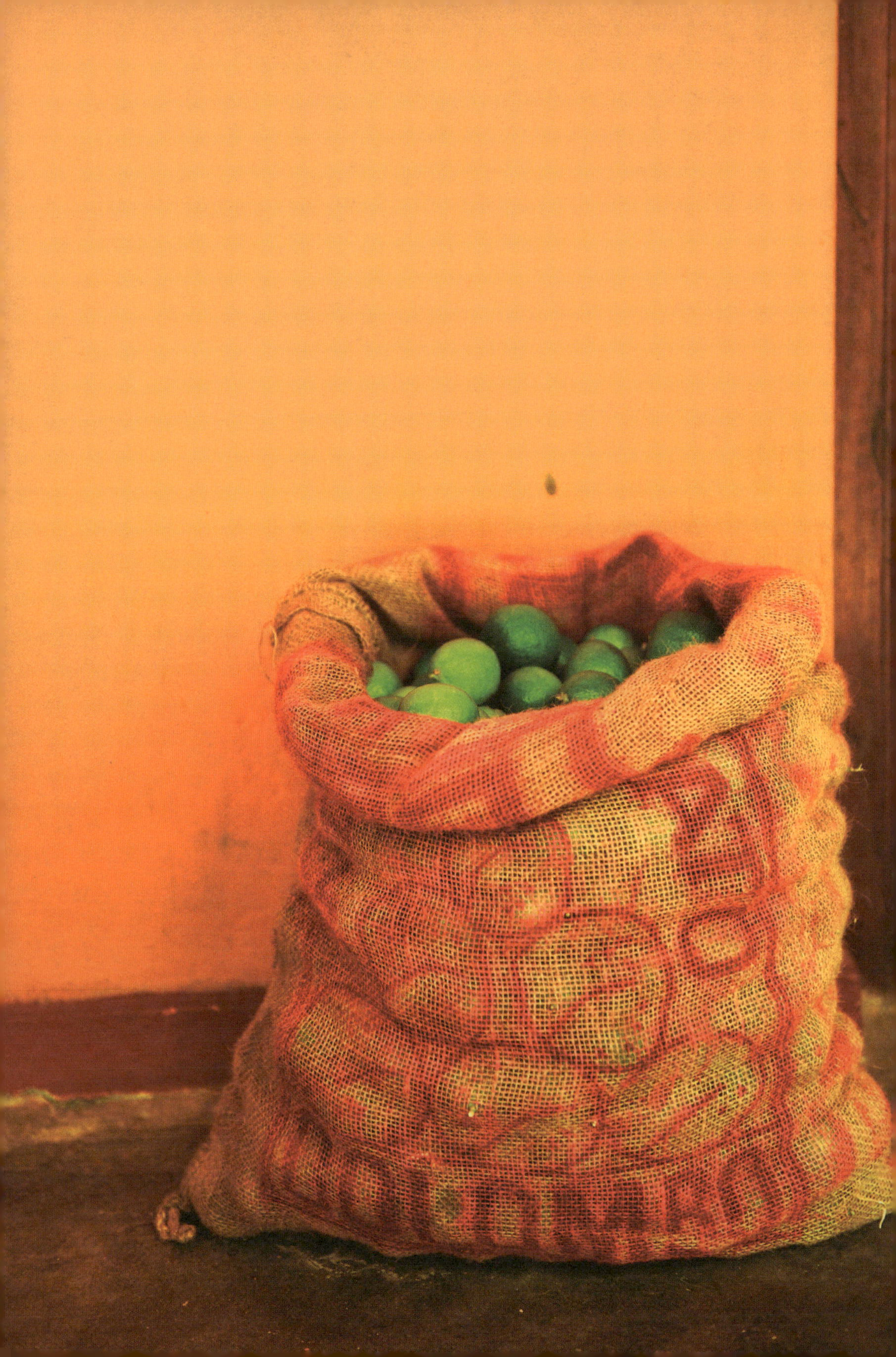

MINT & LIME SAMBOL

Sambols are the accessories to food, they aren't necessary but totally enhance the meal. I added red peppercorns, not just for their colour but also for an extra dynamic. They need to be moist in texture.

SERVES FOUR TO SIX

250g of desiccated/fresh coconut

2 shallots, finely chopped

1/2 green chilli, deseeded finely chopped

2 limes, juiced

1 handful of fresh mint leaves, finely chopped

1 pinch of red peppercorns

1 large pinch of sea salt flakes

In a mortar pound all the ingredients well, taste.

Add more seasoning or more lime to taste and serve as an accompaniment.

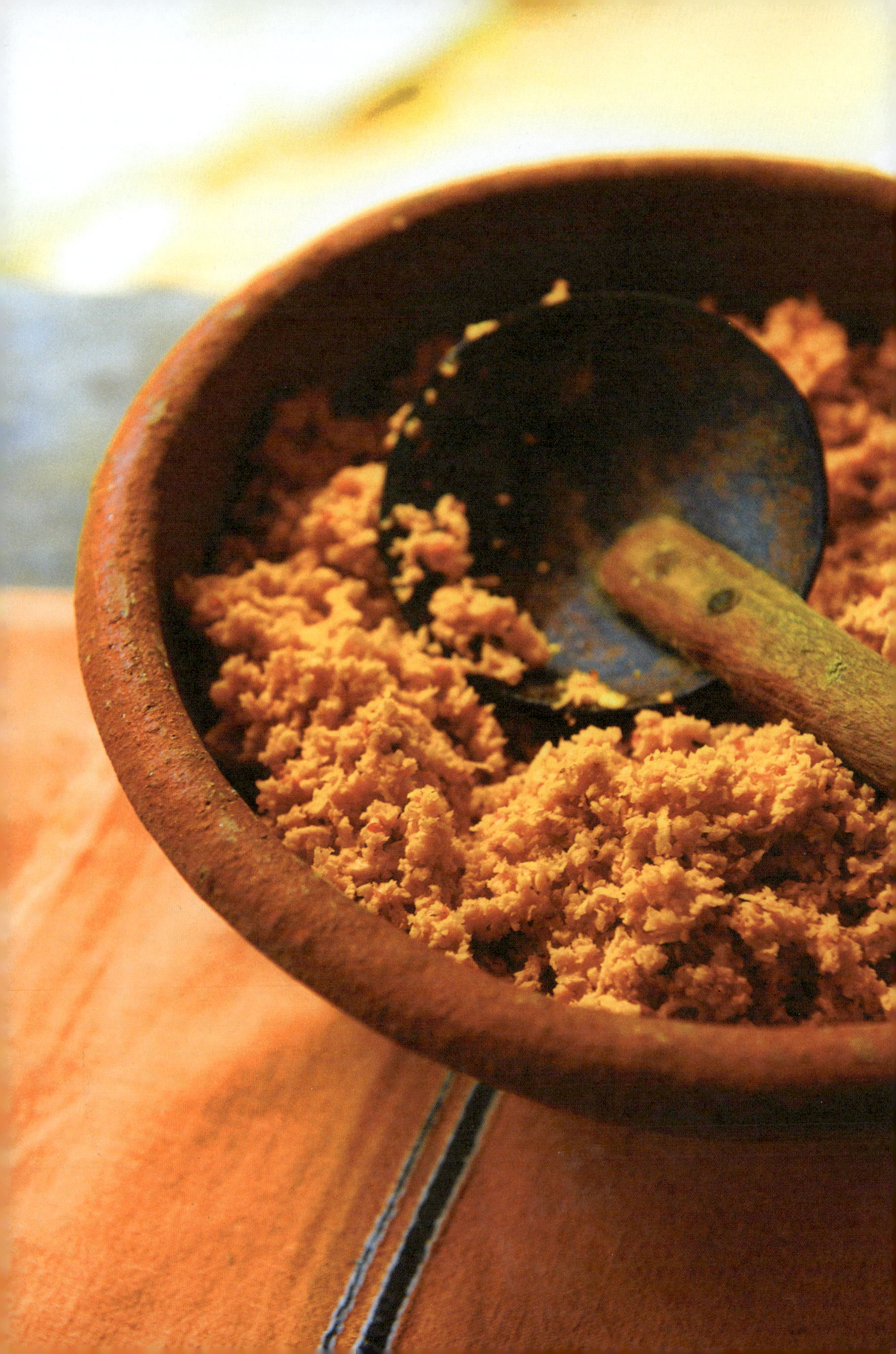

POL SAMBOL

Pol Sambol is basically coconut sambol. To give it the traditional orange colour add more paprika, rather than chilli powder as this might be a little too fiery for a western tongue. If the desiccated coconut is too dry, soak in coconut milk for an hour or so and then squeeze out any excess liquid.

SERVES FOUR TO SIX

250g desiccated/fresh coconut

1/2 teaspoon of chilli powder

1 teaspoon of paprika

2 shallots, finely chopped

2 limes, juiced

Sea salt flakes

In a mortar, pound all the ingredients together well and season to taste.

Serve as an accompaniment.

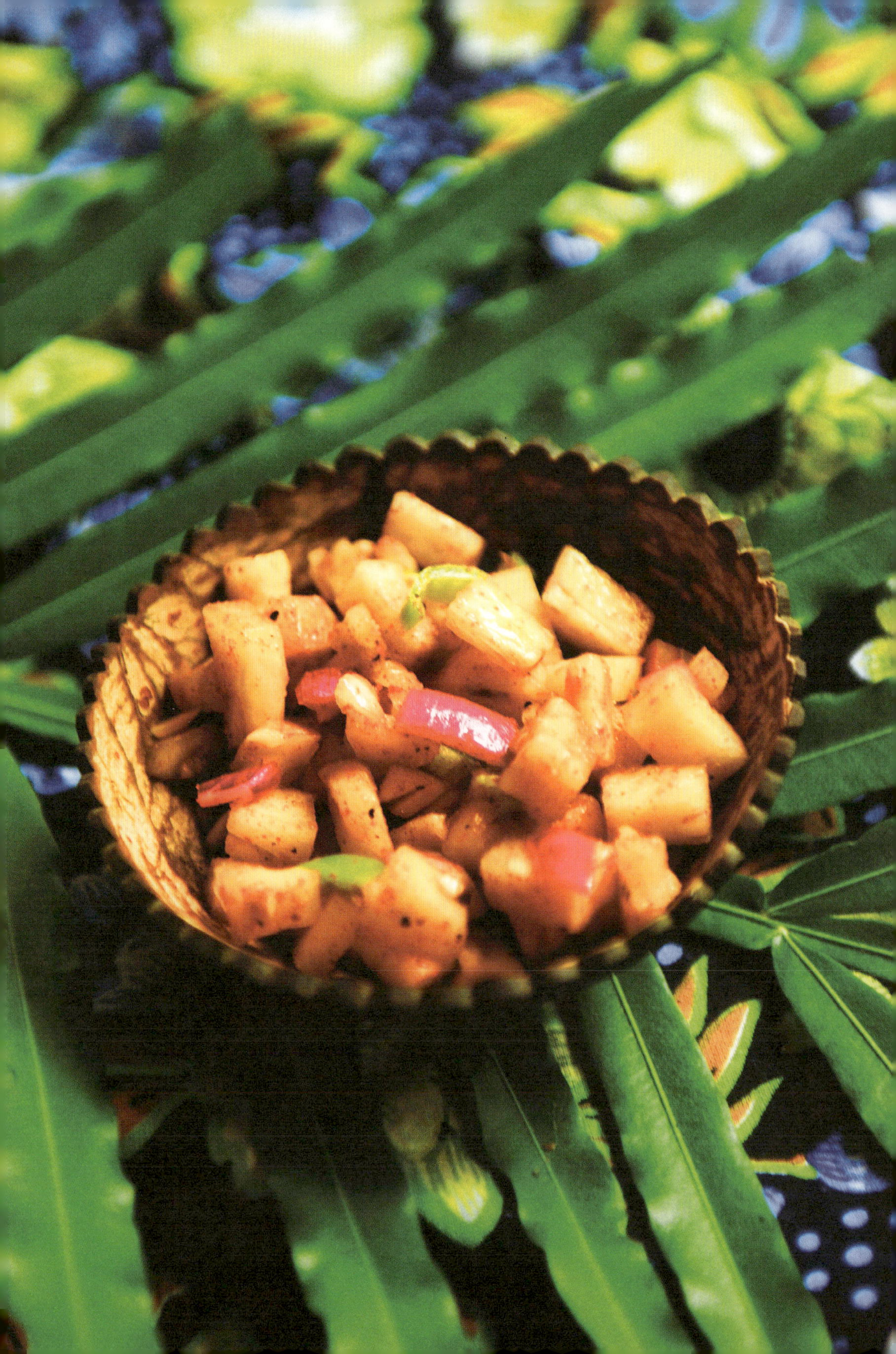

PINEAPPLE & CHILLI CHUTNEY

This is a delicious zingy little side dish to serve with any of the curries or dishes.

SERVES FOUR TO SIX

1 medium ripe pineapple peeled, cored & chopped

1 pinch of chilli powder

1 small green pepper, seeded, finely chopped

1/2 white onion roughly chopped

8 green beans, finely chopped, blanched for 1 minute, cooled

1 tablespoon grated jaggery or muscovado brown sugar

1 tablespoon lime juice

Sea salt flakes

Combine all ingredients well and season to taste.

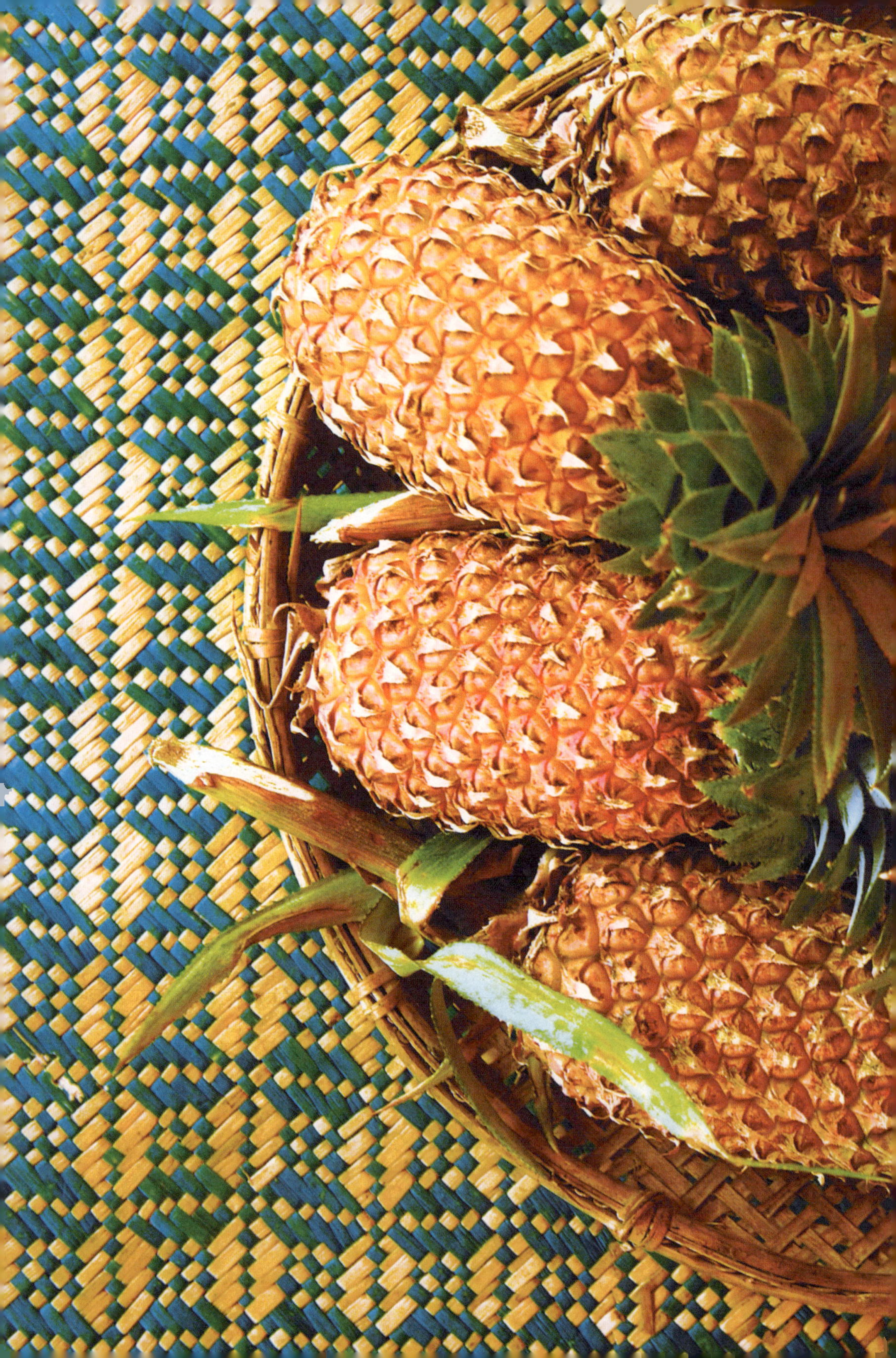

PUDDINGS

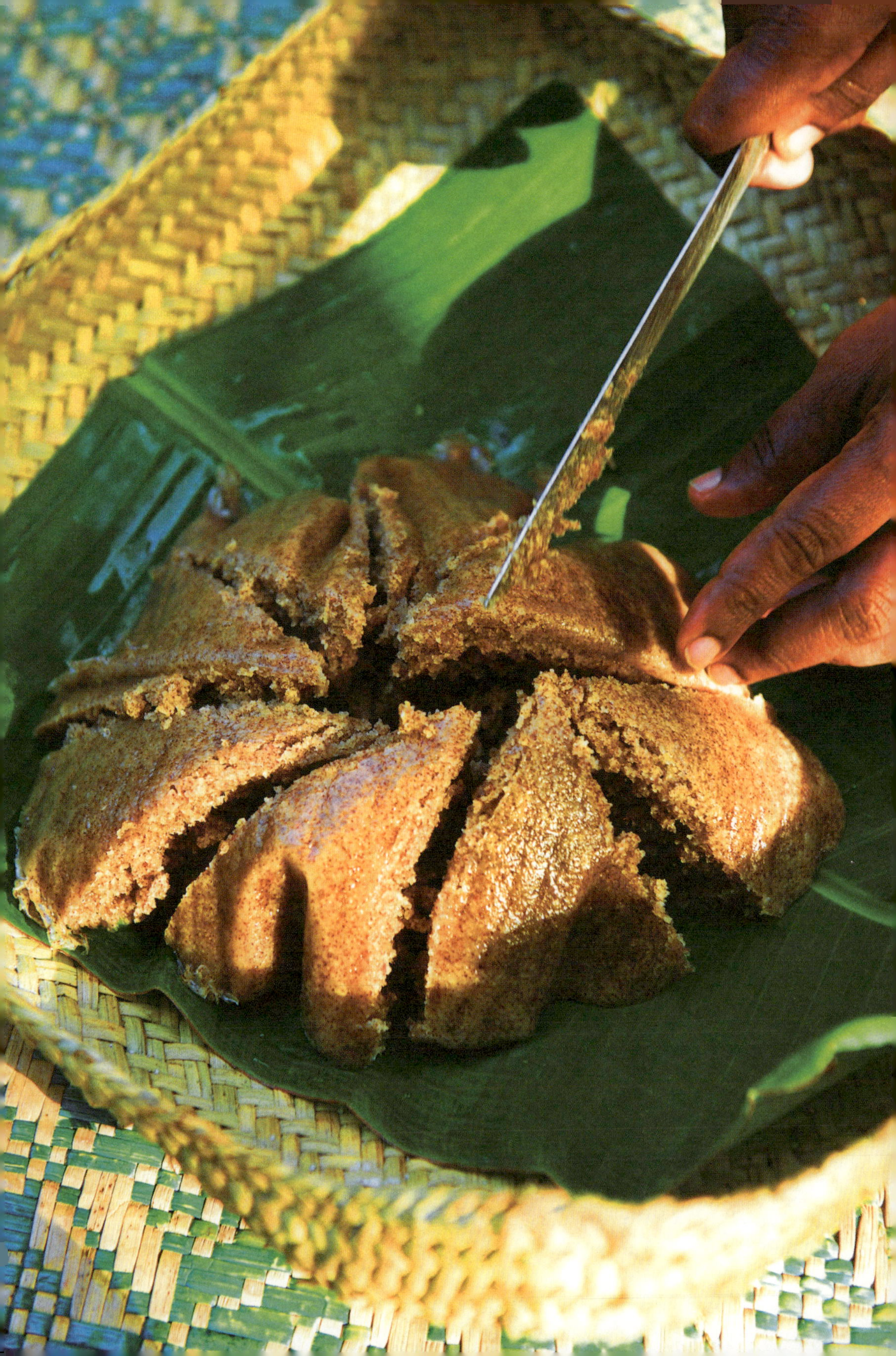

COCONUT CAKE

This is usually wrapped in a banana leaf and steamed over a clay pot of bubbling hot water. I used a tea towel instead. This is delicious served at breakfast with mashed banana.

SERVES FOUR TO FIVE

50g of rice flour and enough water to make a dough

200g fresh grated/ desiccated coconut

6 tablespoons tree syrup

200ml coconut milk

Place the rice flour in a large mixing bowl, make a well in the middle and add enough water to make a smooth paste.

Mix together the grated coconut and the tree syrup in a frying pan and cook well for about 10 minutes on a low heat. Then add to the rice dough. Stir in the coconut milk.

Fill a large saucepan a third full with water. Place a colander on top. Line the colander with a thin tea towel or muslin cloth. Pour on the mixture, fold over the ends of the tea towel. Place a lid on top and steam for 30 minutes or until the mixture thickens, it will remain gooey. Remove from the colander and gently peel off the tea towel. Serve in slices when cool.

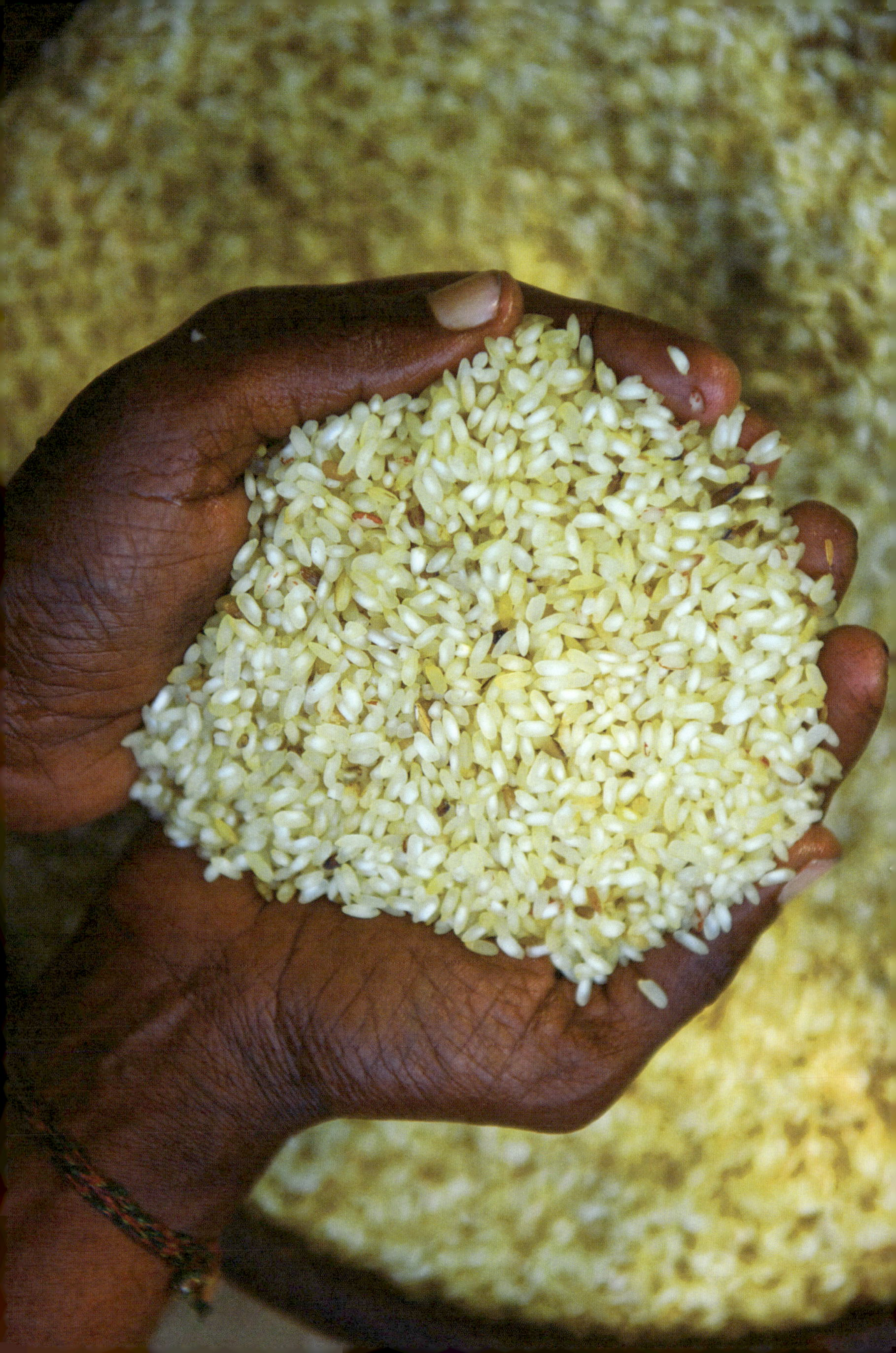

KIRI BATH
MILK RICE

This is a simple tradition of rice cooked in coconut milk. Auspicious Kiri bath is used as the first food on New Year's day as well as the food served on the first of day of each month. If you want to enhance it you can add cinnamon/grated mace, cardamom or raisins. I've given the recipe in its most basic form.

SERVES FOUR

500g long-grain white rice

400ml coconut milk

1 large tablespoon coconut cream

Sea salt flakes

Wash and drain the rice. Place in a heavy-based saucepan. Cover with the coconut milk and a pinch of salt. Cover and bring to simmering point, remove the lid and cook, stirring occasionally until all the milk is absorbed.

Stir in the coconut cream, cook for a few minutes longer. Turn out the rice on to a flat plate.

When cool, cut into squares or diamond shapes.

Serve either warm or cold.

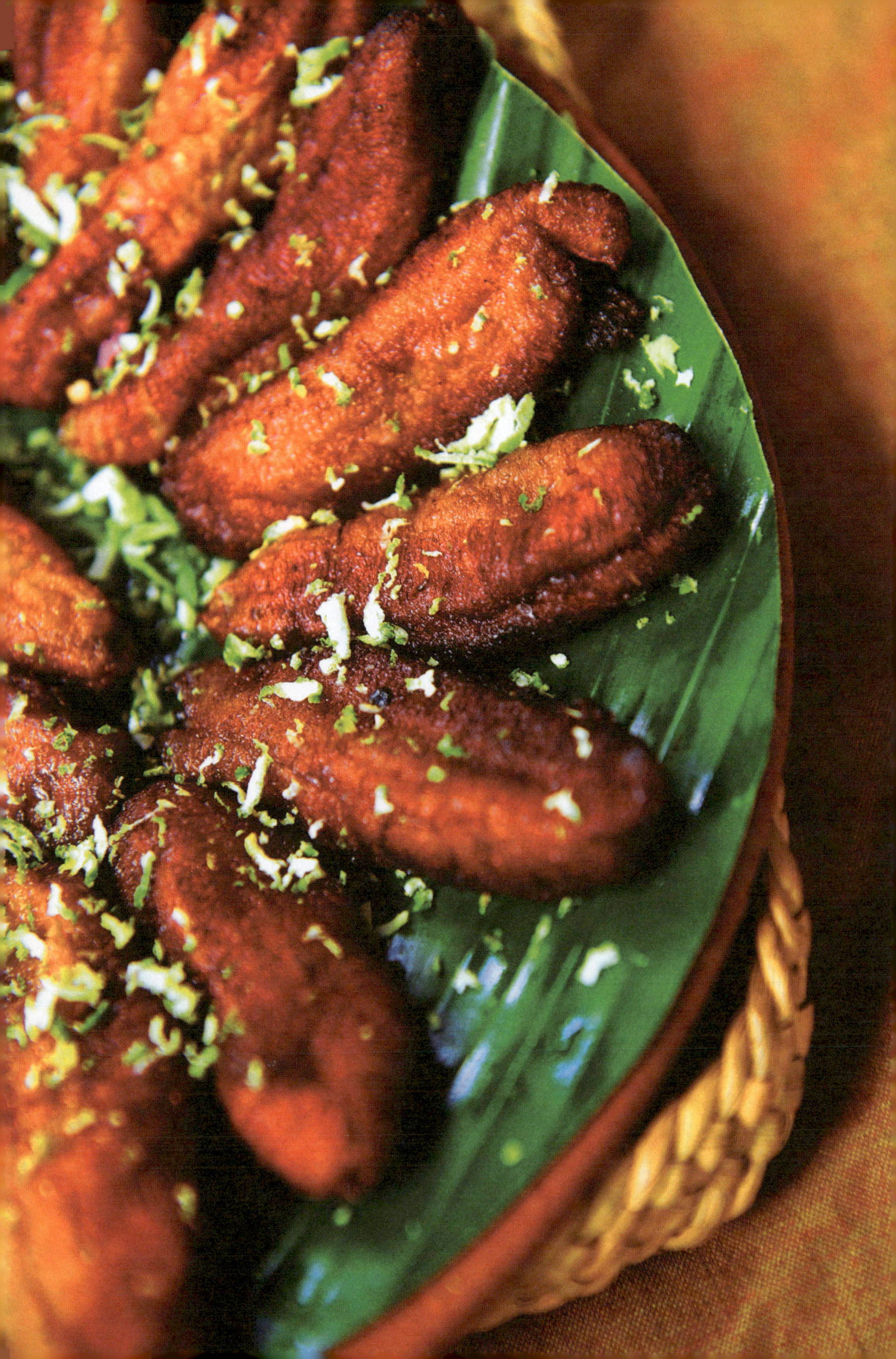

BANANAS WITH CARDAMOM, PISTACHIO & COCONUT

This is a very easy and quick pudding. I like the bananas on the less mushy side. It's delicious with thick yogurt or crème fraîche.

SERVES FOUR

4 bananas, sliced vertically

1 dessertspoon of ghee

1 tablespoon of jaggery/muscovado sugar

A few cardamom seeds, crushed

A handful of desiccated coconut

A handful of pistachios, crushed

In a frying pan melt the ghee on a low heat.

Add the jaggery or muscovado sugar, blend together as best as you can. Lay in the bananas, sprinkle over the coconut and cardamom. Let the bananas cook for a couple of minutes then turn them over.

When they are cooked through but still firm, remove to a serving plate and sprinkle with the pistachios.

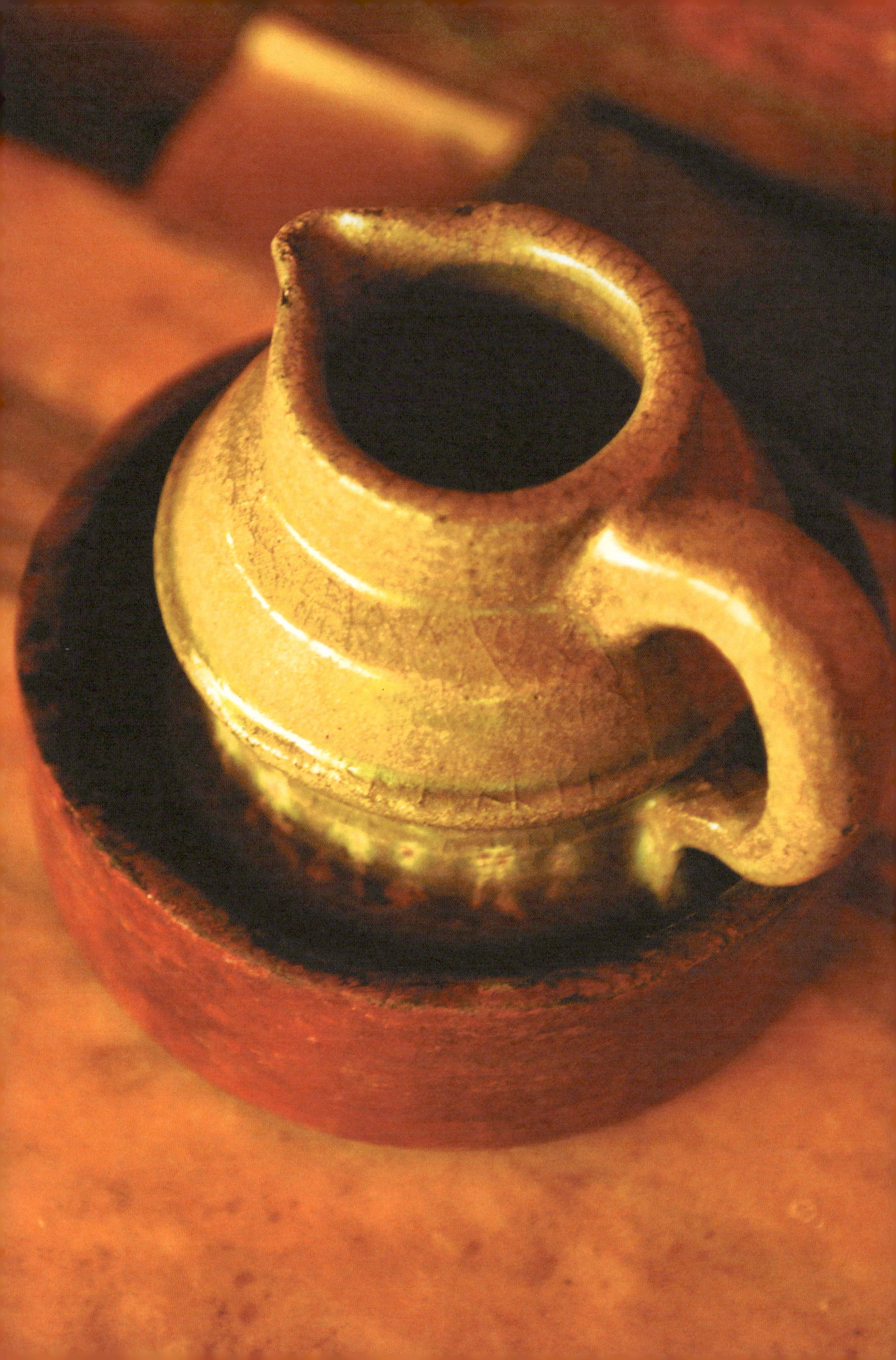

CURD & KITUL TREACLE

Curd, which is like a creamy yogurt, comes from the buffalo. Kitul treacle is a tree sap from the Kitul palm tree. If ever two ingredients were meant to be together, it's these two.

SERVES FOUR

500ml of Greek yoghurt

Tree syrup or maple syrup

I've substituted the curd for Greek yogurt, and I have found tree syrup in my local health food shop, but failing that use maple syrup, and throw some grated or dessicated coconut on top.

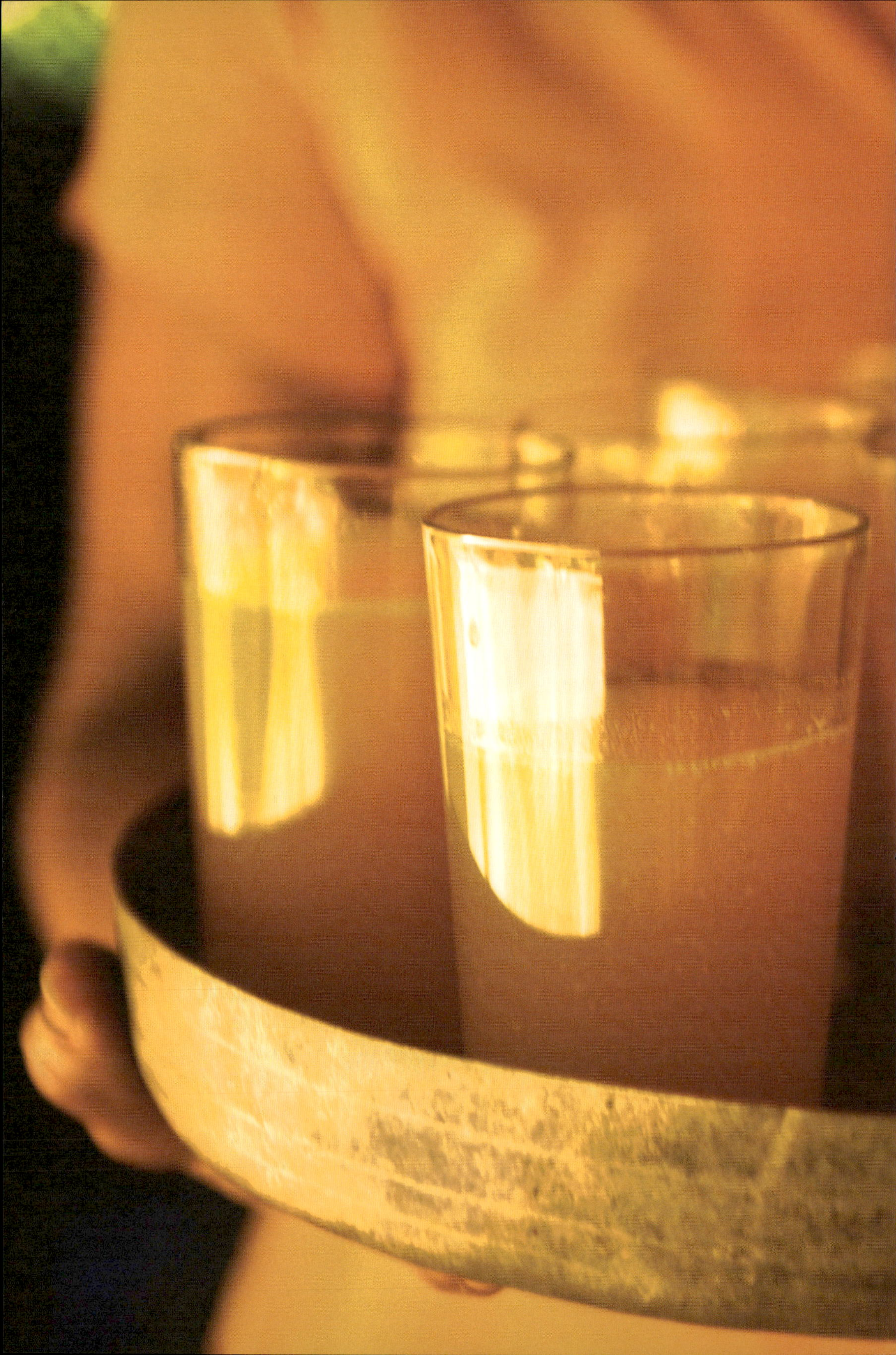

DRINKS

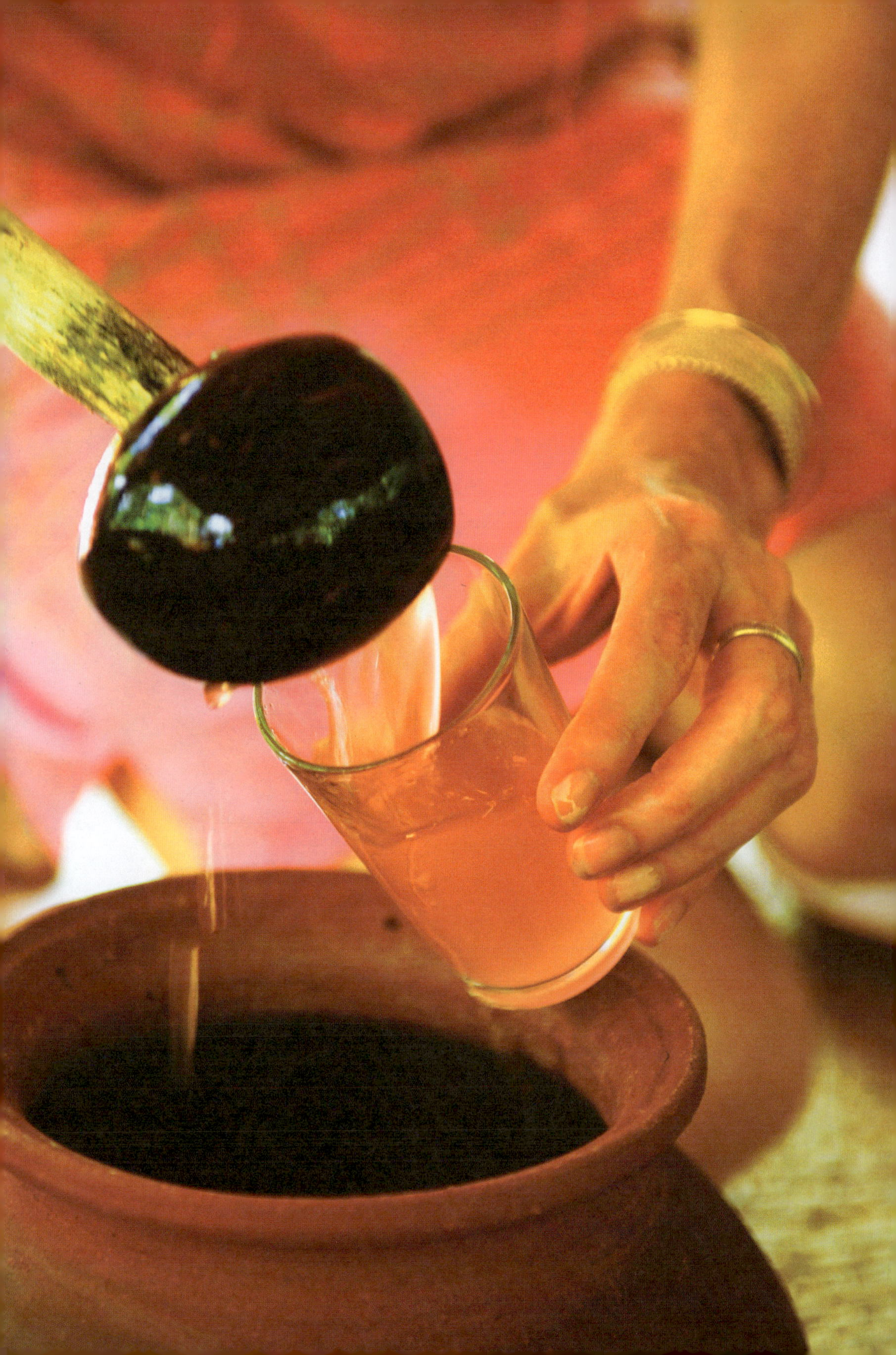

ULPOTHA
WATERMELON JUICE

Because of the heat in Sri Lanka, juices are often made with a little salt. I've omitted this from the recipe. Instead I've added a squeeze of lime, which has a wonderful effect with the sweetness of the watermelon.

SERVES APPROXIMATELY FOUR

1 medium sized water melon seeds removed

1 lime squeezed

Place the watermelon in a blender, juice and blend.

Pour through a sieve into a jug.

Add the fresh lime and serve.

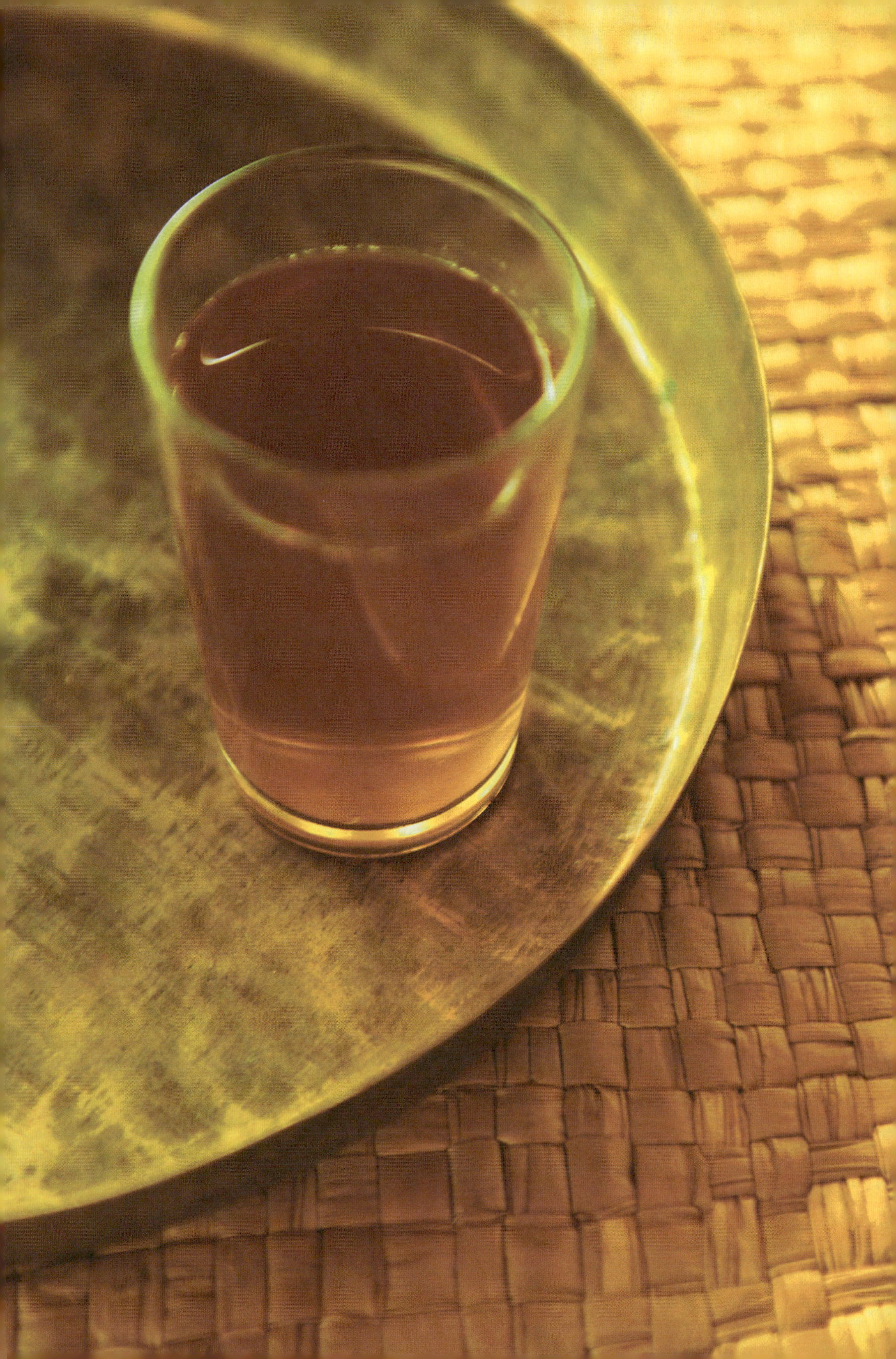

GINGER & LIME TEA

This tea is served after meals and totally hits the spot. I tend to be quite cautious with the amount of ginger and the black tea so as to make it not too strong.

SERVES FOUR

2 teaspoons of loose Ceylon Tea

50g sliced ginger

2 limes, juiced

Boiling water

Pound the ginger in a mortar. Place in a teapot with the lime juice. Add the black tea.

Pour in the boiling water and let sit for five minutes.

Let it cool for another minute or so, strain and serve.

CORIANDER TEA

This tea is soothing on the digestive system.

SERVES FOUR

1/2 cup of coriander seeds washed and dried

Boiling water

In a heavy-based frying pan dry roast the coriander seeds. Whilst the seeds are still hot grind in a pestle and mortar to a powder (extra can be stored for later use).

Place the ground coriander seed in a teapot and pour on the boiling water.

Let brew for five minutes and strain and serve.

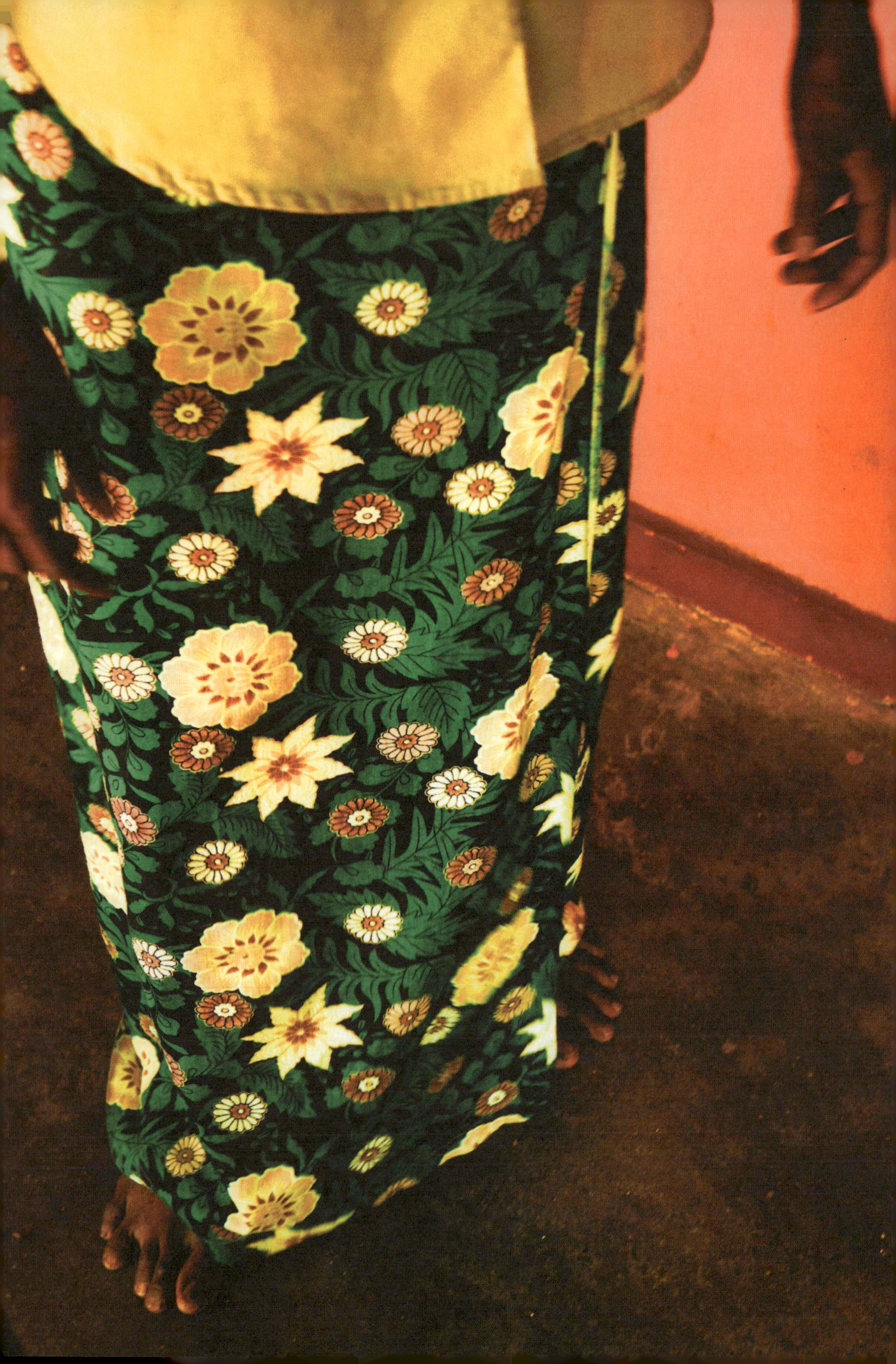

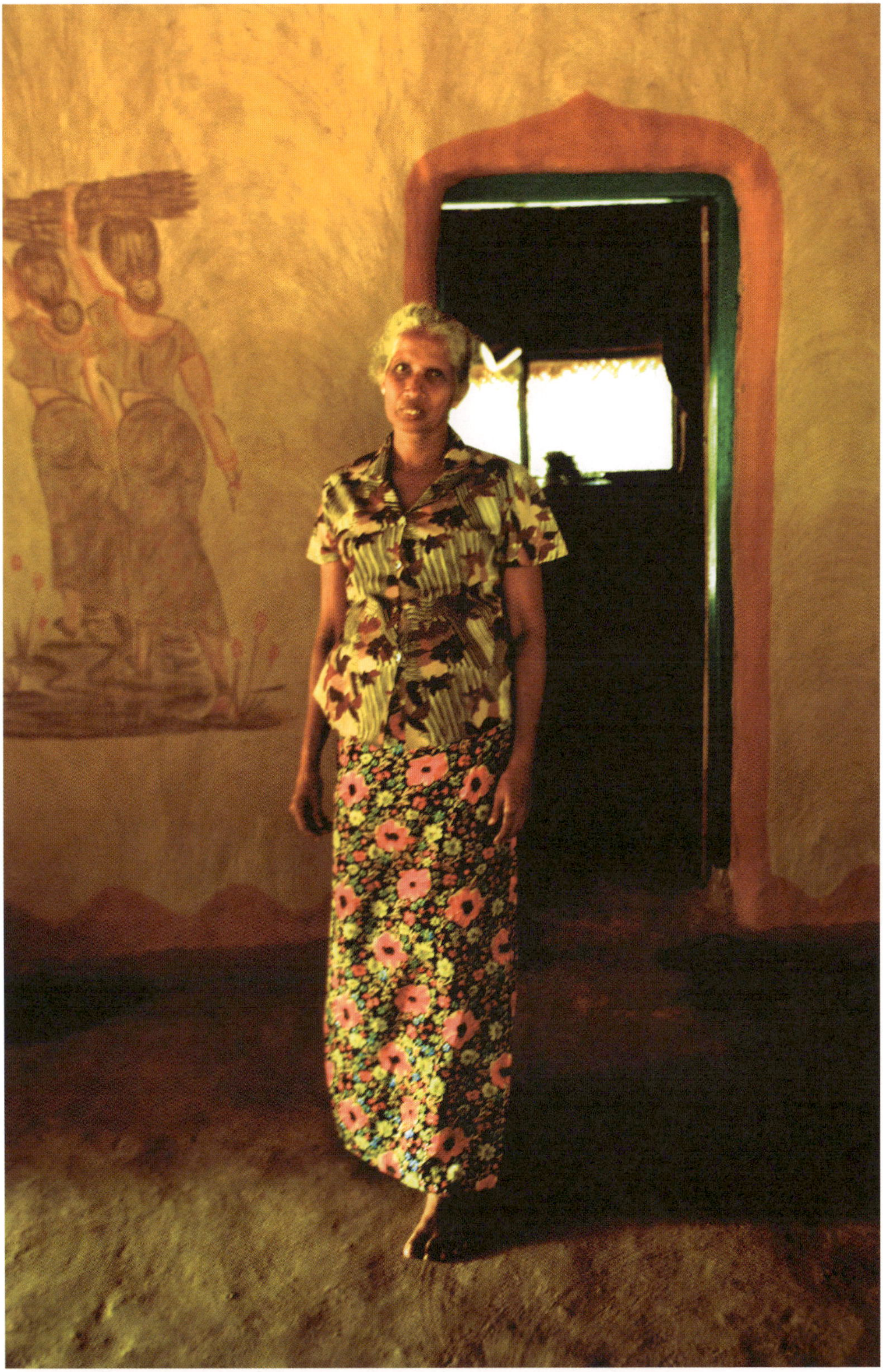

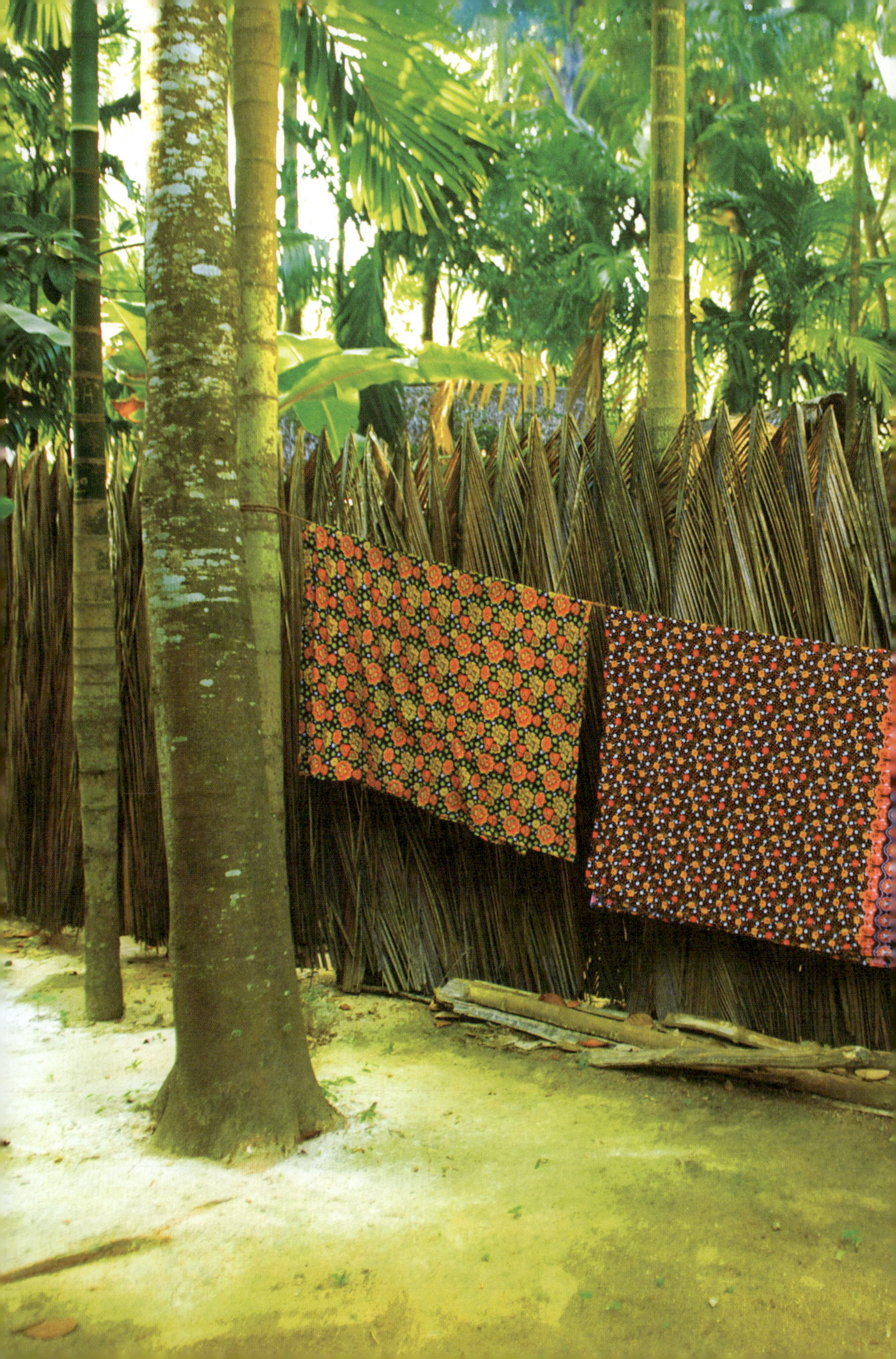

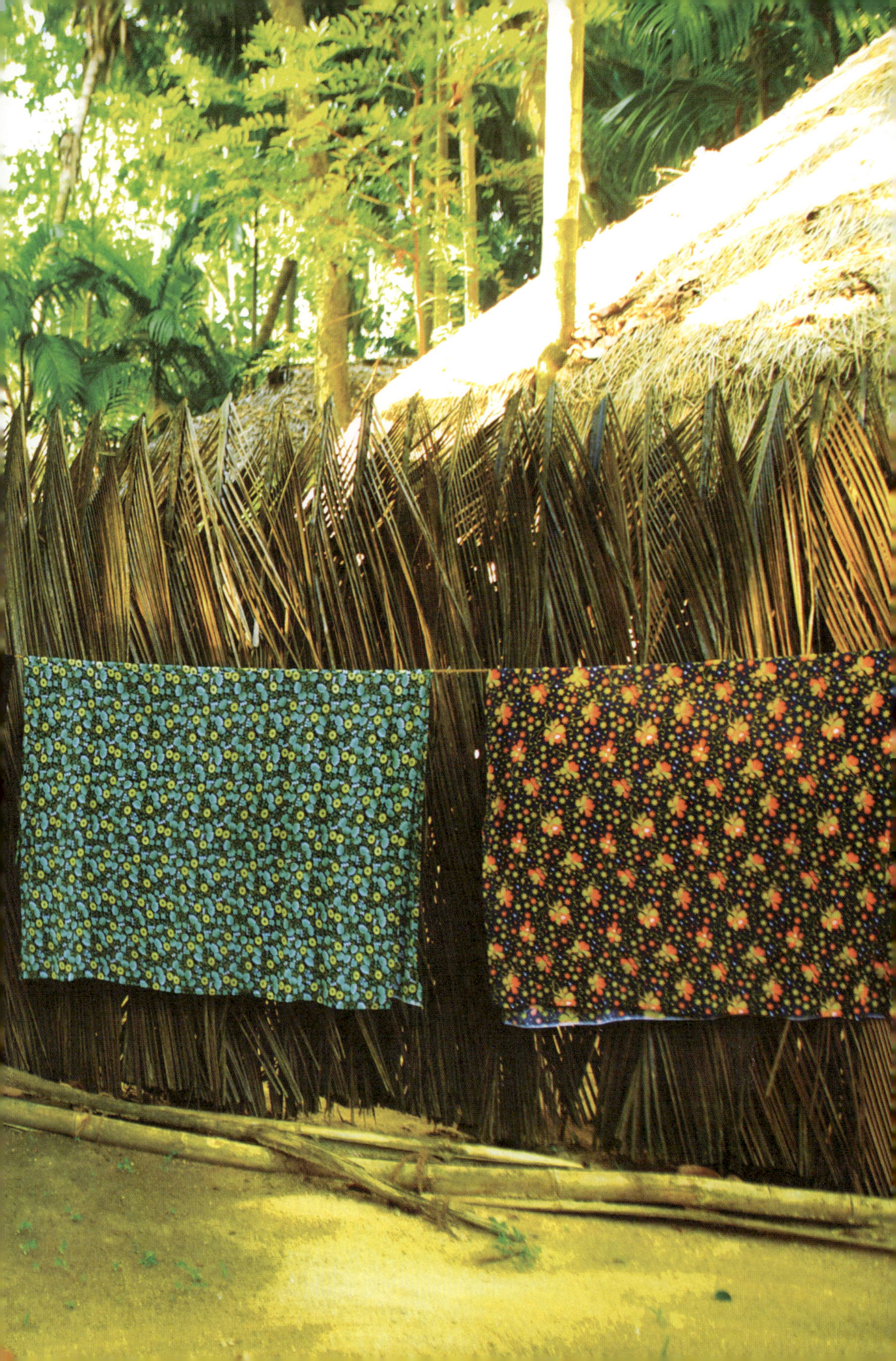

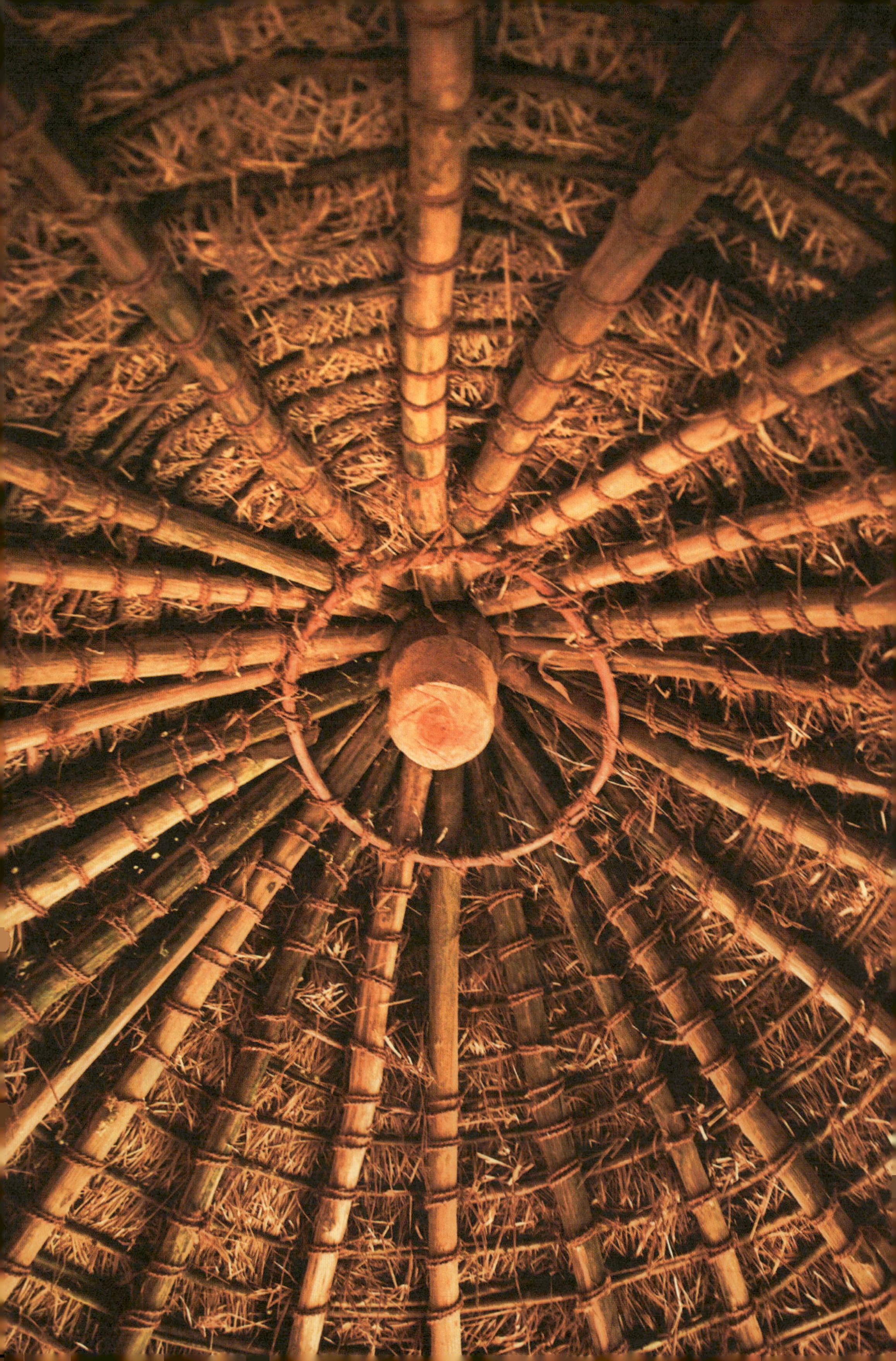

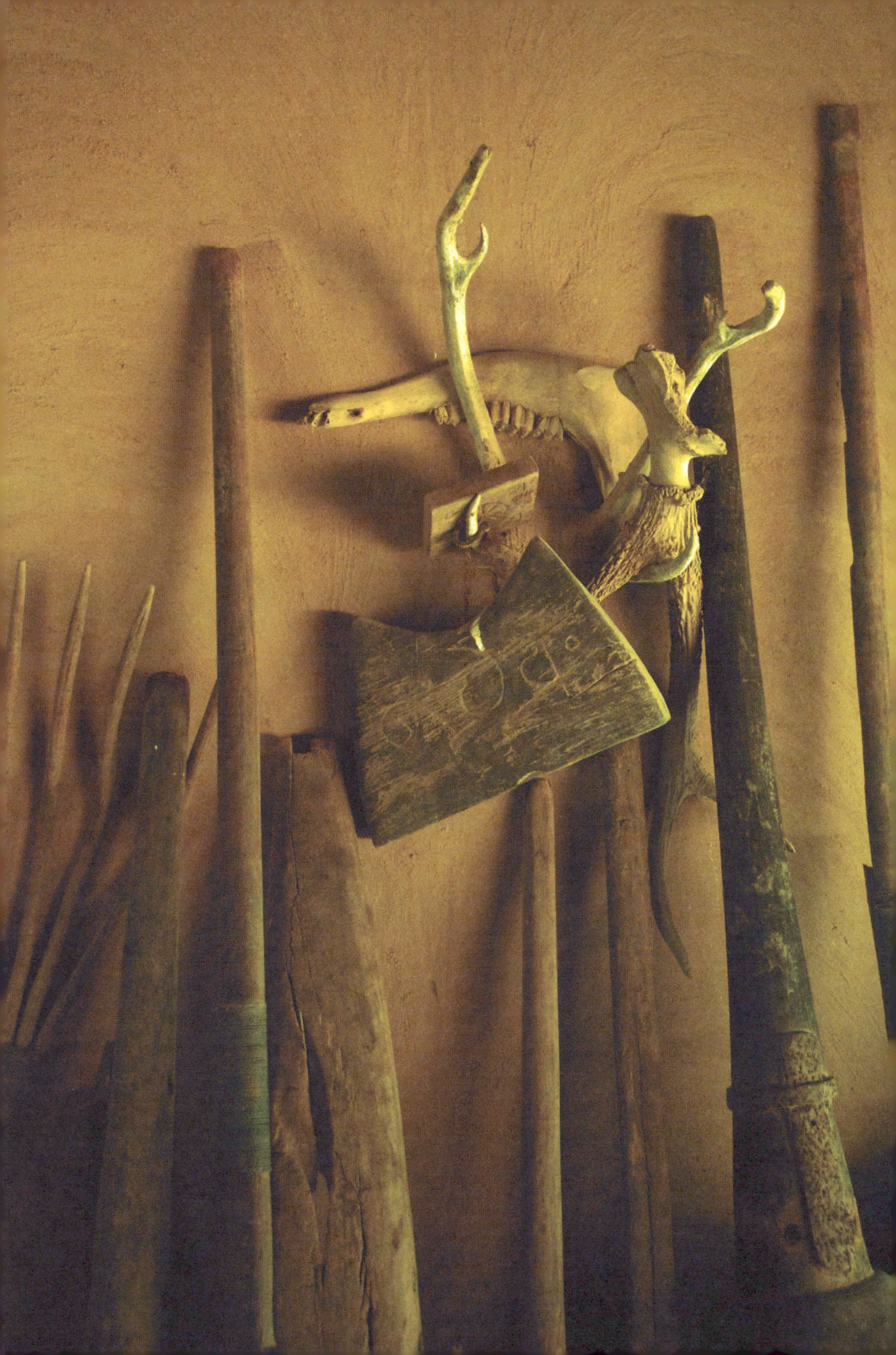

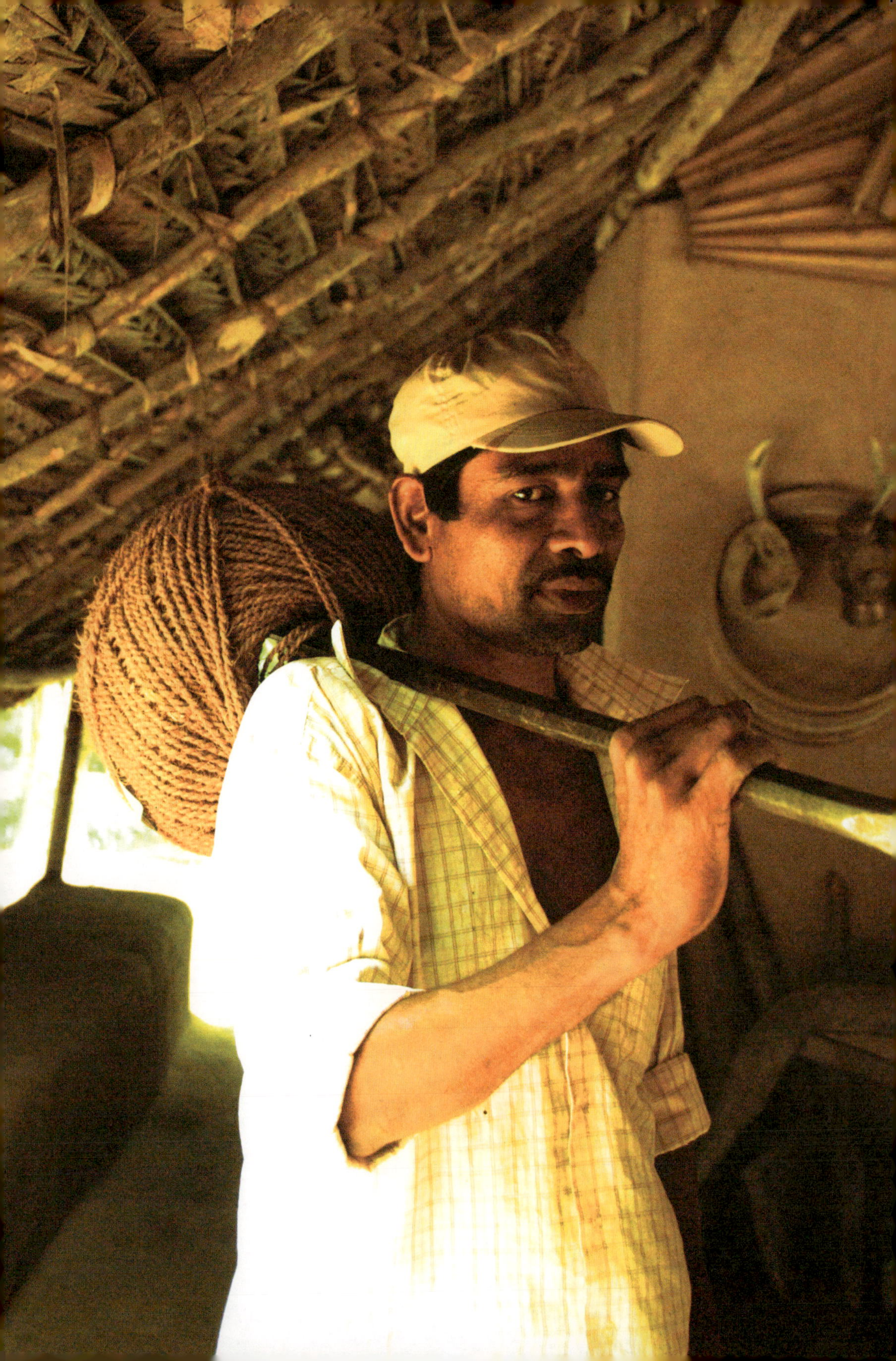

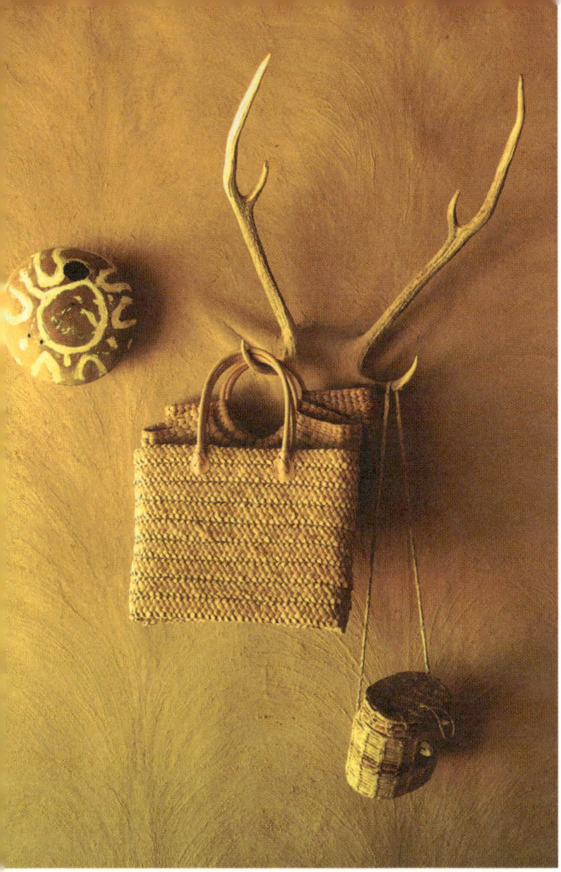
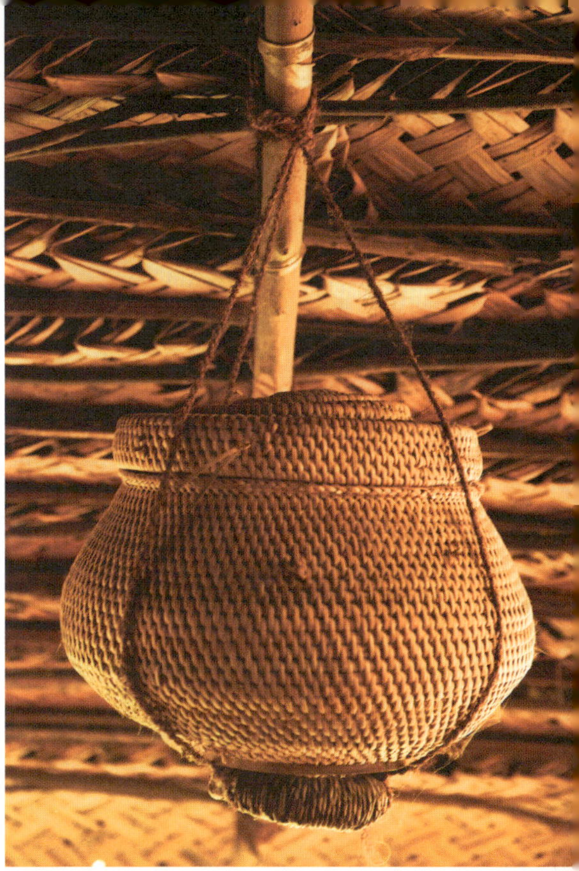
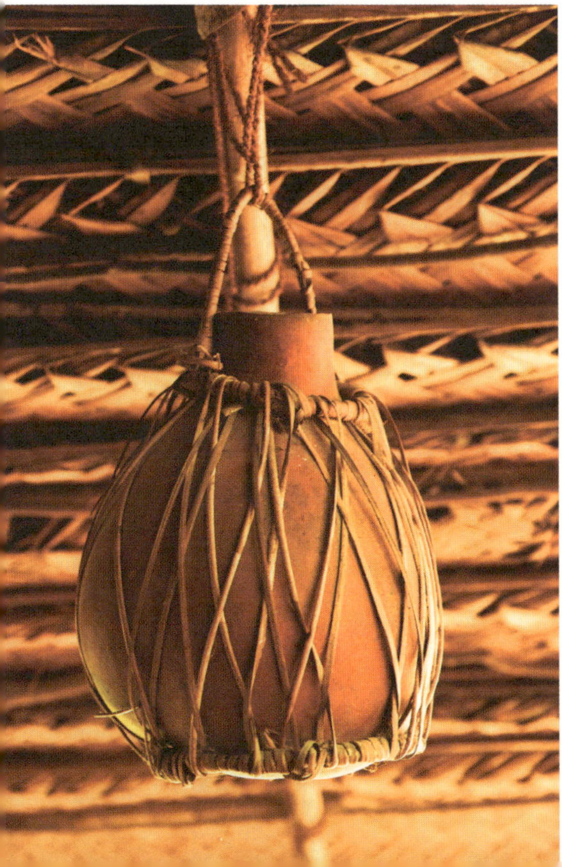
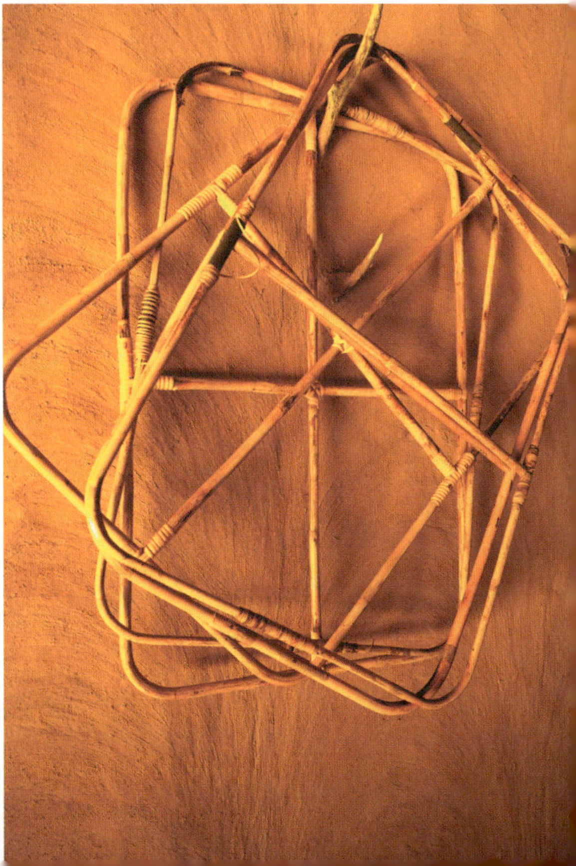

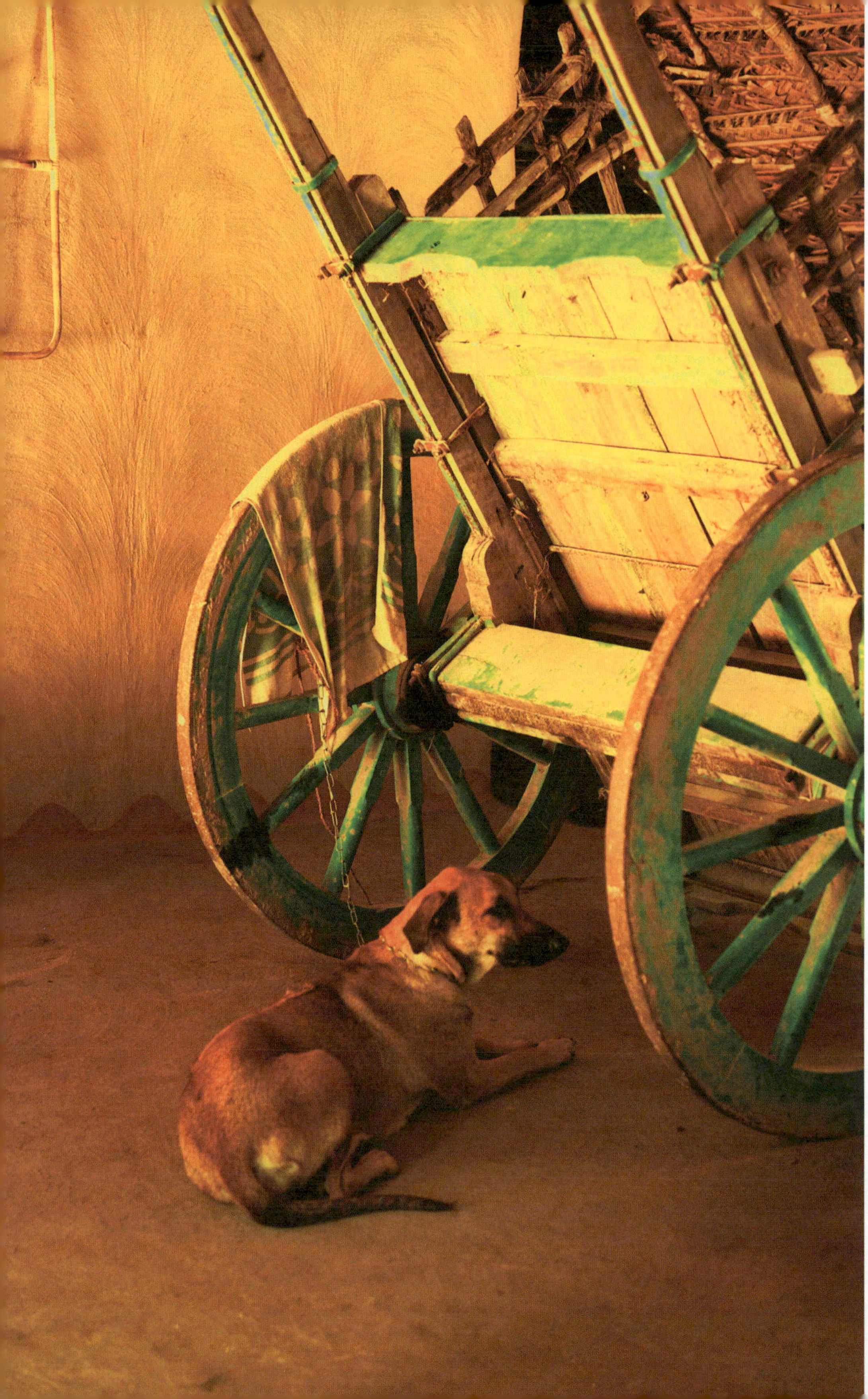

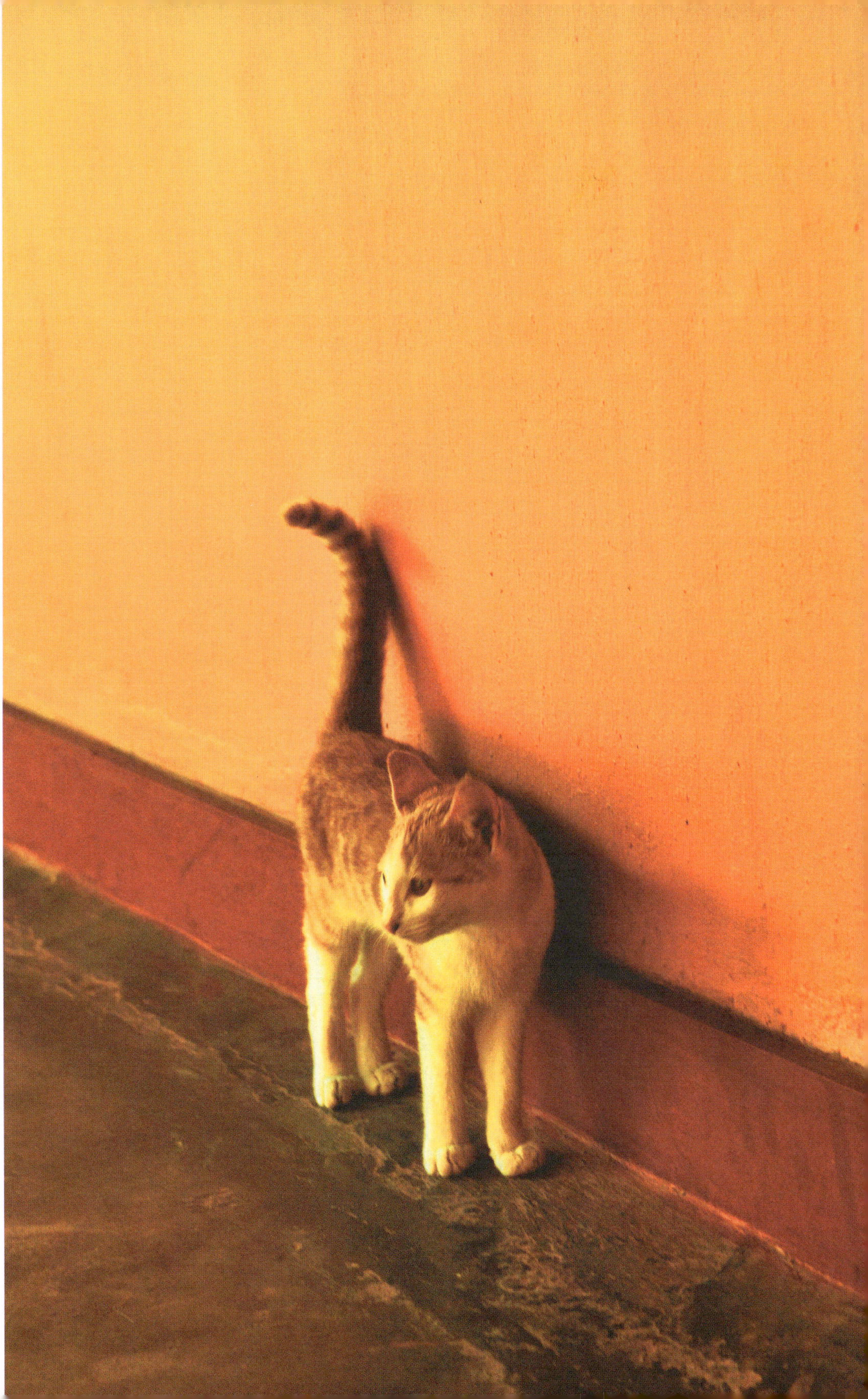

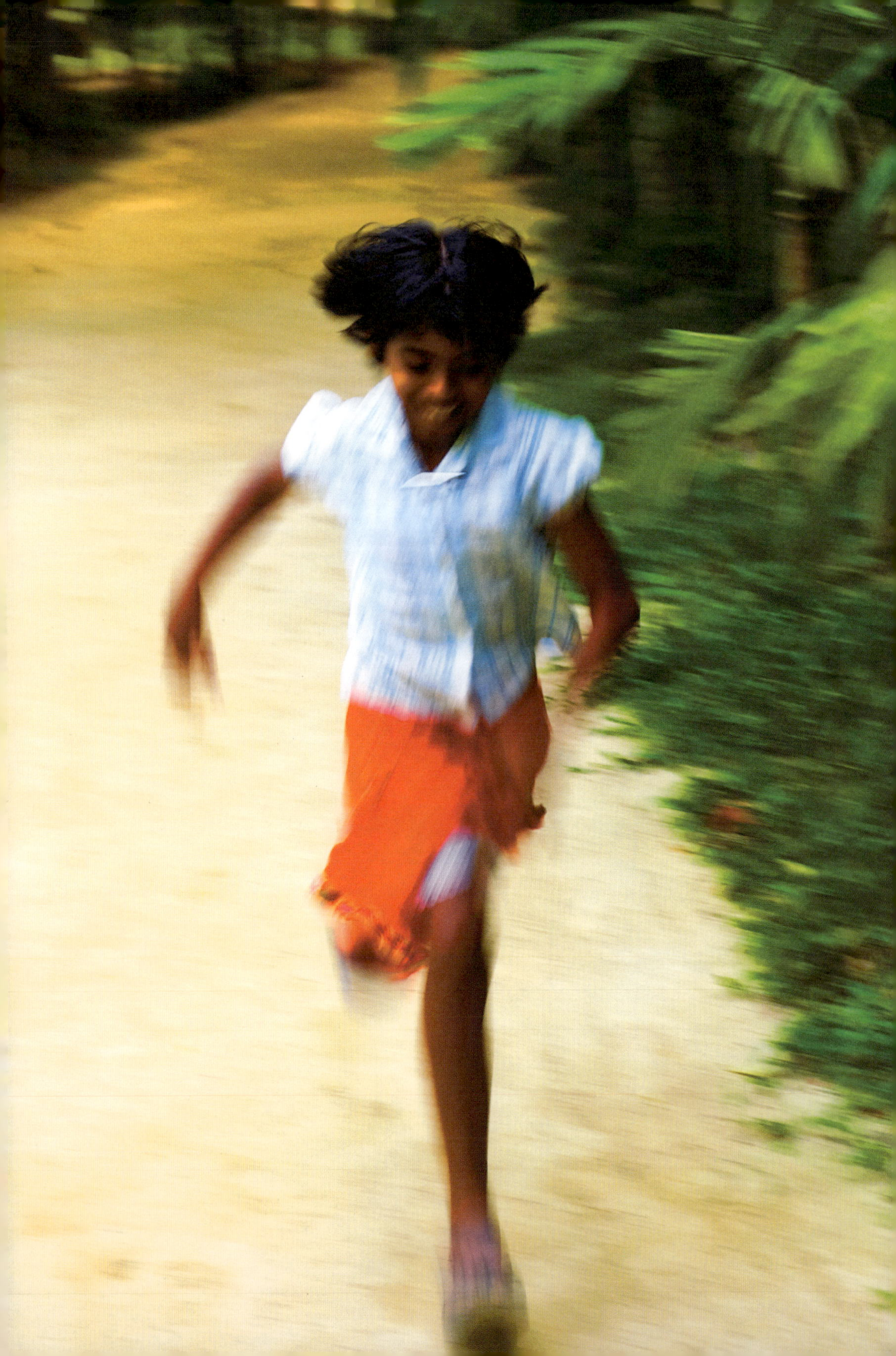

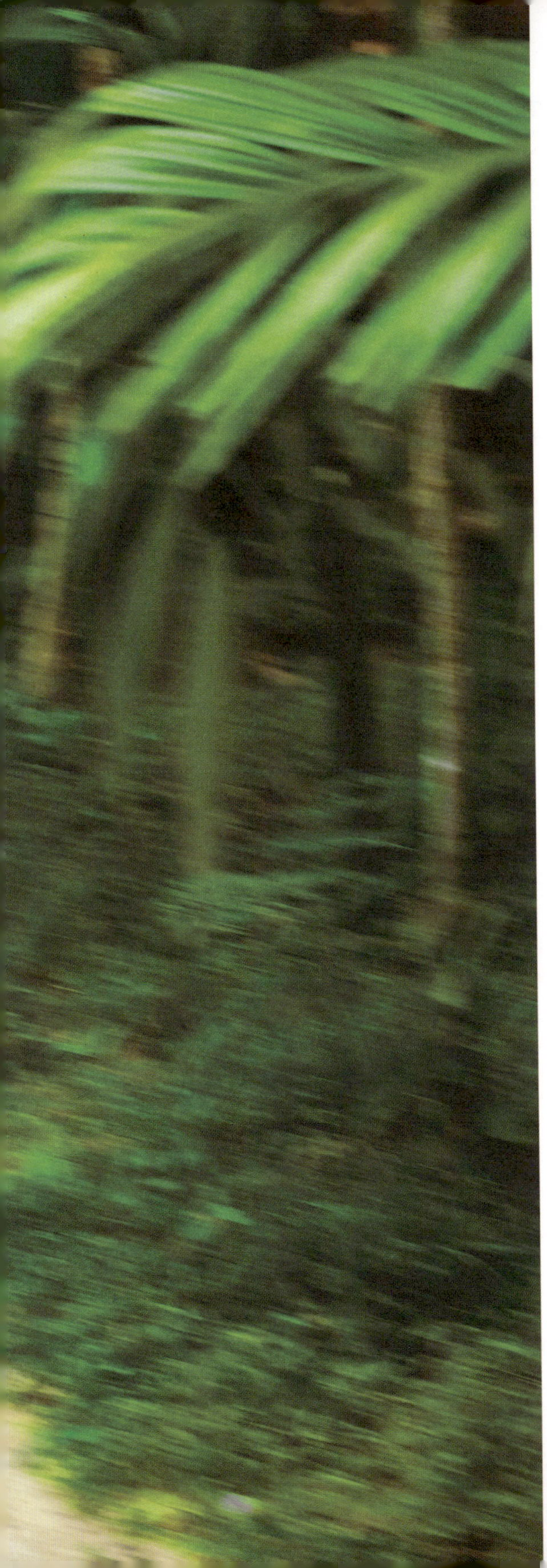

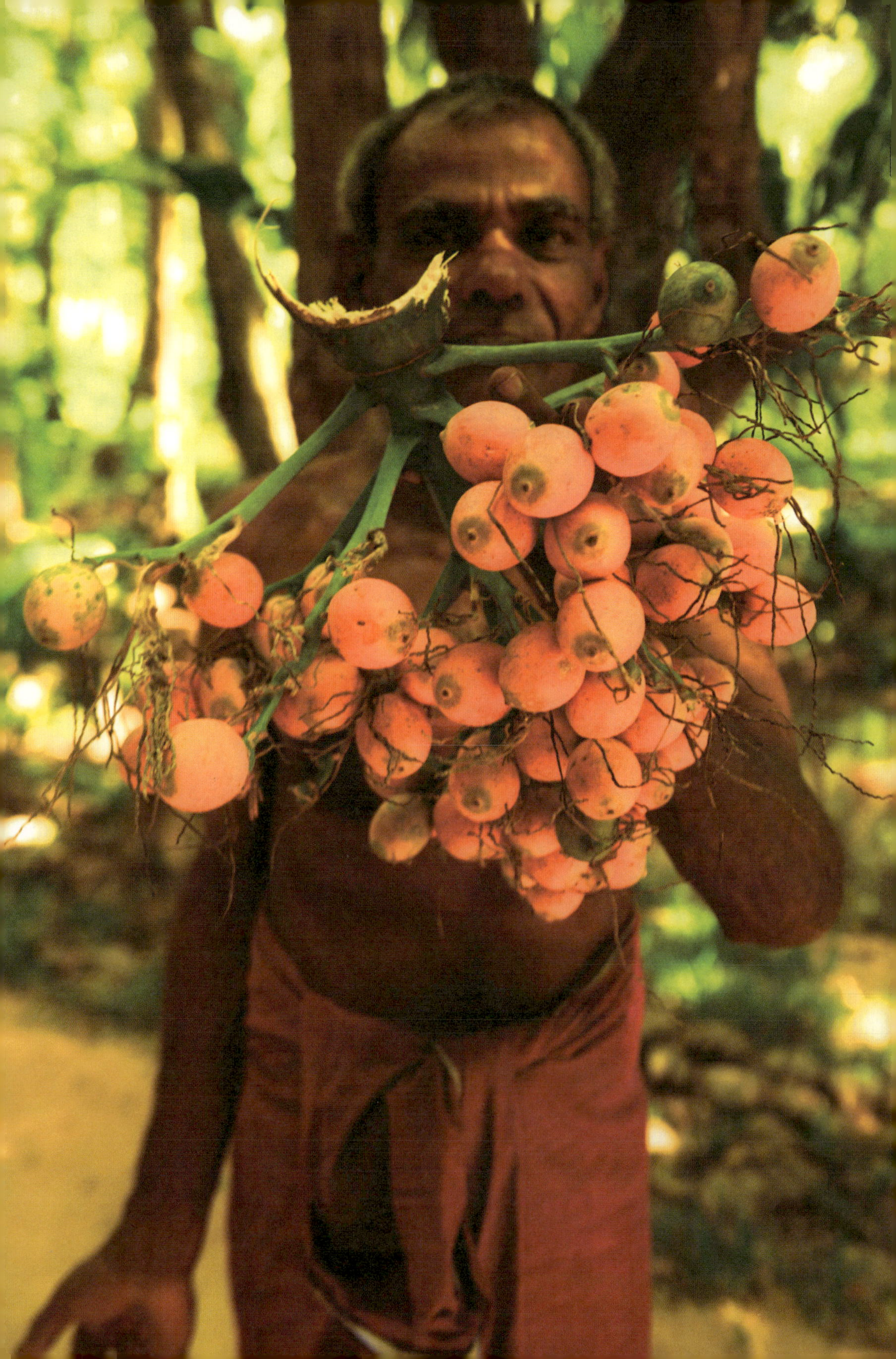

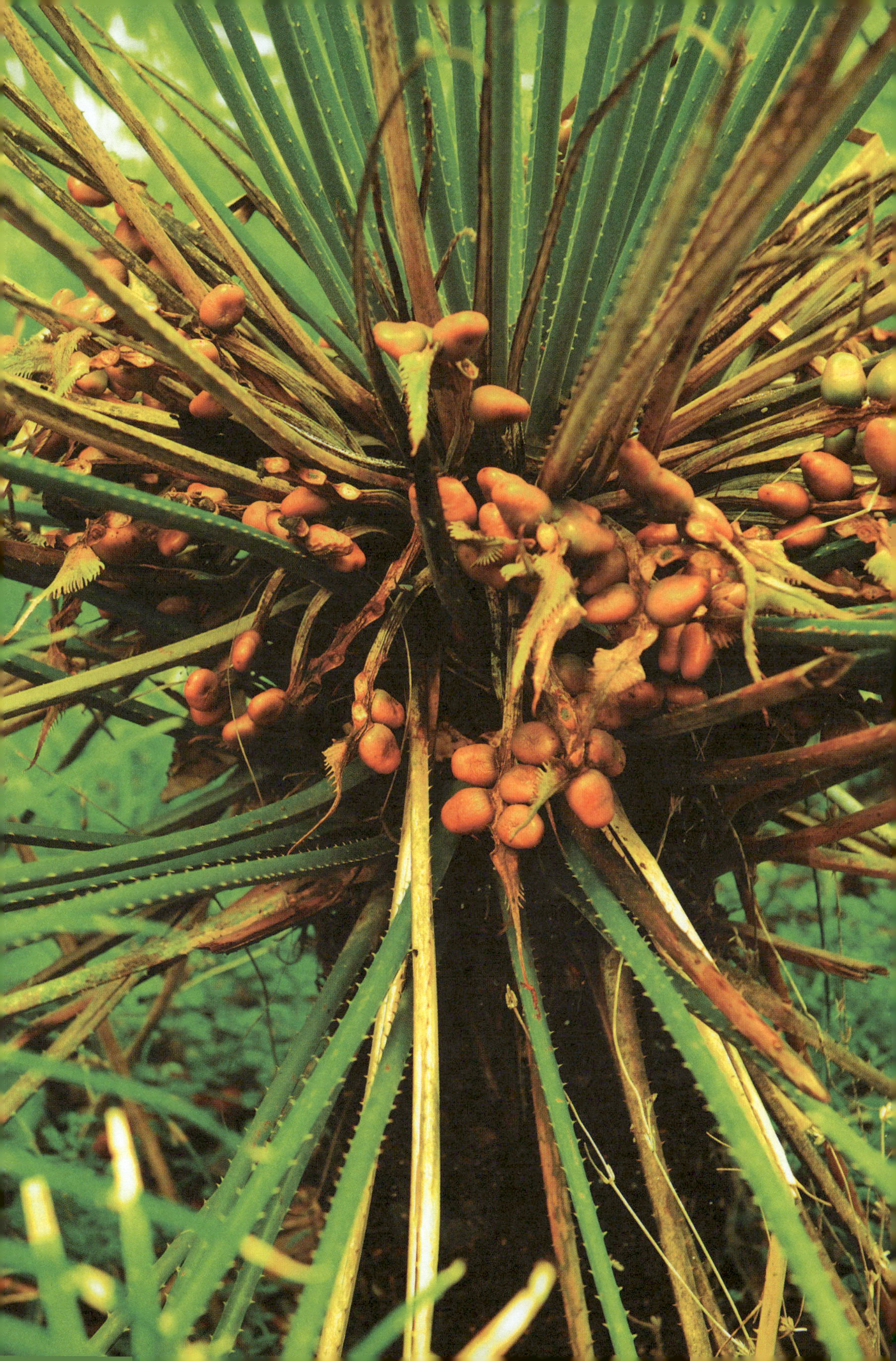

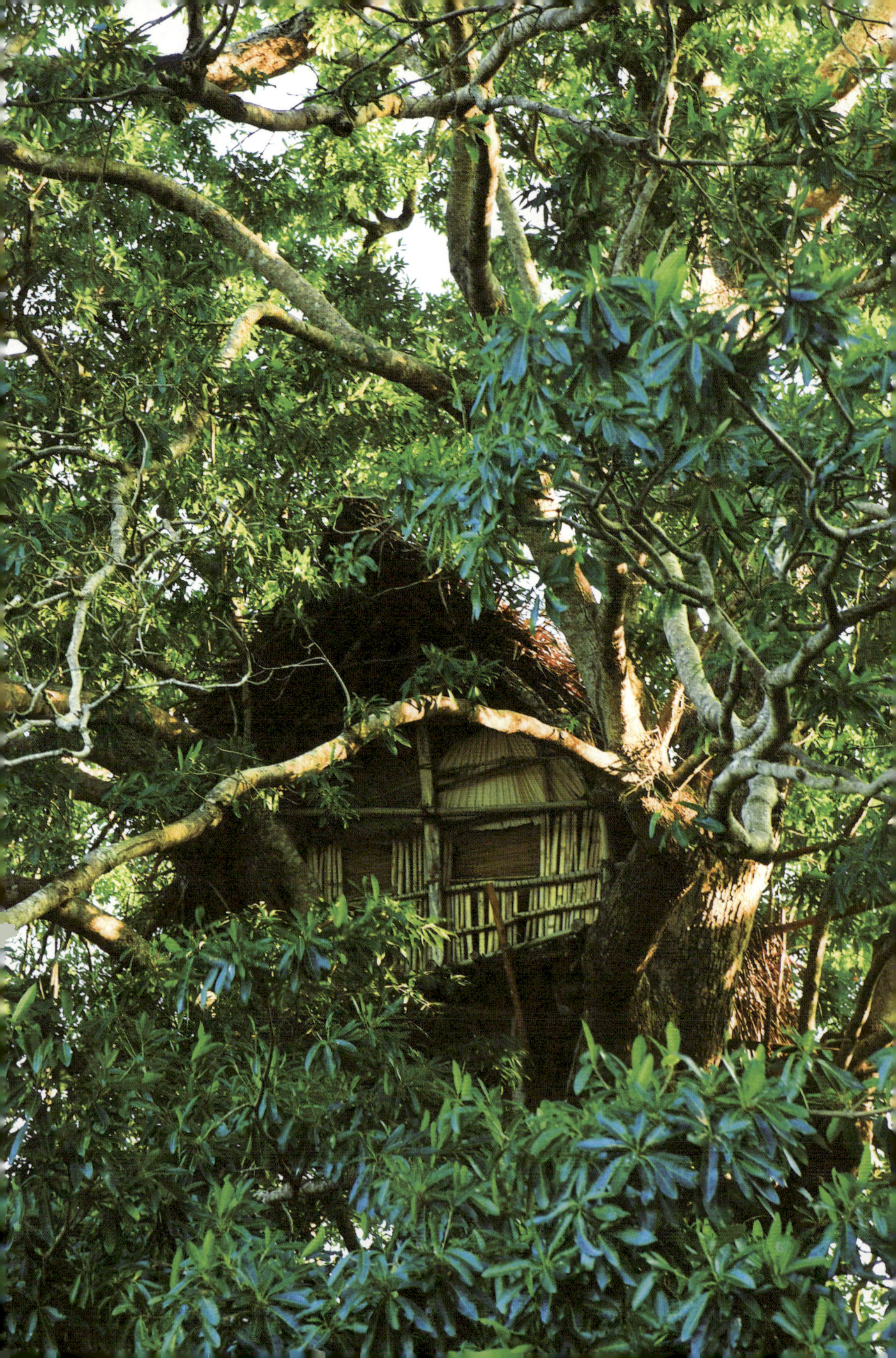

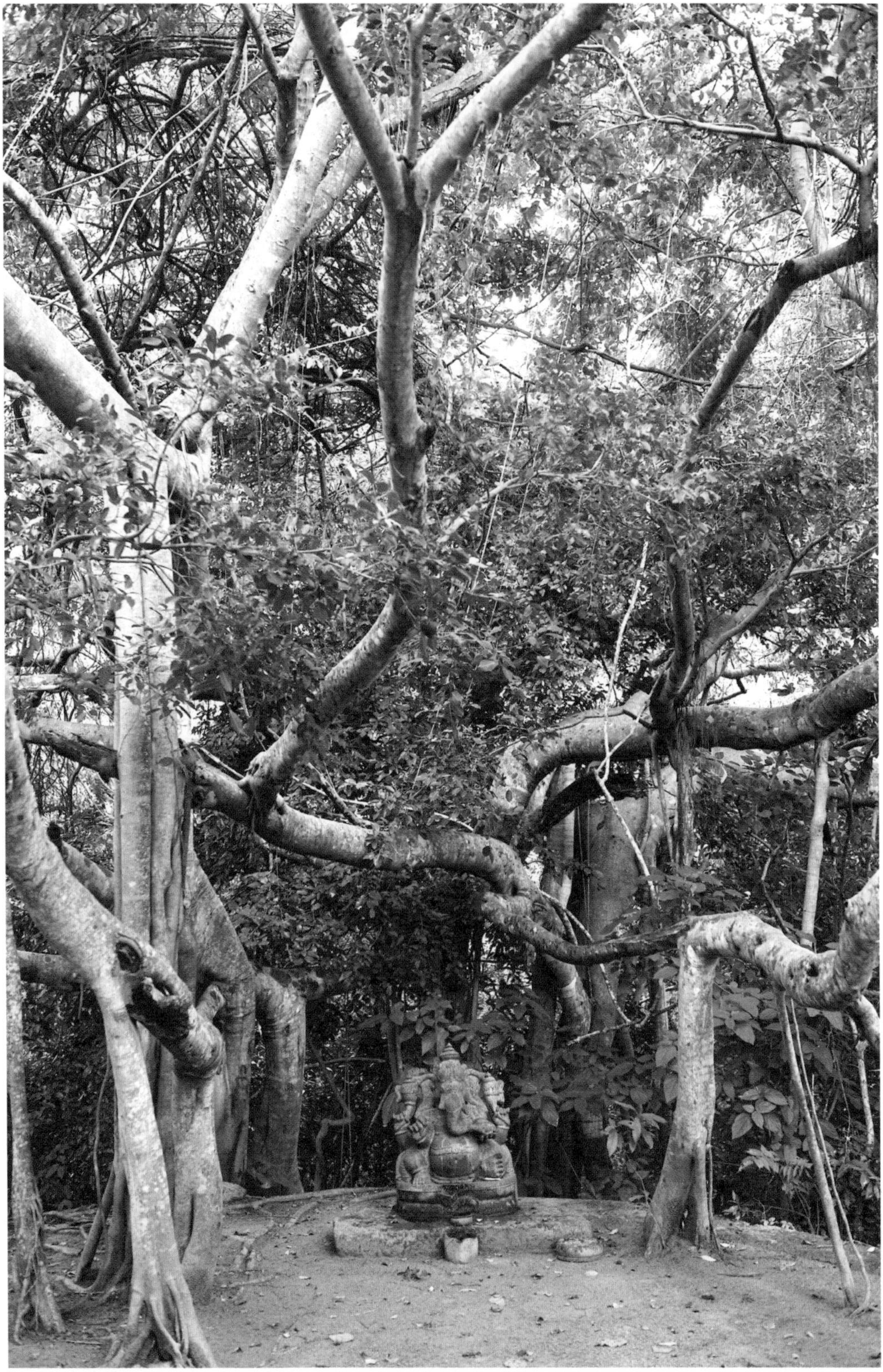

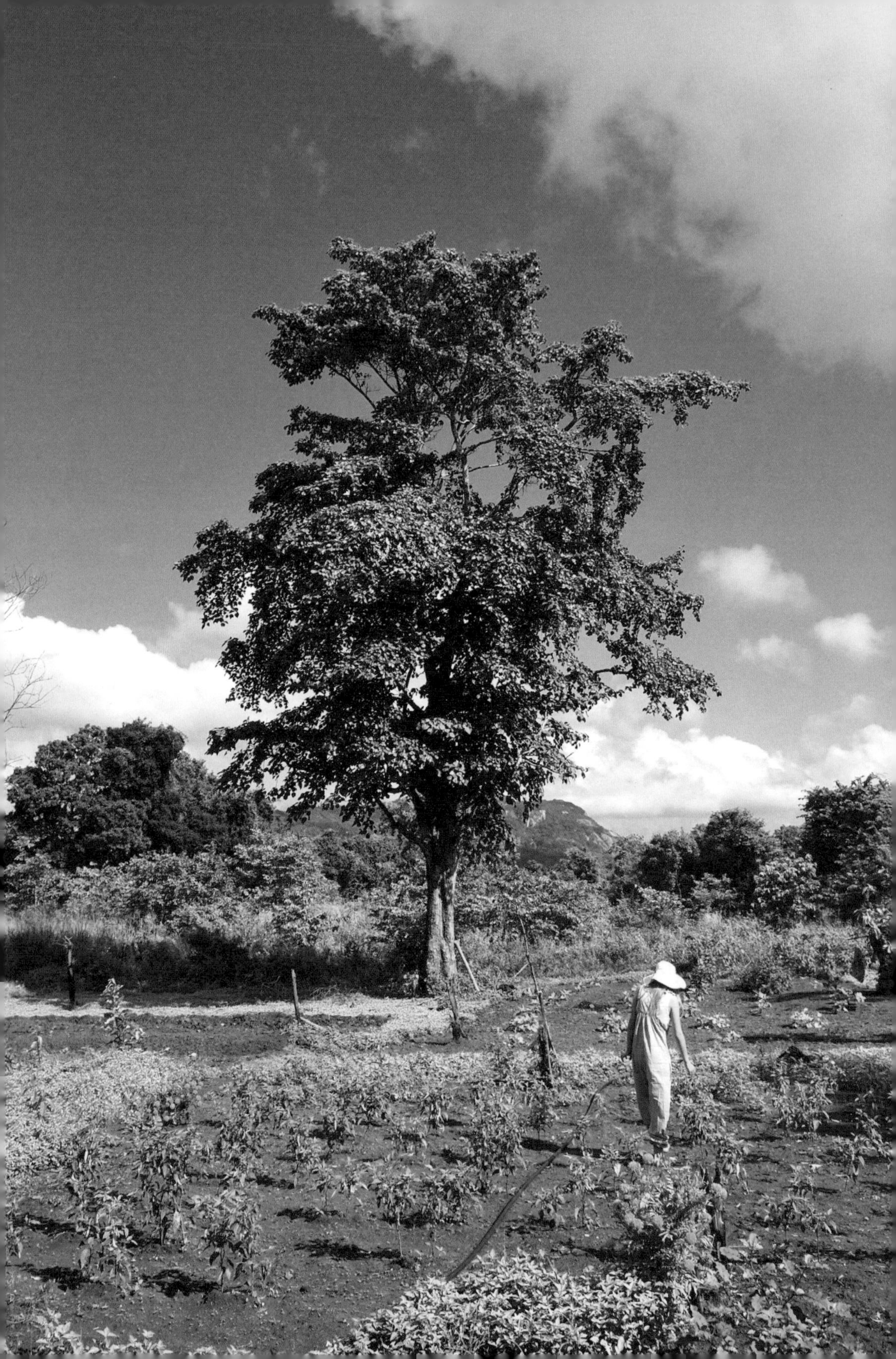

KITCHEN GARDEN

Take a bike ride a couple of kilometres or so down toward Tennekoongama and turn right before the Runamukgama railway station. Along a dirt track you will find Ulpotha's two-acre kitchen garden.

The visitor will be greeted by rows of yams, melons, gotukola, green beans, beetroots, cabbage and chillies which have been companion planted alongside banana, mango, jackfruit and breadfruit trees. Rory Spowers, author of '*A Year In Green Tea And Tuks Tuks*', bought some rocket seeds over from Europe, which grow remarkably well and are always a welcome surprise in salads along with ruby tomatoes and crisp cucumbers.

The produce from Ulpotha's kitchen garden, tended by the villagers and graced with nurture and positive attention, can only come to our plate with the utmost of goodness and wellbeing, as a herd of five elephants might have felt when they swept in one late afternoon to raid the vegetables.

They sucked up the manioc (a sweet potato) and dug up the carrots. In their rush to get away, a baby elephant fell down the well. The villagers came to his rescue and pulled him out as his mother trumpeted and threatened to charge. She calmed as soon as they were reunited. They all trotted off into the sunset only for seven to return a week later hunting down the cucumber and papaya. They seemed to have tip-toed through the betel leaf arches leaving them curiously intact, but head-butted the shed leaving an obvious opening.

The Ulpotha kitchen garden yields a constant crop of organically grown food planted in adherence to lunar cycles for planting and harvesting. This is also a time for celebration, communal singing and dancing and where fertility rights are performed honouring deities of the land.

Crops are protected from bugs, pests and other infestations using traditional methods, such as the use of powdered neem seeds, dried makra leaves, crushed coconut shavings, sap from the jackfruit, cactus milk, branches of the kadura tree, bamboo leaves and riverbed sand.

Ploughing and threshing are carried out using buffalo. Not only do they produce fertilizer and nourishing milk, they reproduce themselves. Tractors tend to break through the crust in paddy fields, resulting in the need for greater amounts of irrigation, while digging up the soil too deeply, which brings less fertile soil to the surface.

Growing one's own food is the only involvement of 'having' that comes directly to us, from the seed to the food on our table. Everything we own or use has been passed through so many people and experiences – whilst a simple green bean that has been pushed into the earth with good intention and grown with the combination of the elements soil, sun and water, then picked at an auspicious time, is the most natural and direct practice we can ingest here on this planet. It is the purest and most sacred path from our Mother Earth to all of us.

177   KITCHEN GARDEN

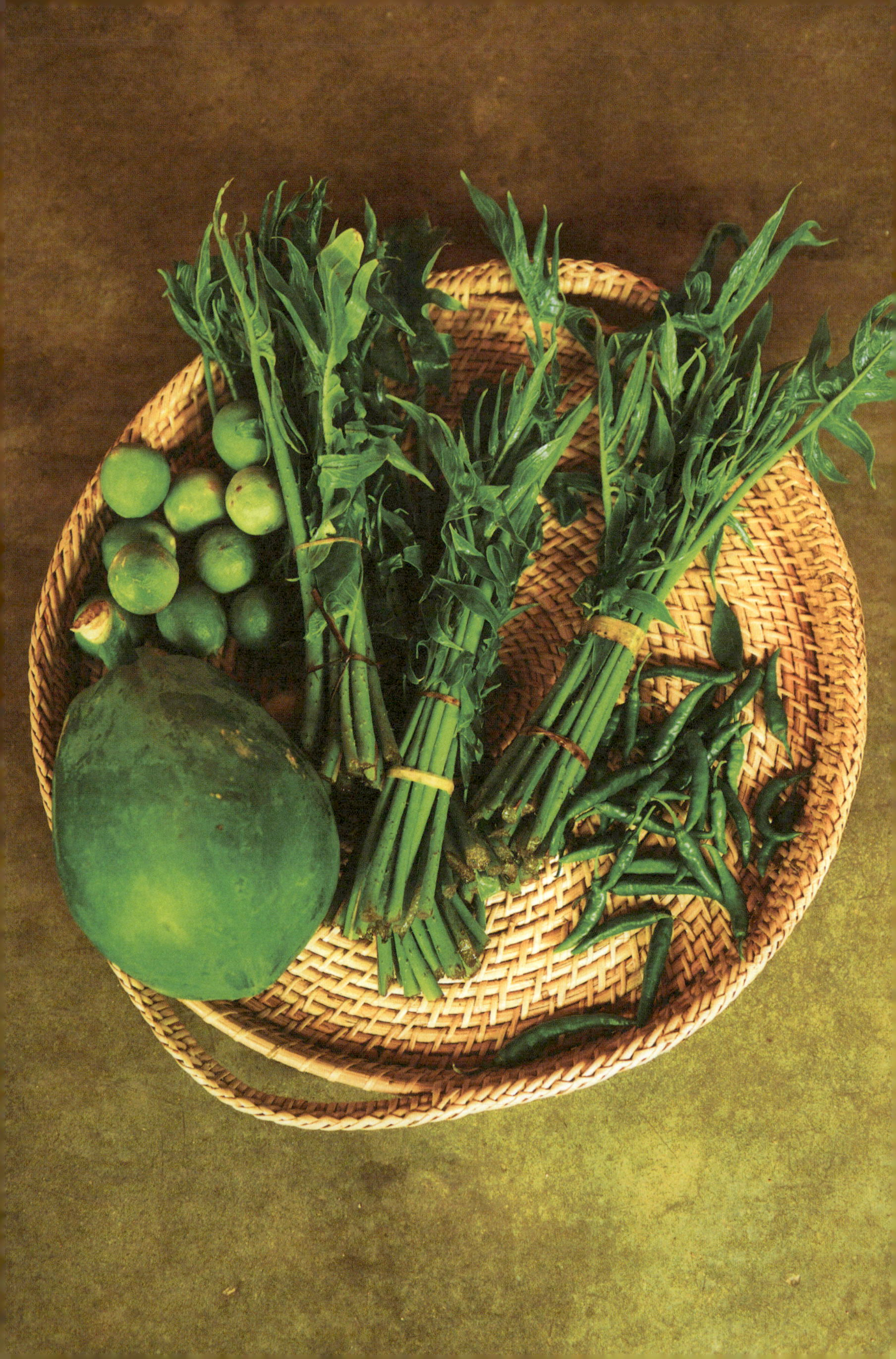

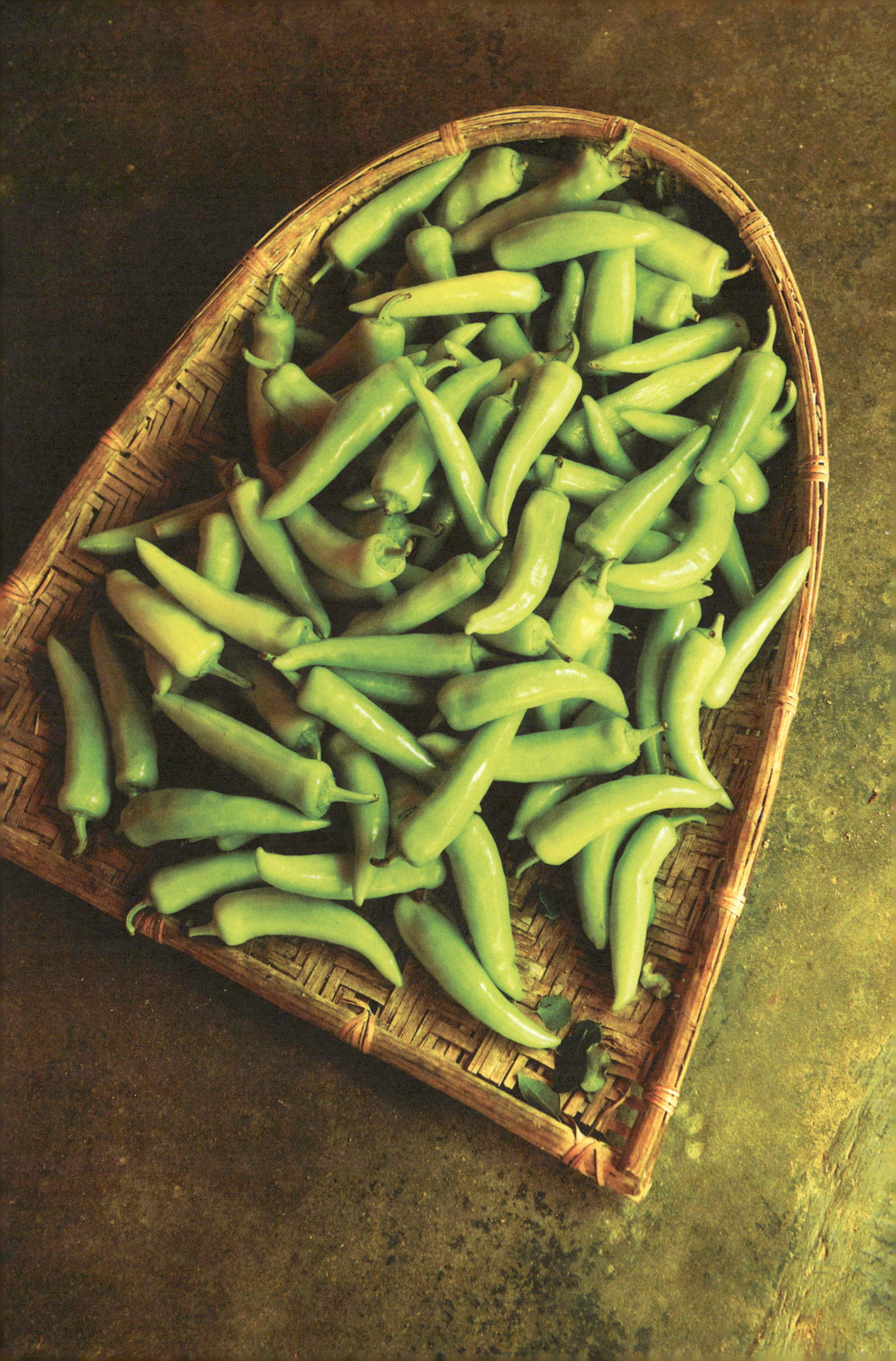

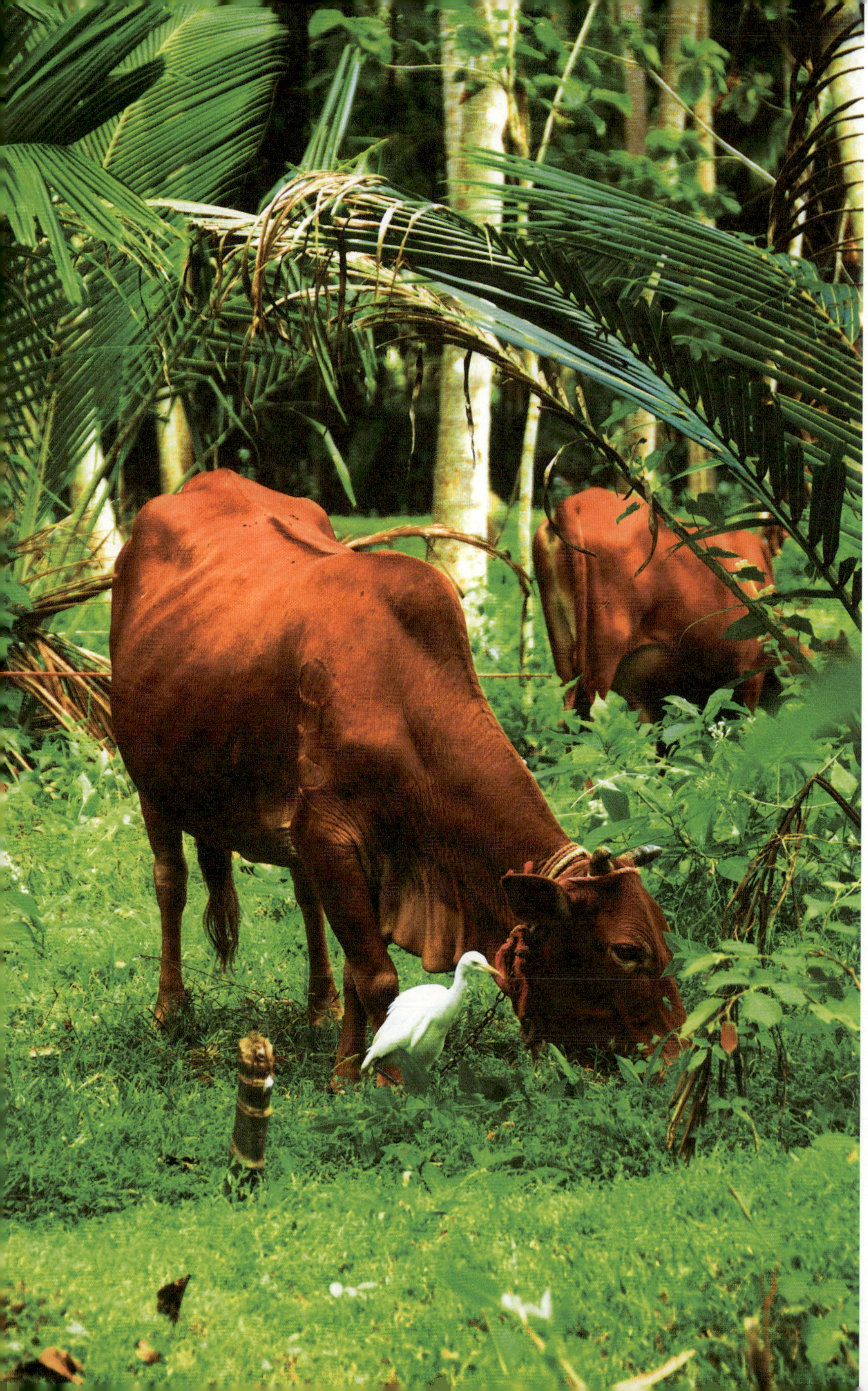

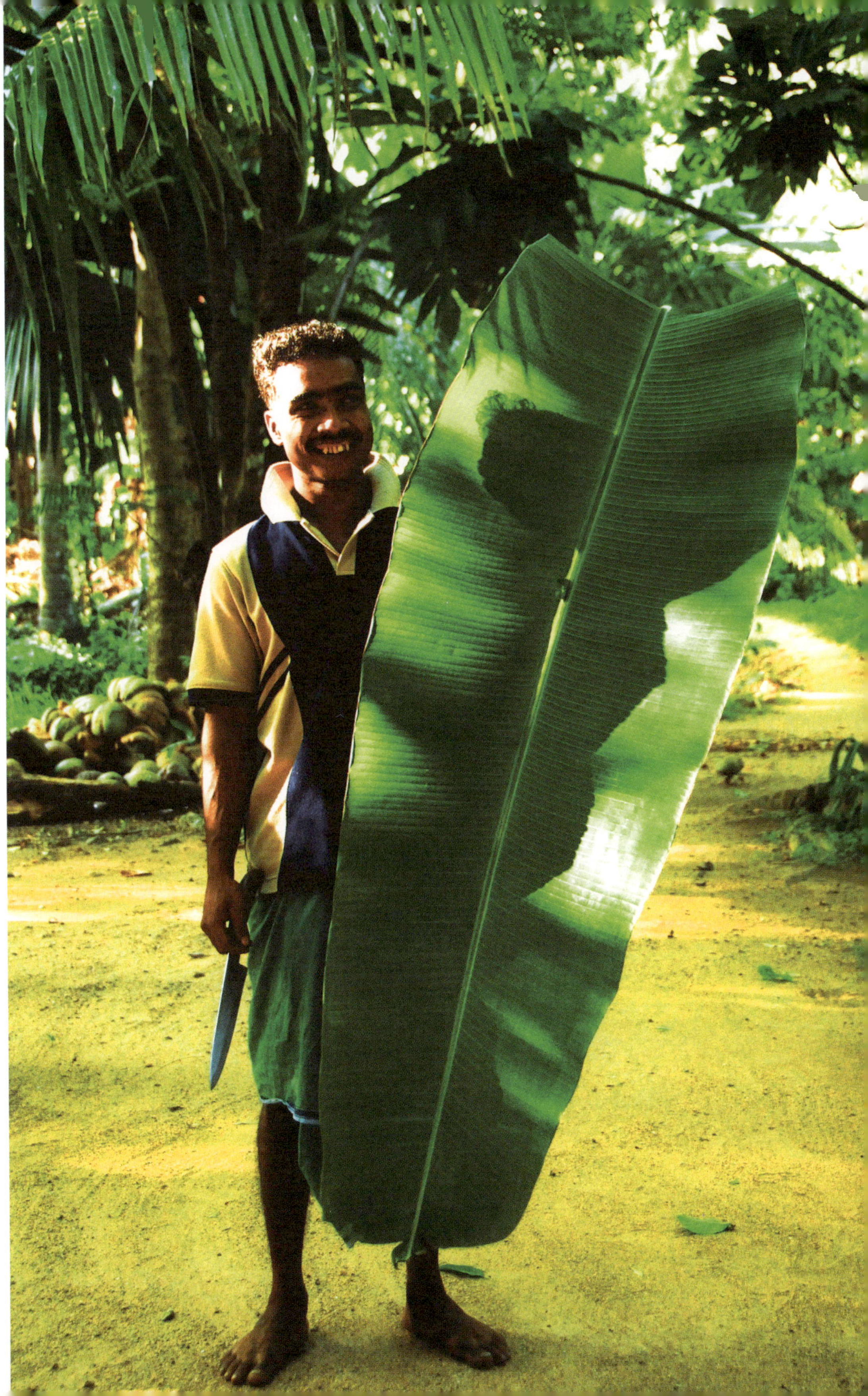

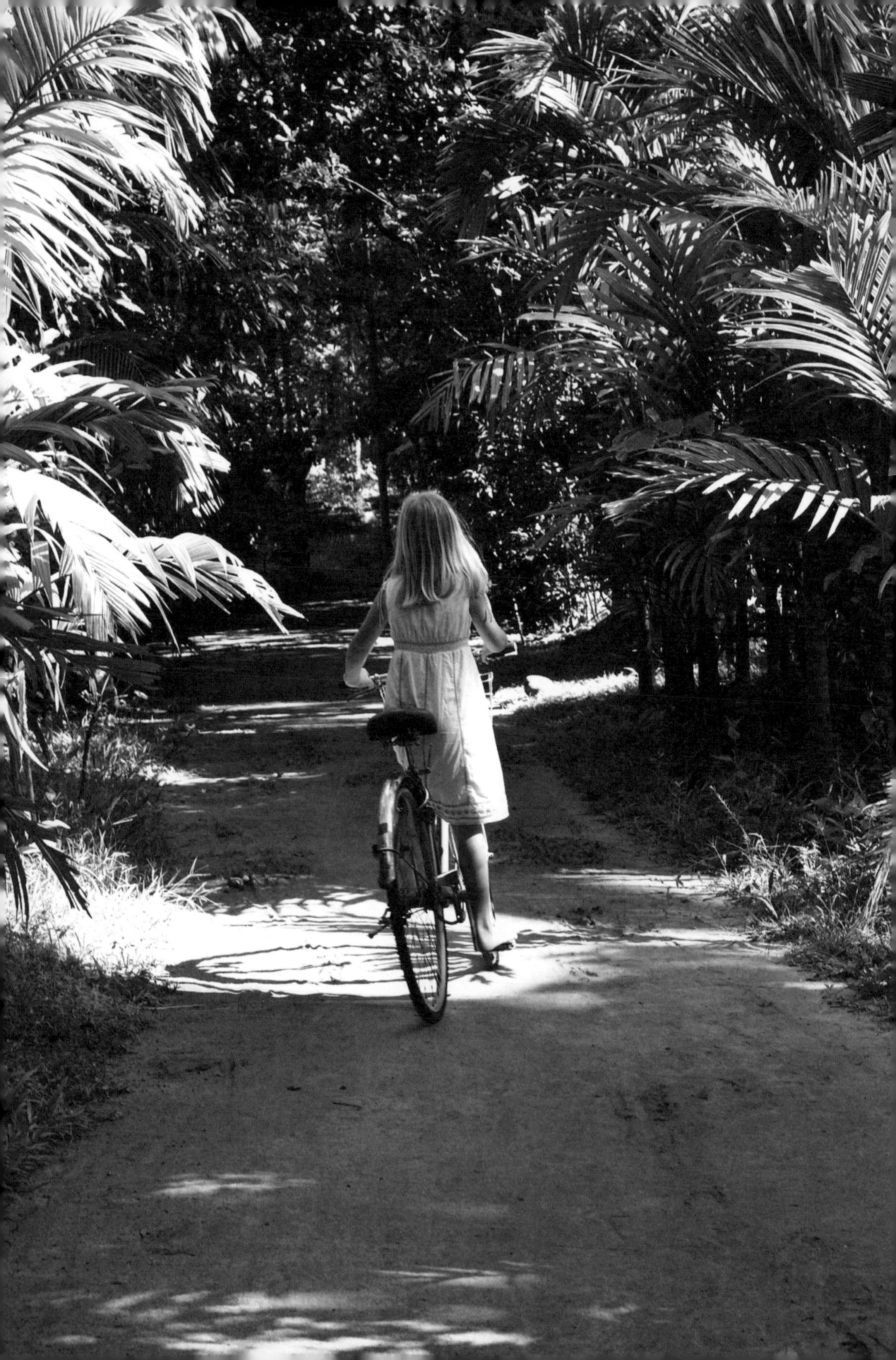

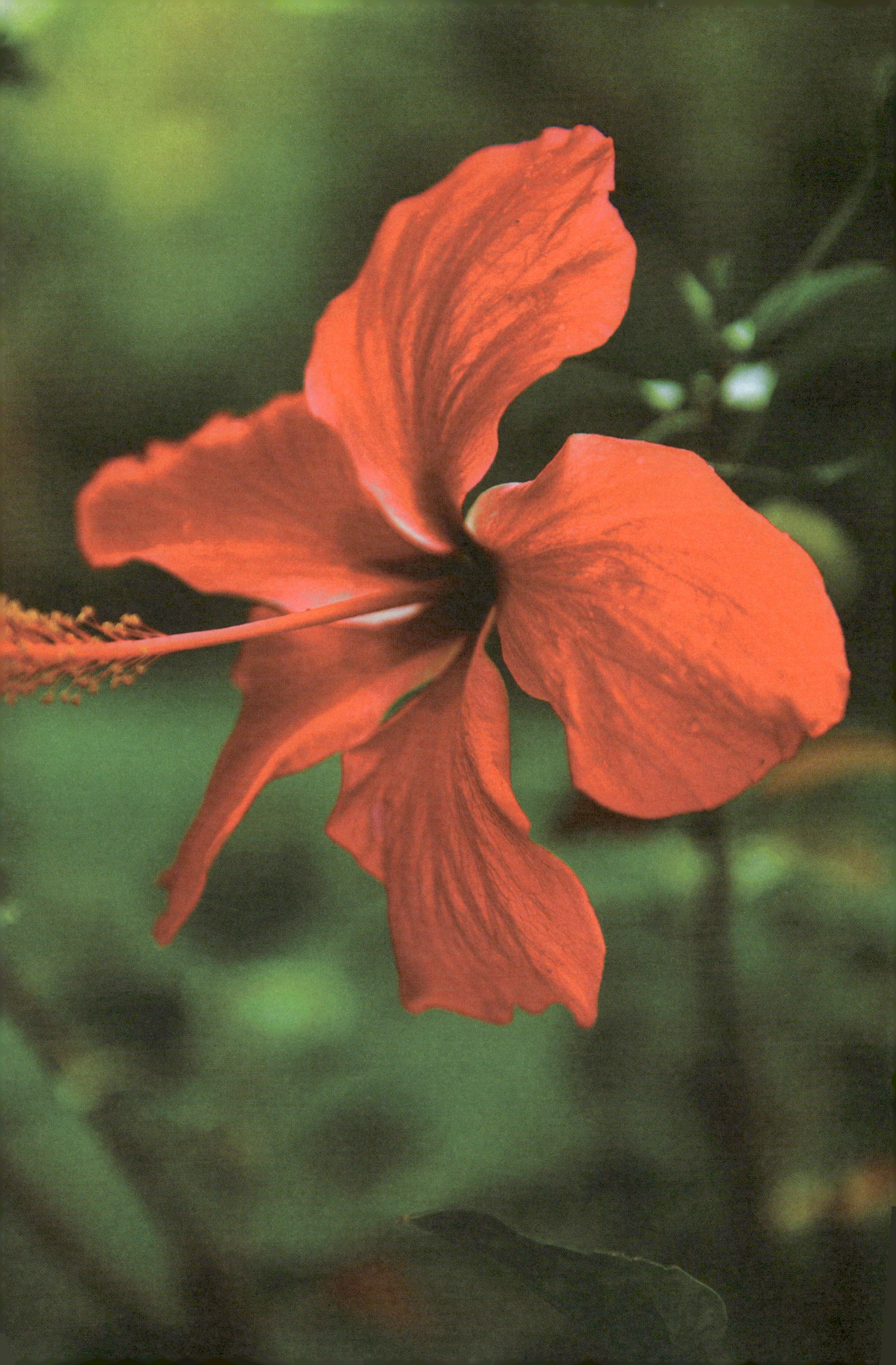

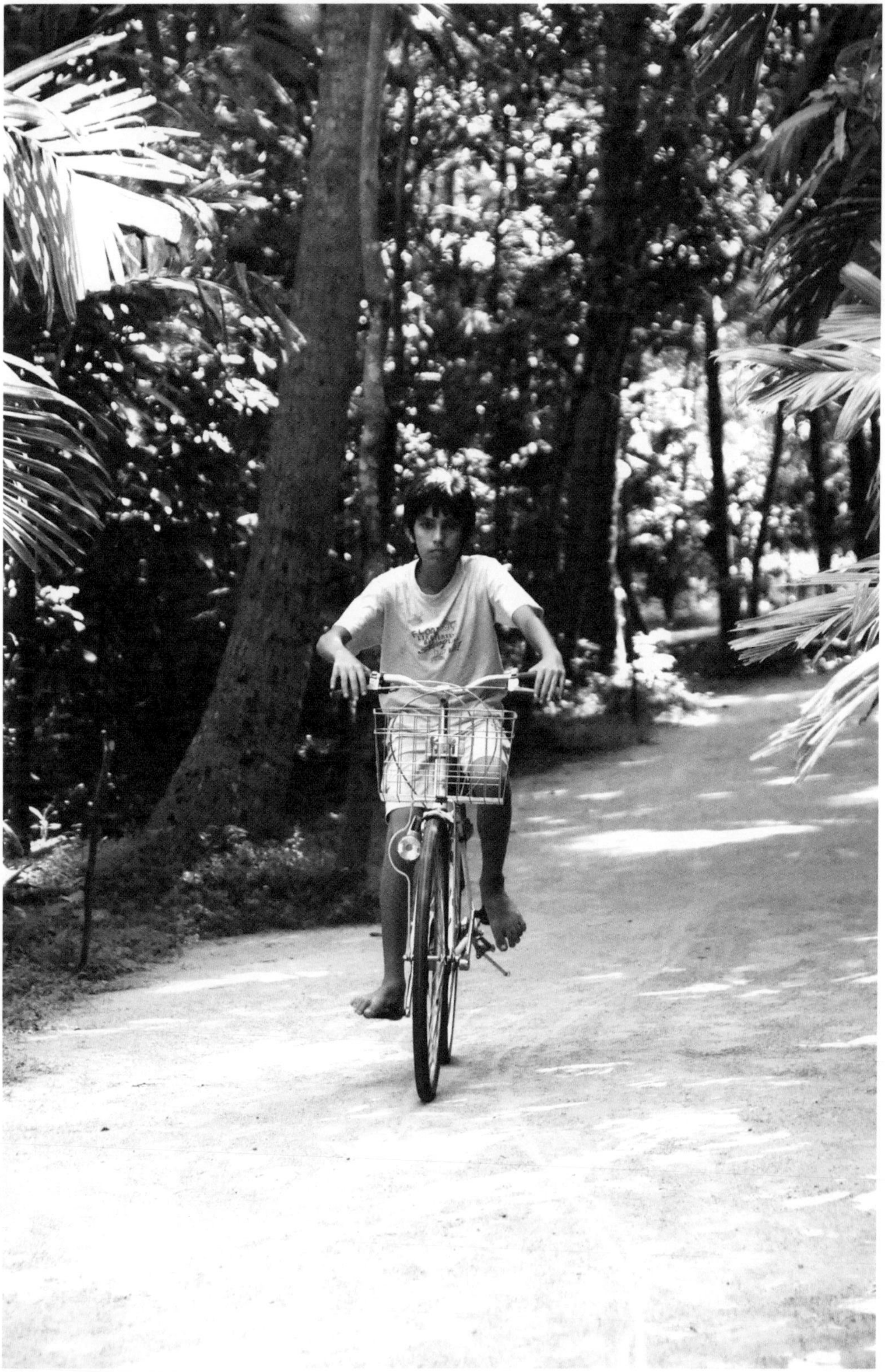

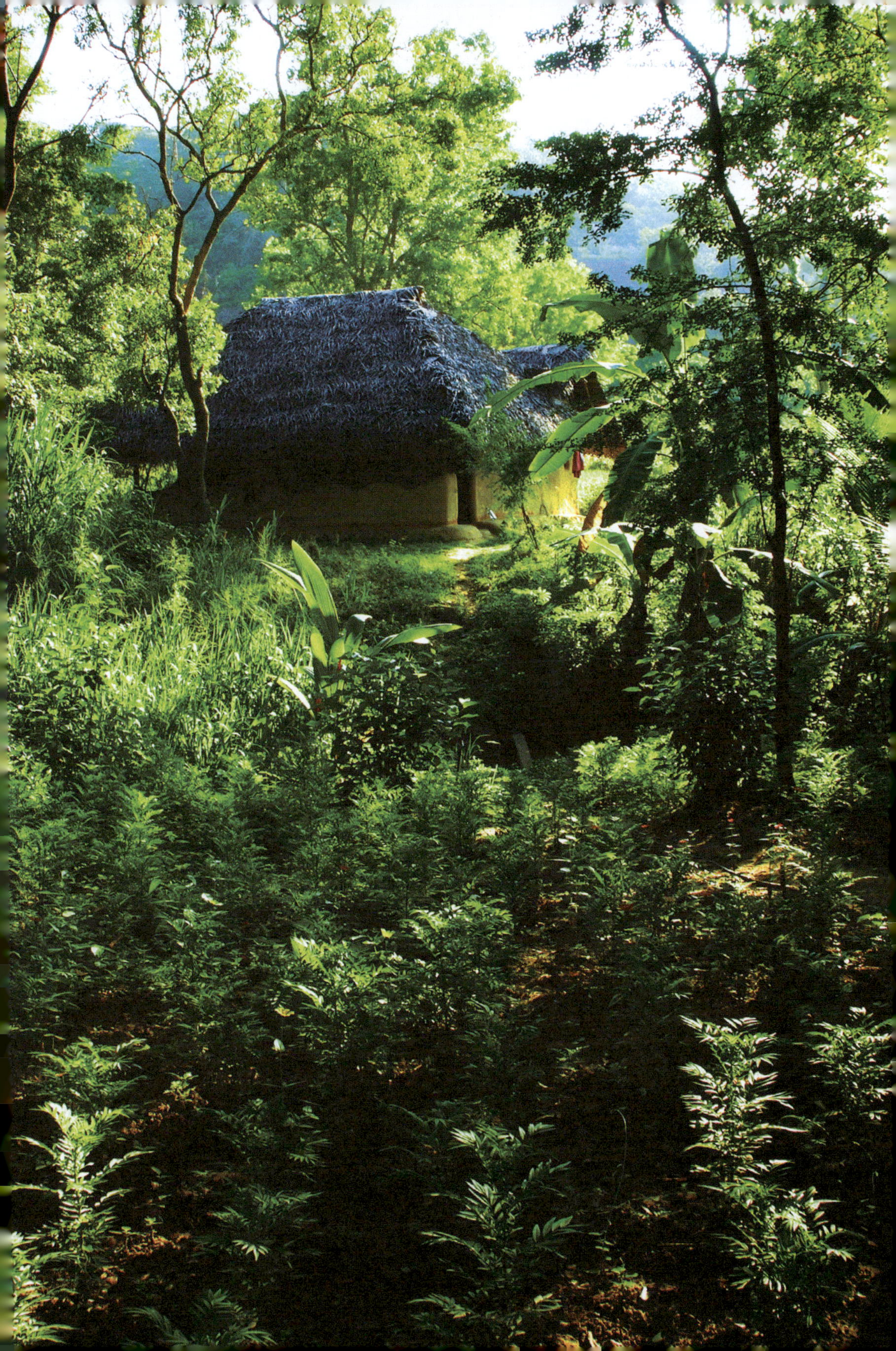

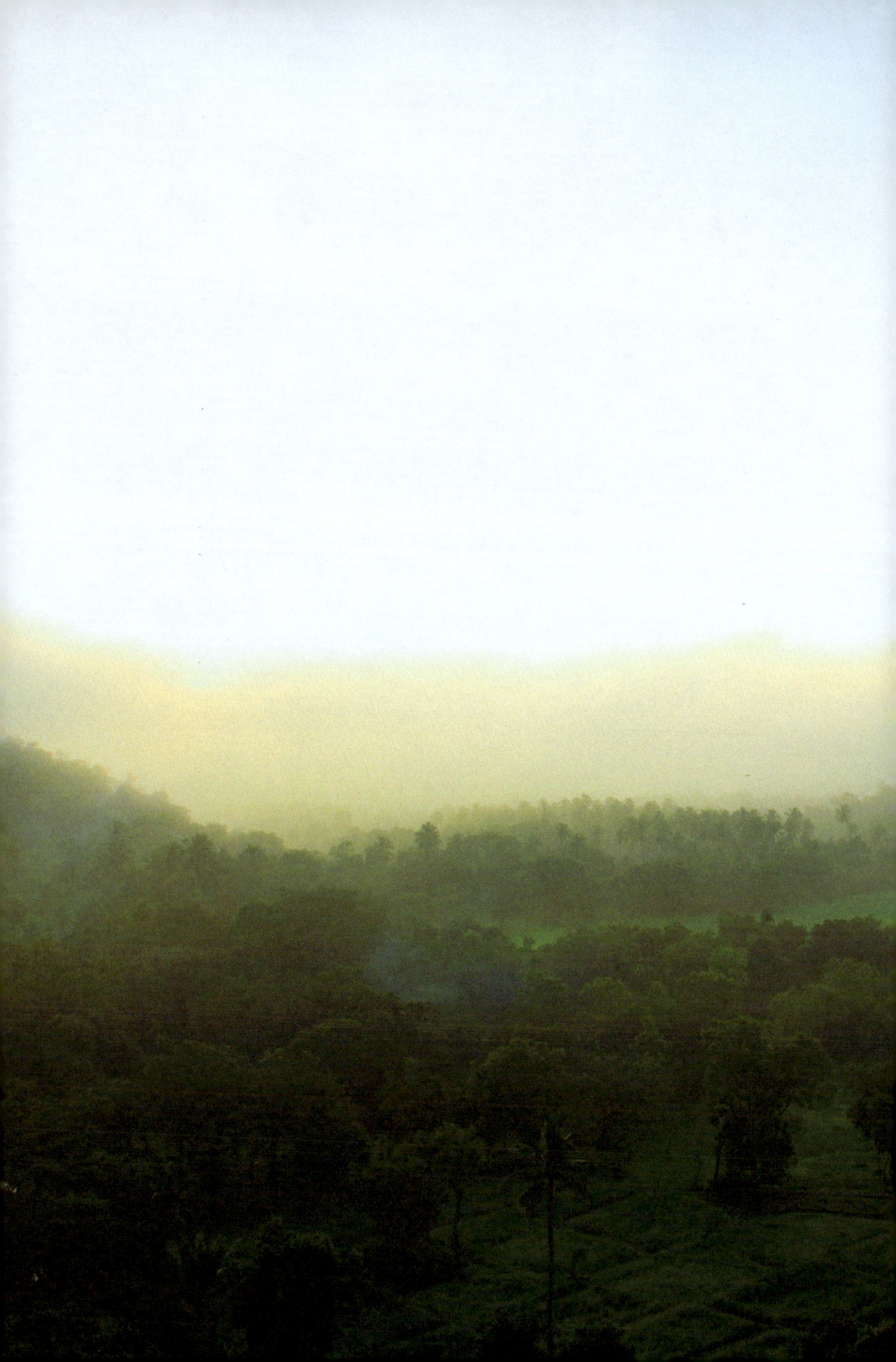

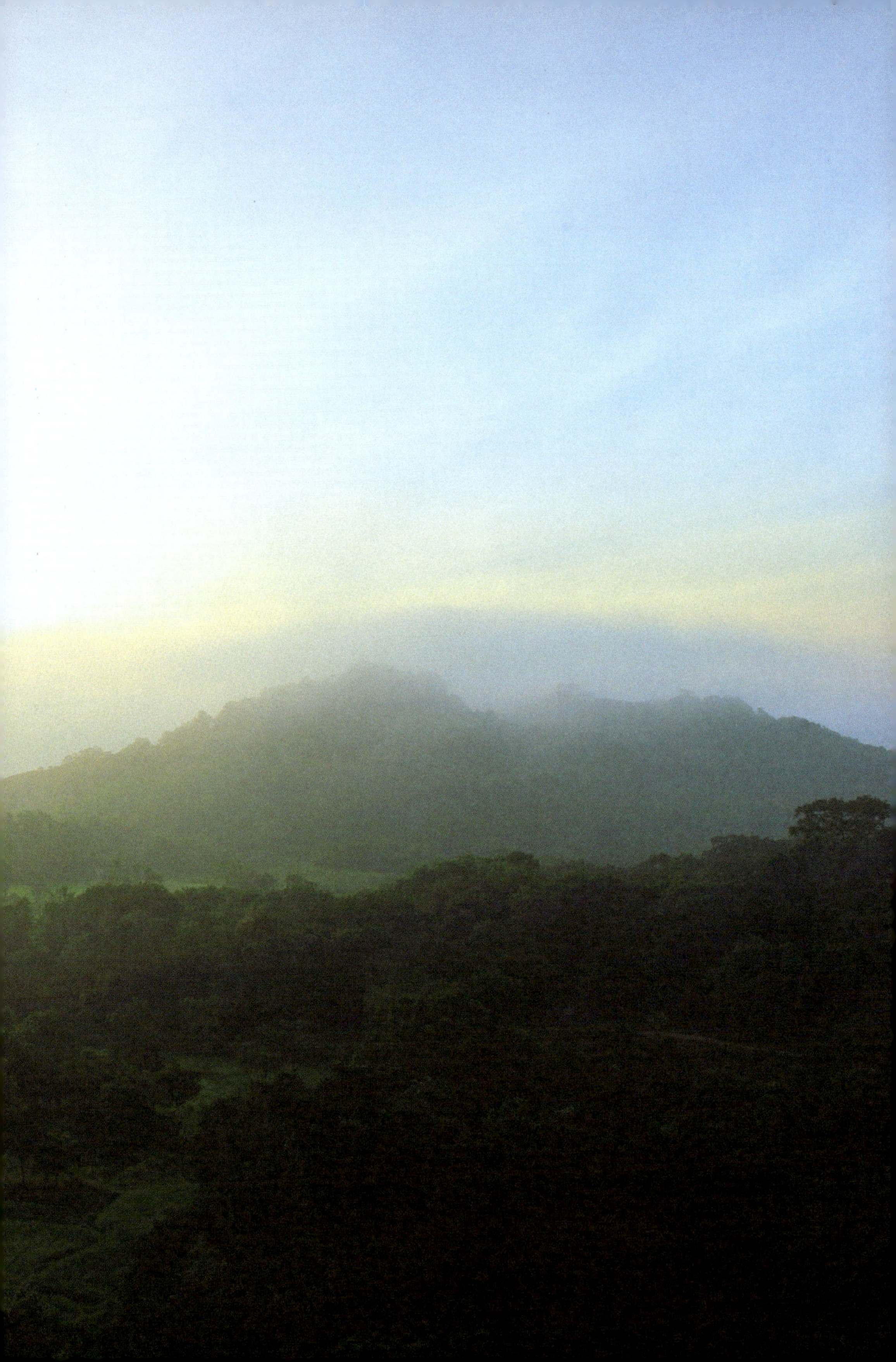

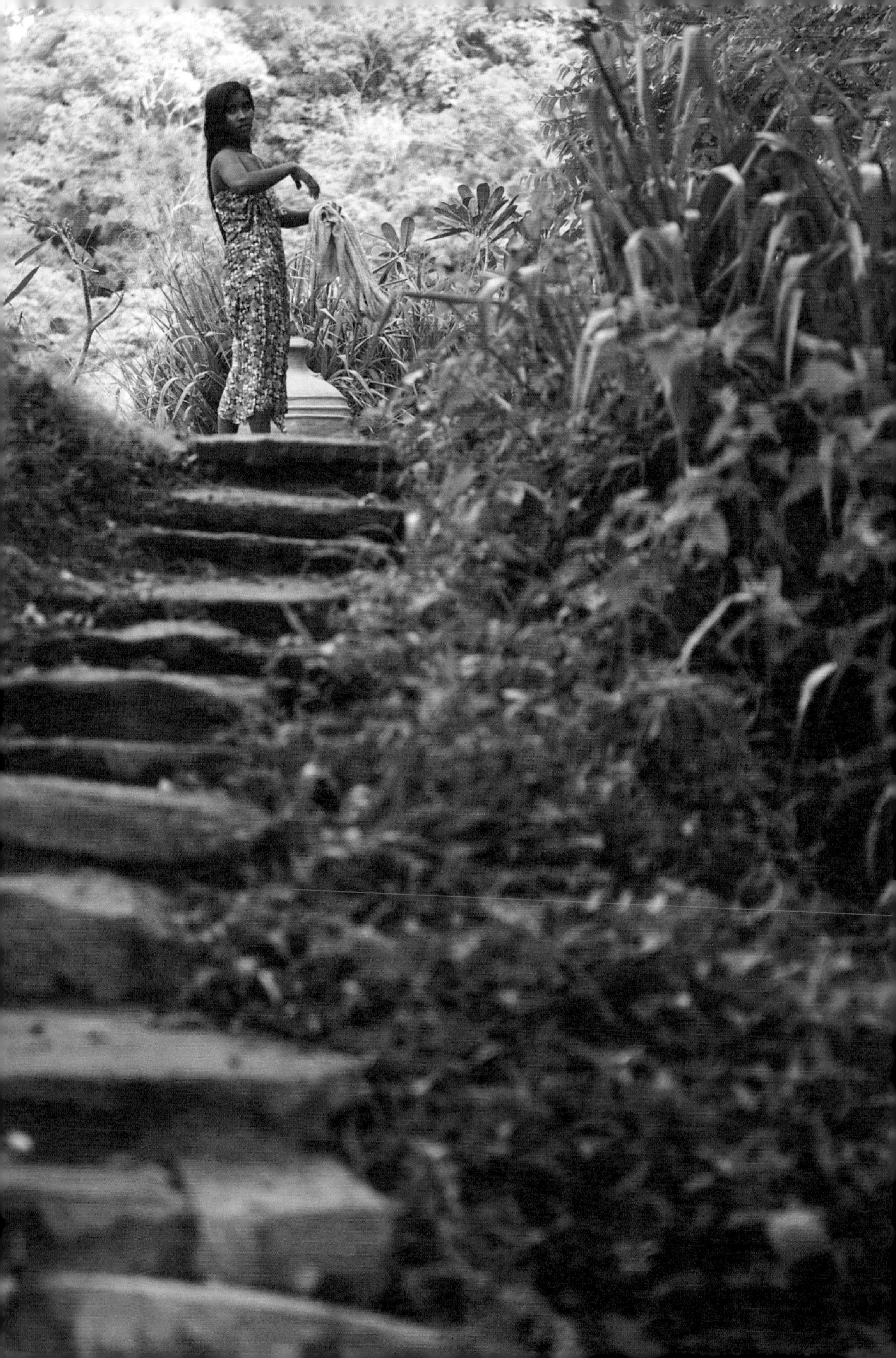

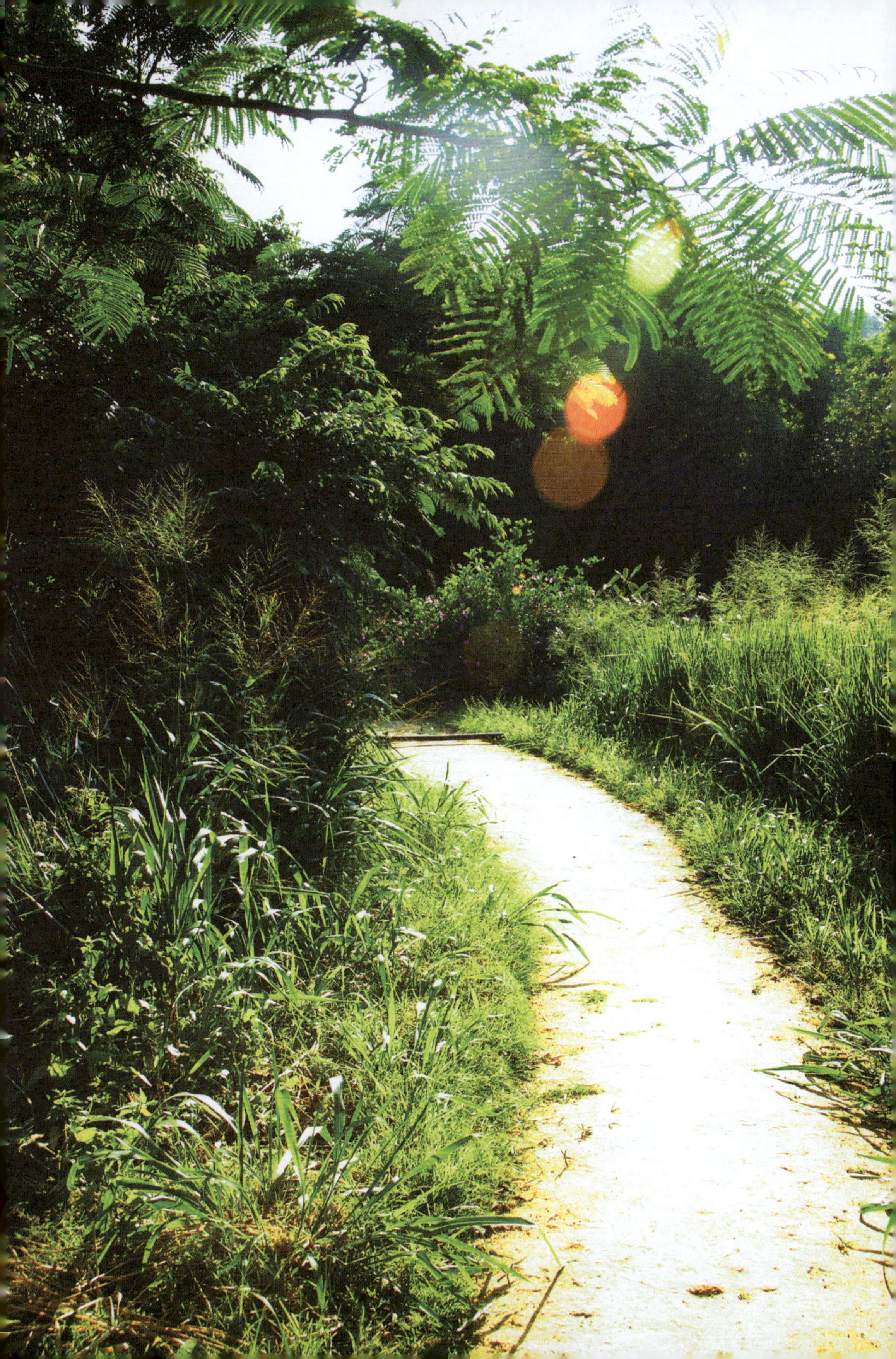

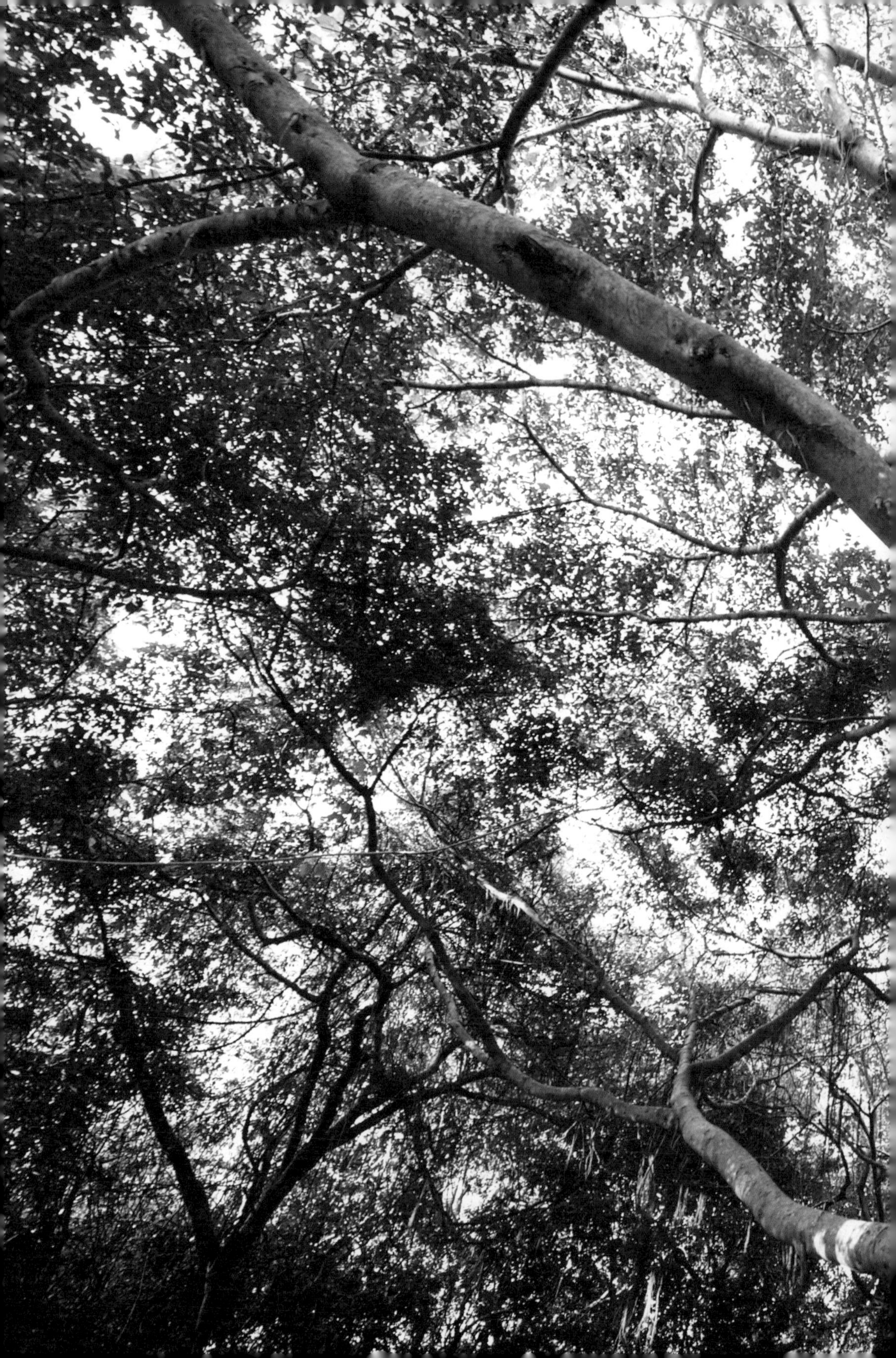

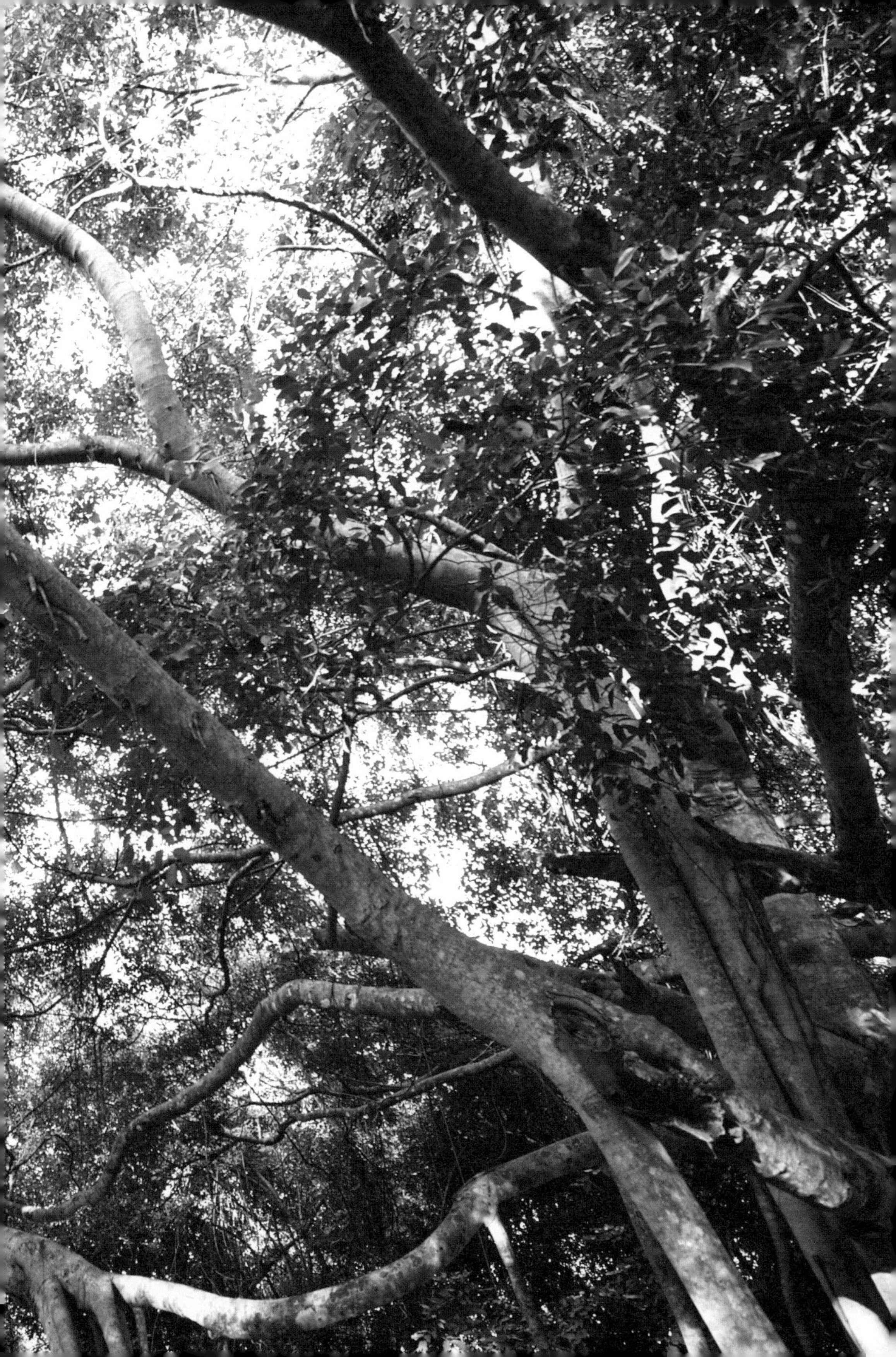

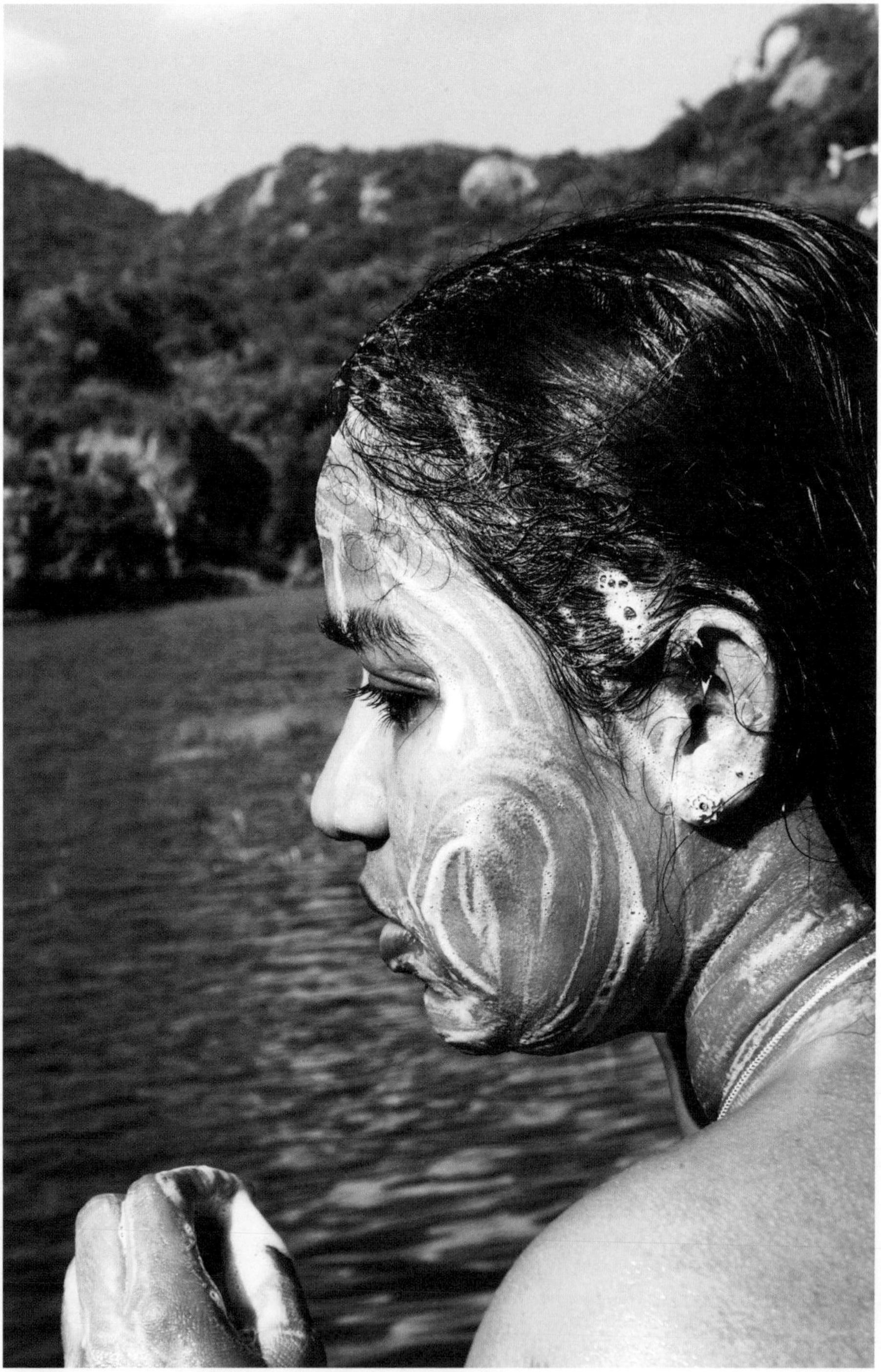

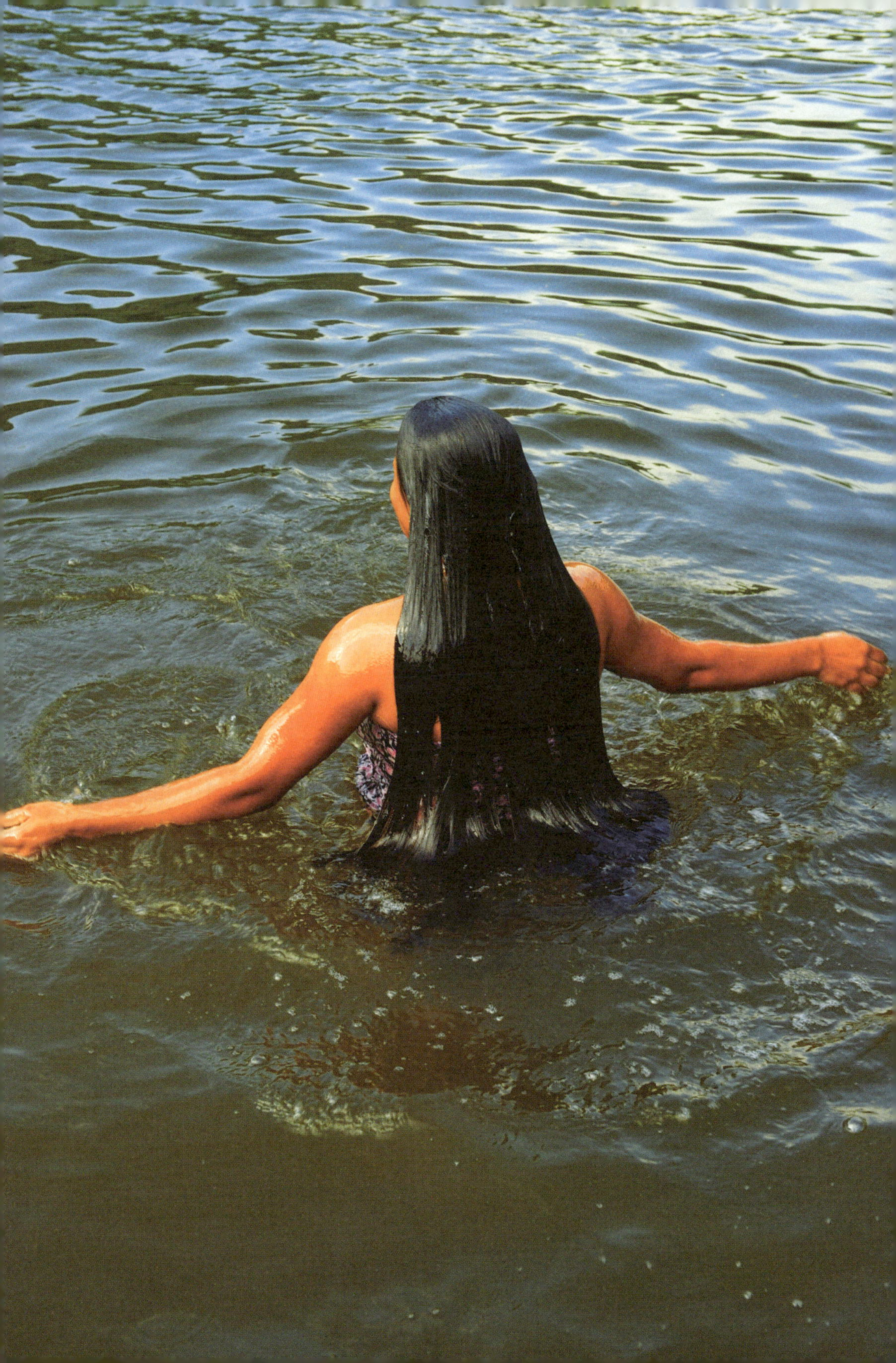

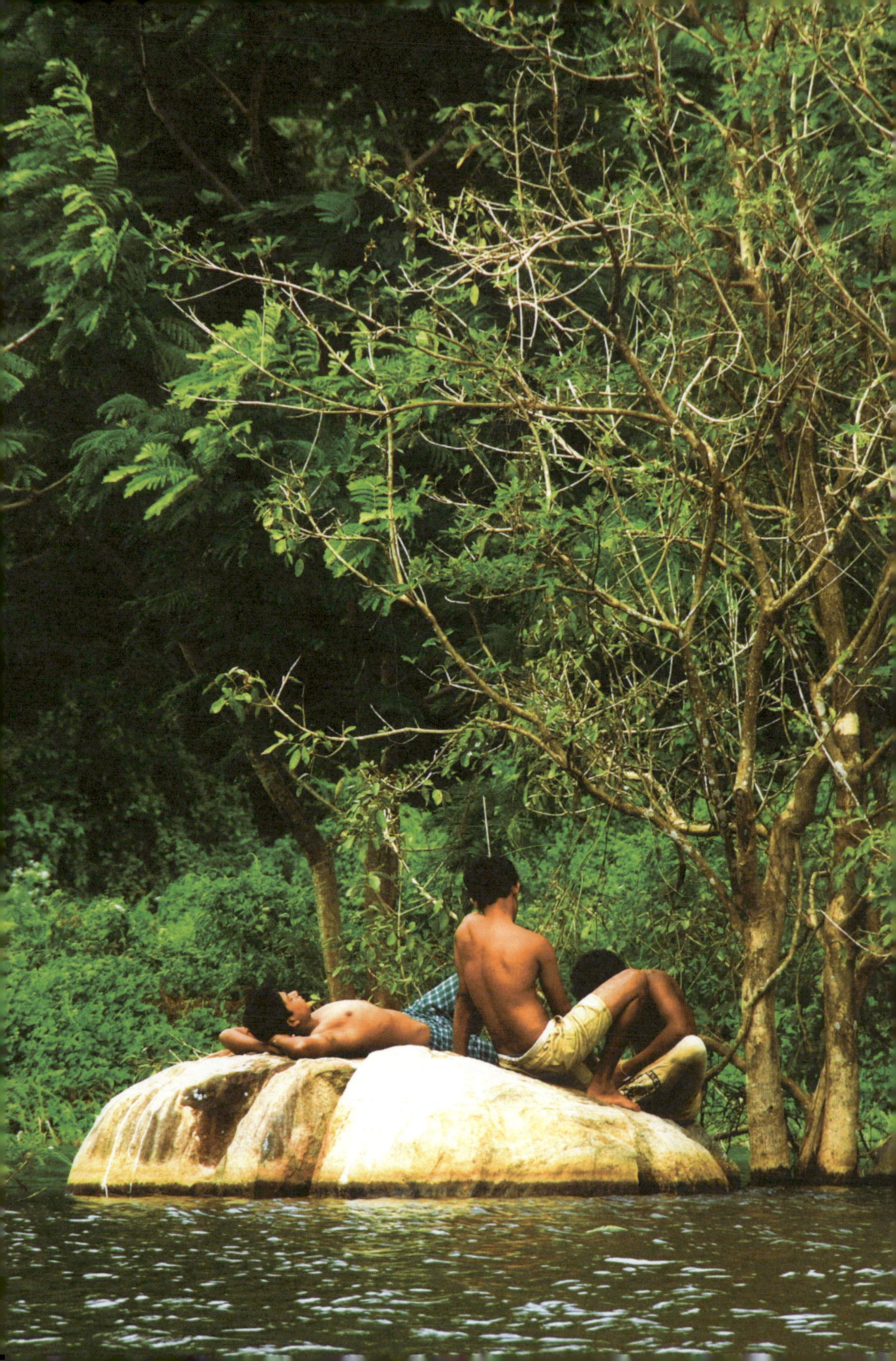

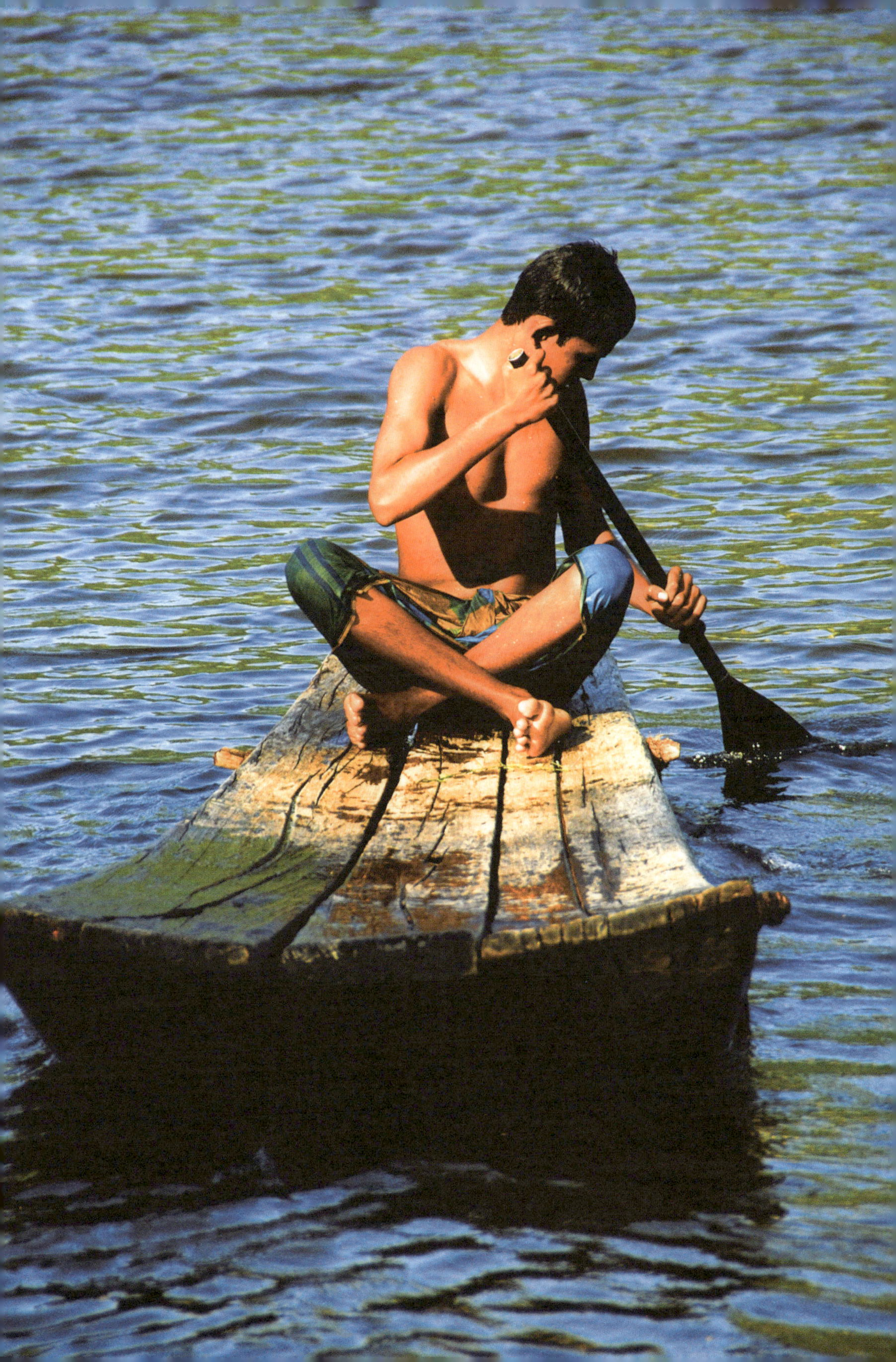

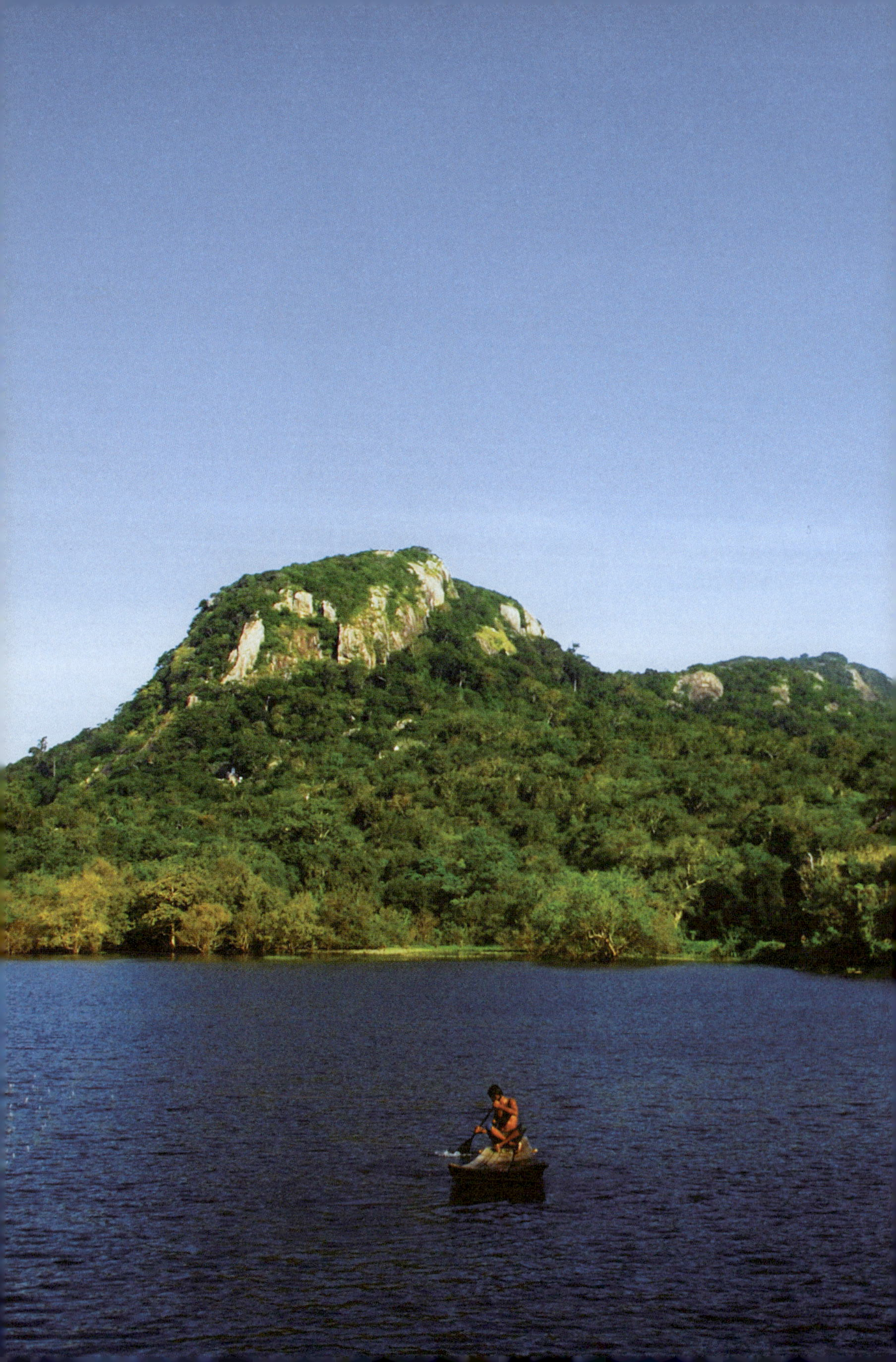

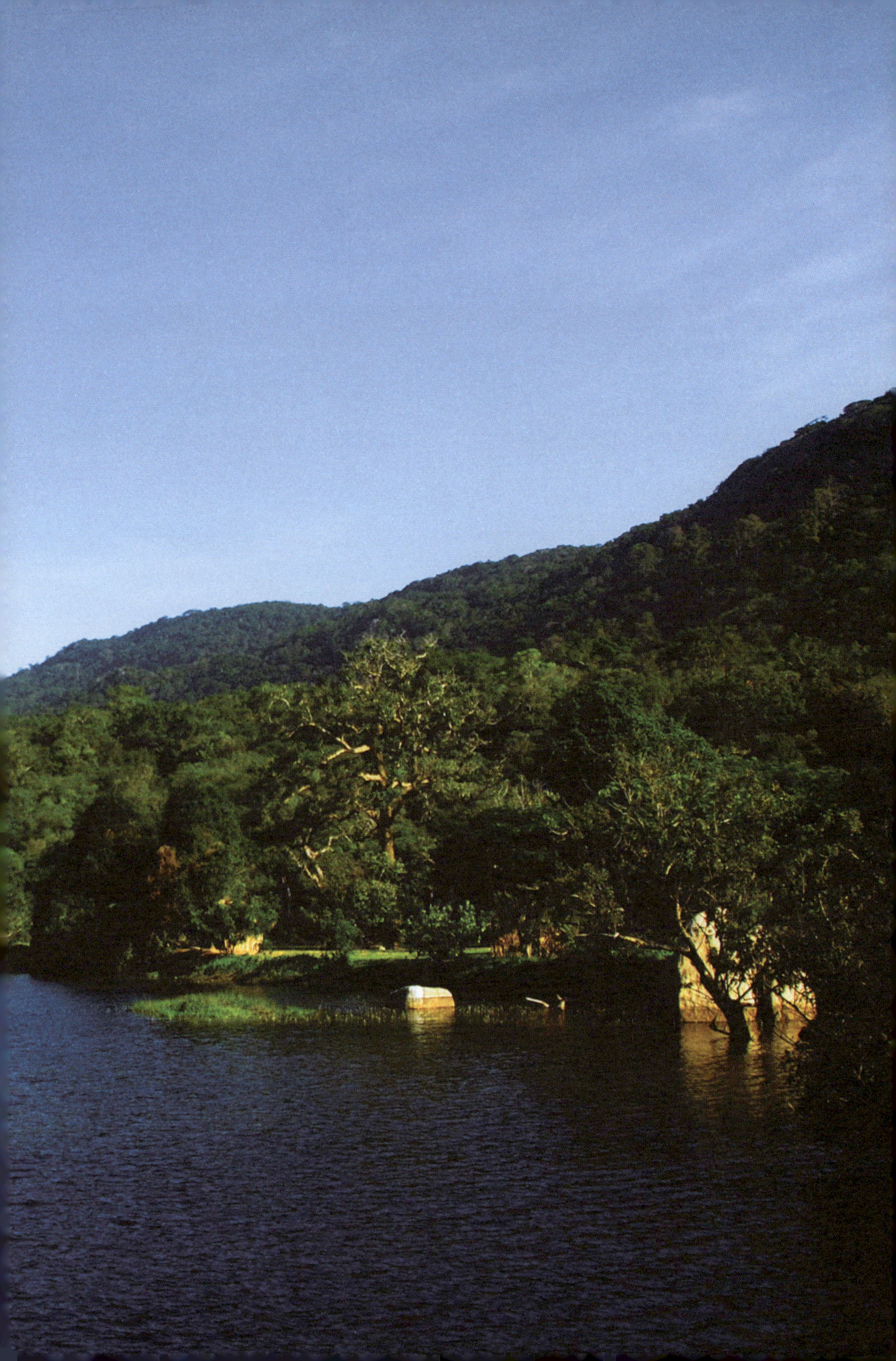

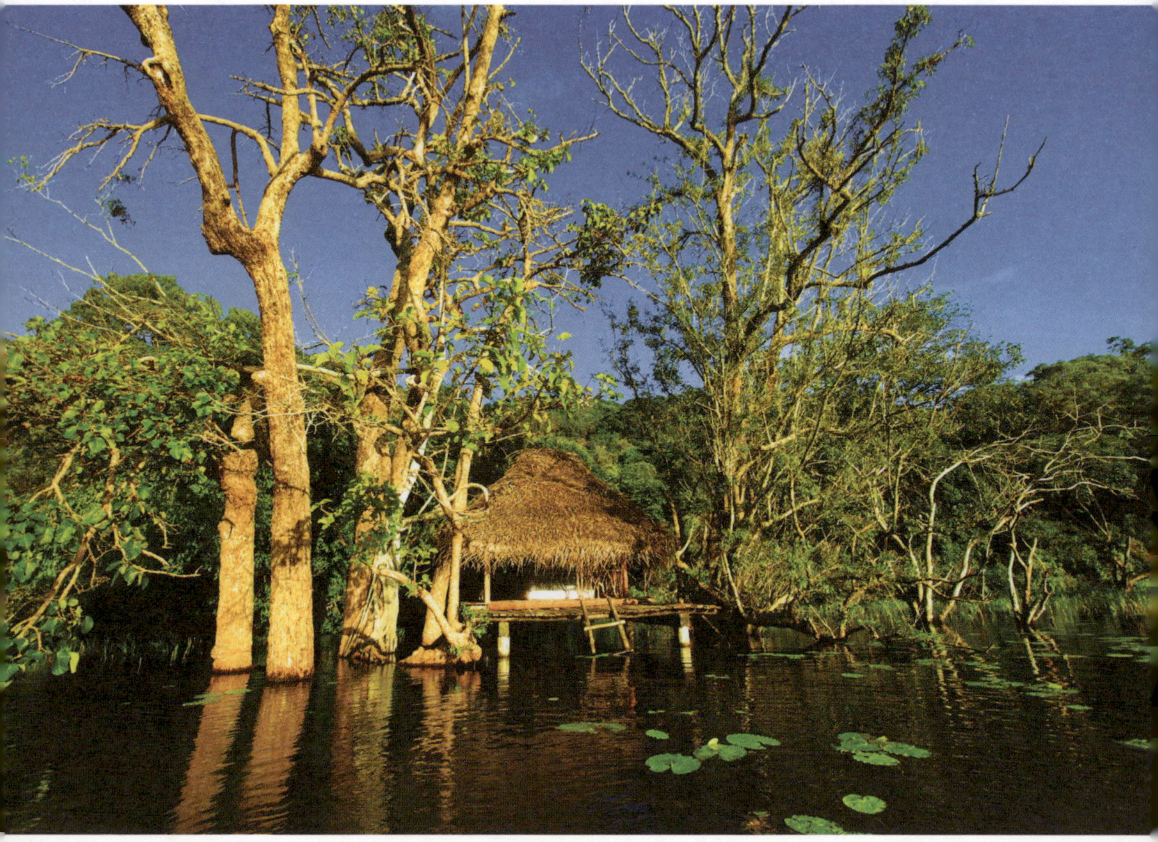

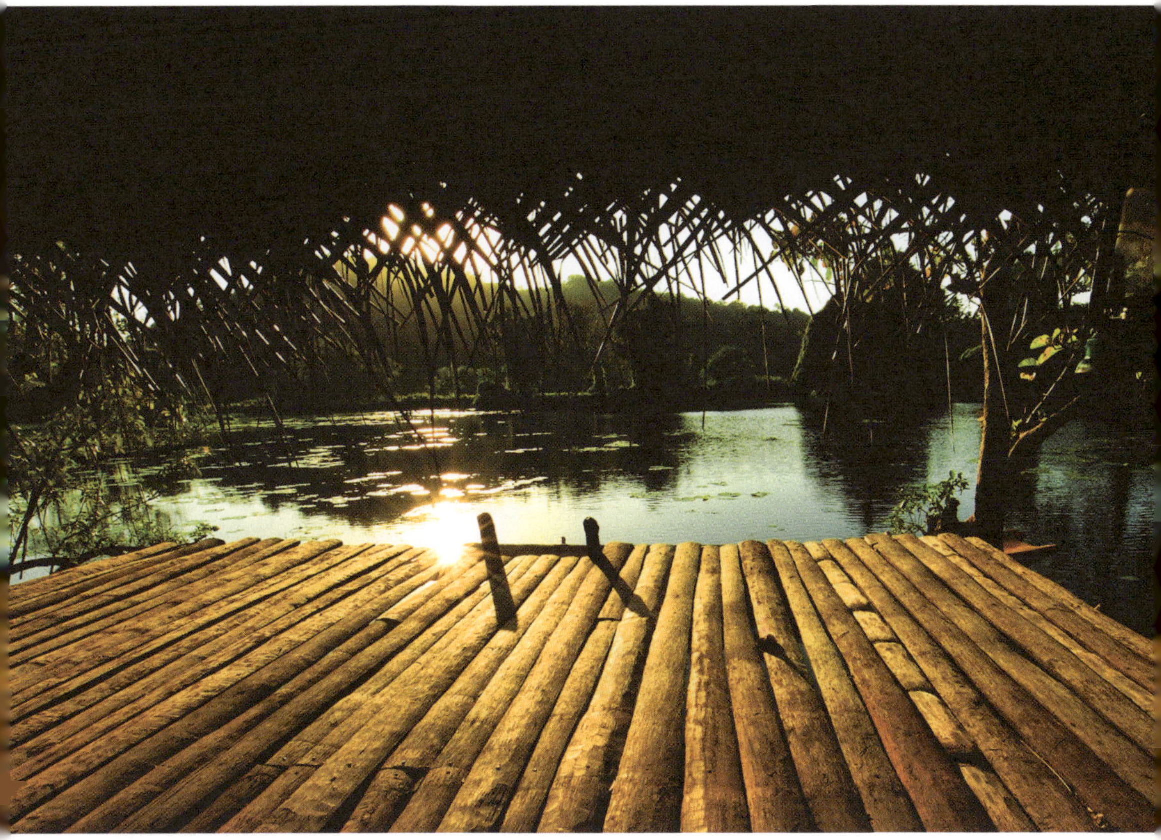

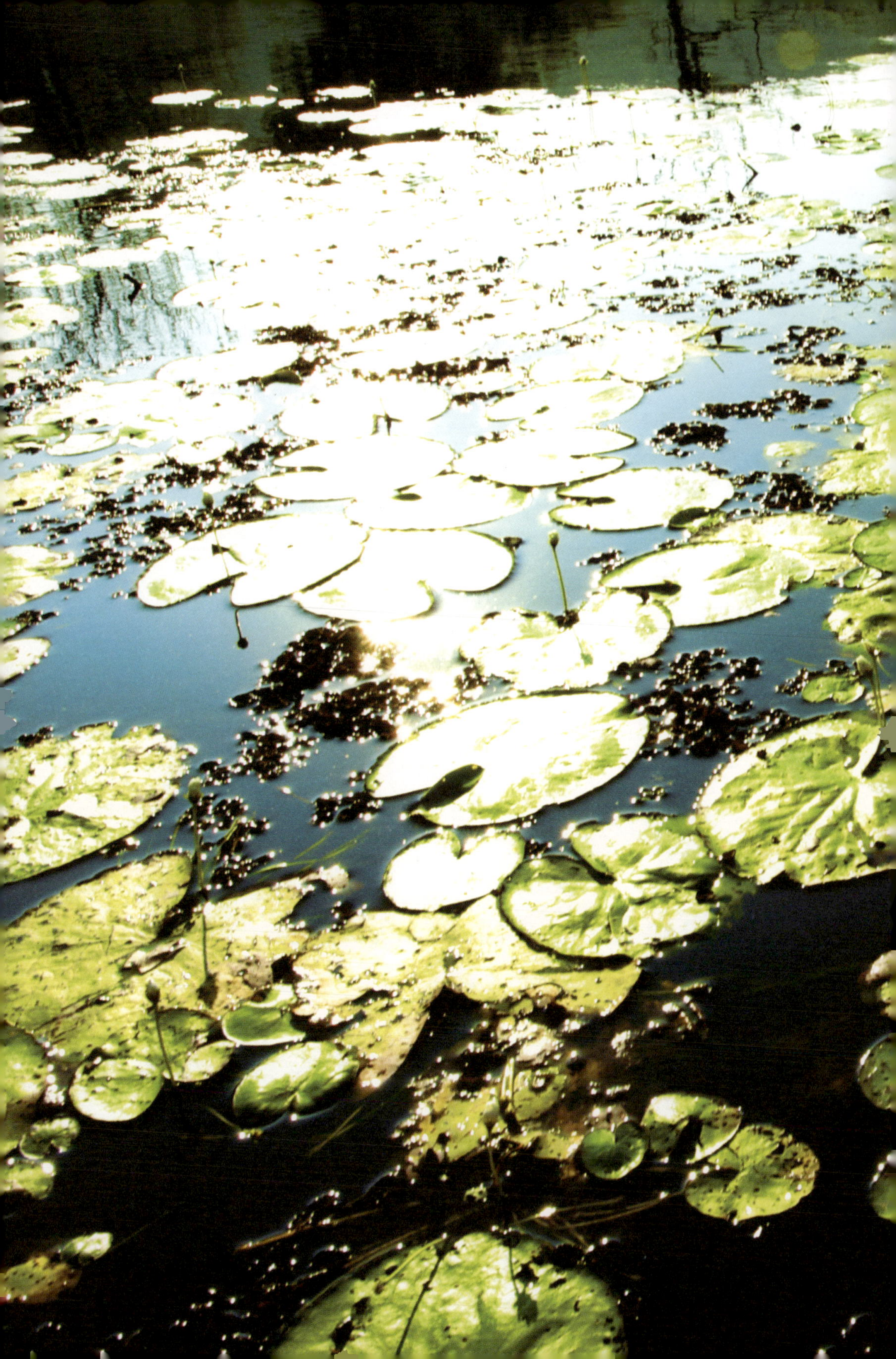

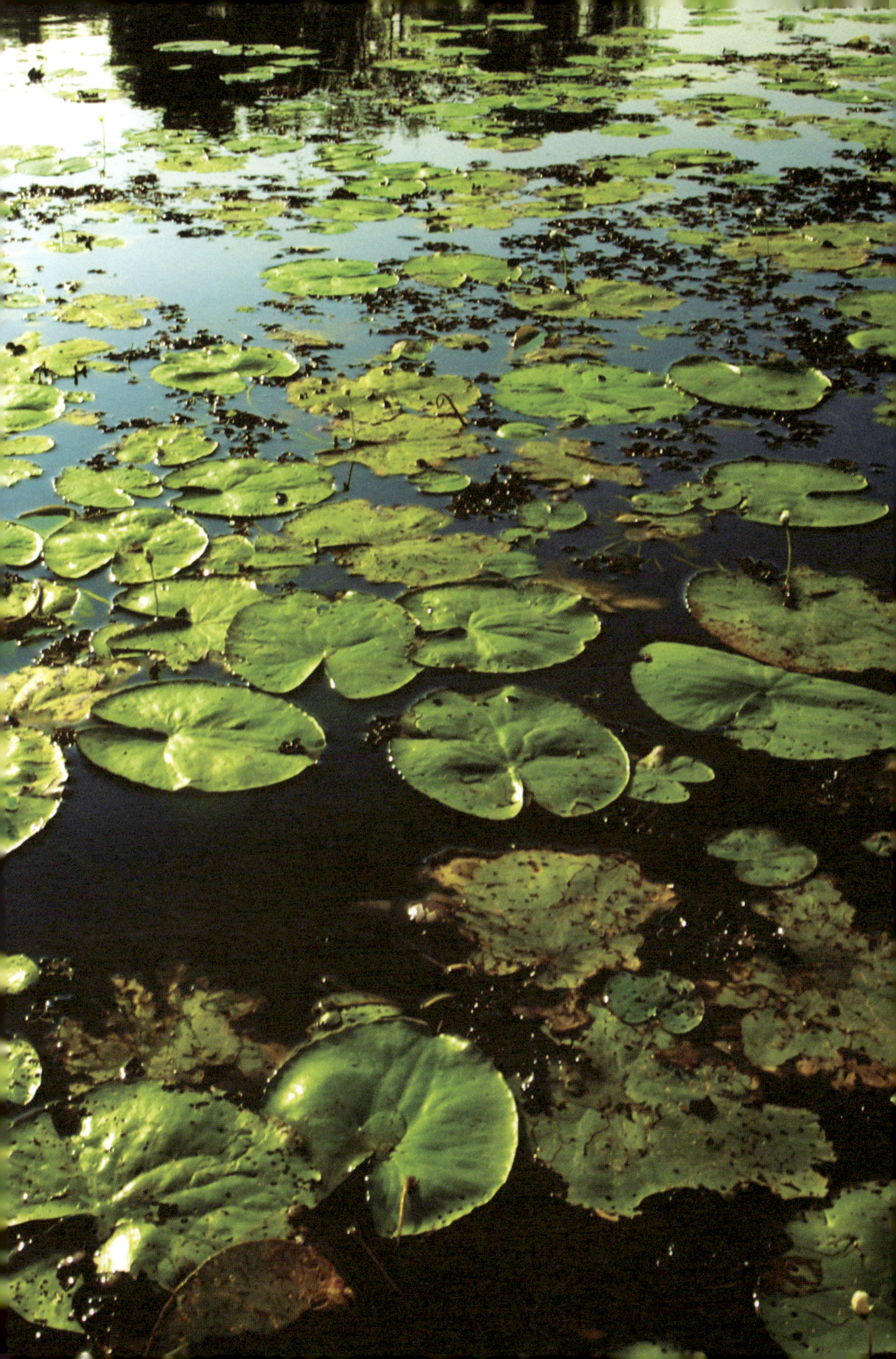

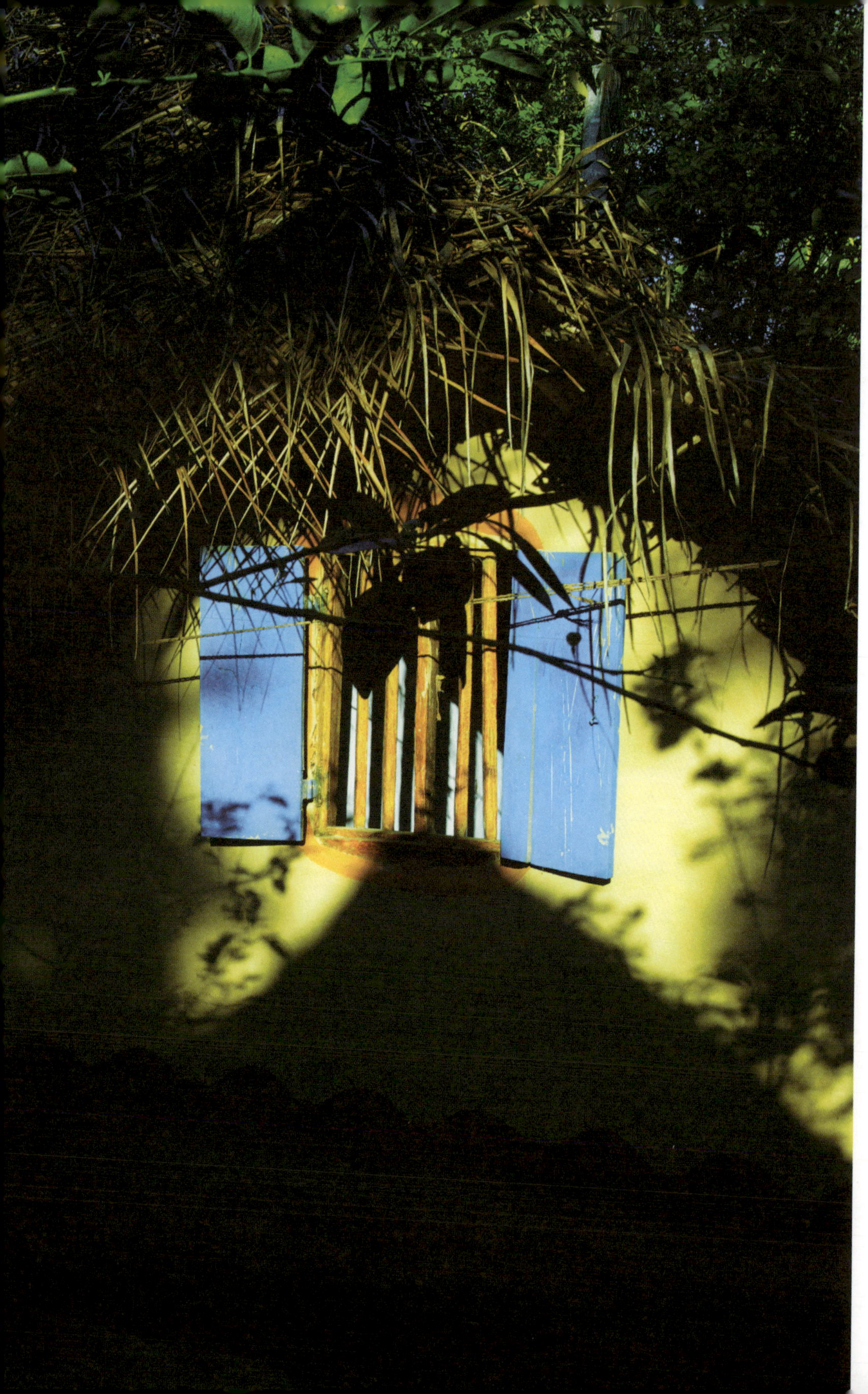

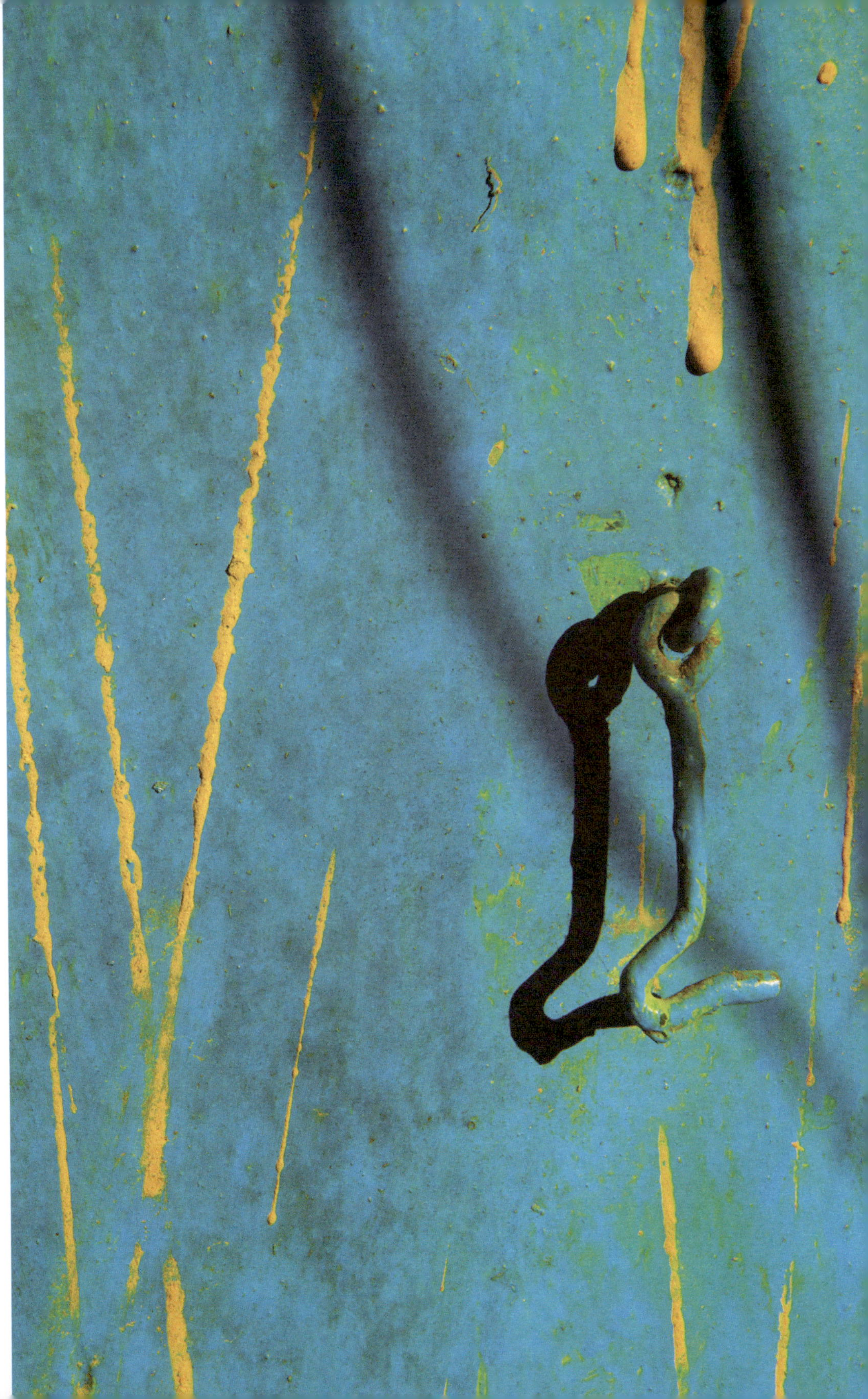

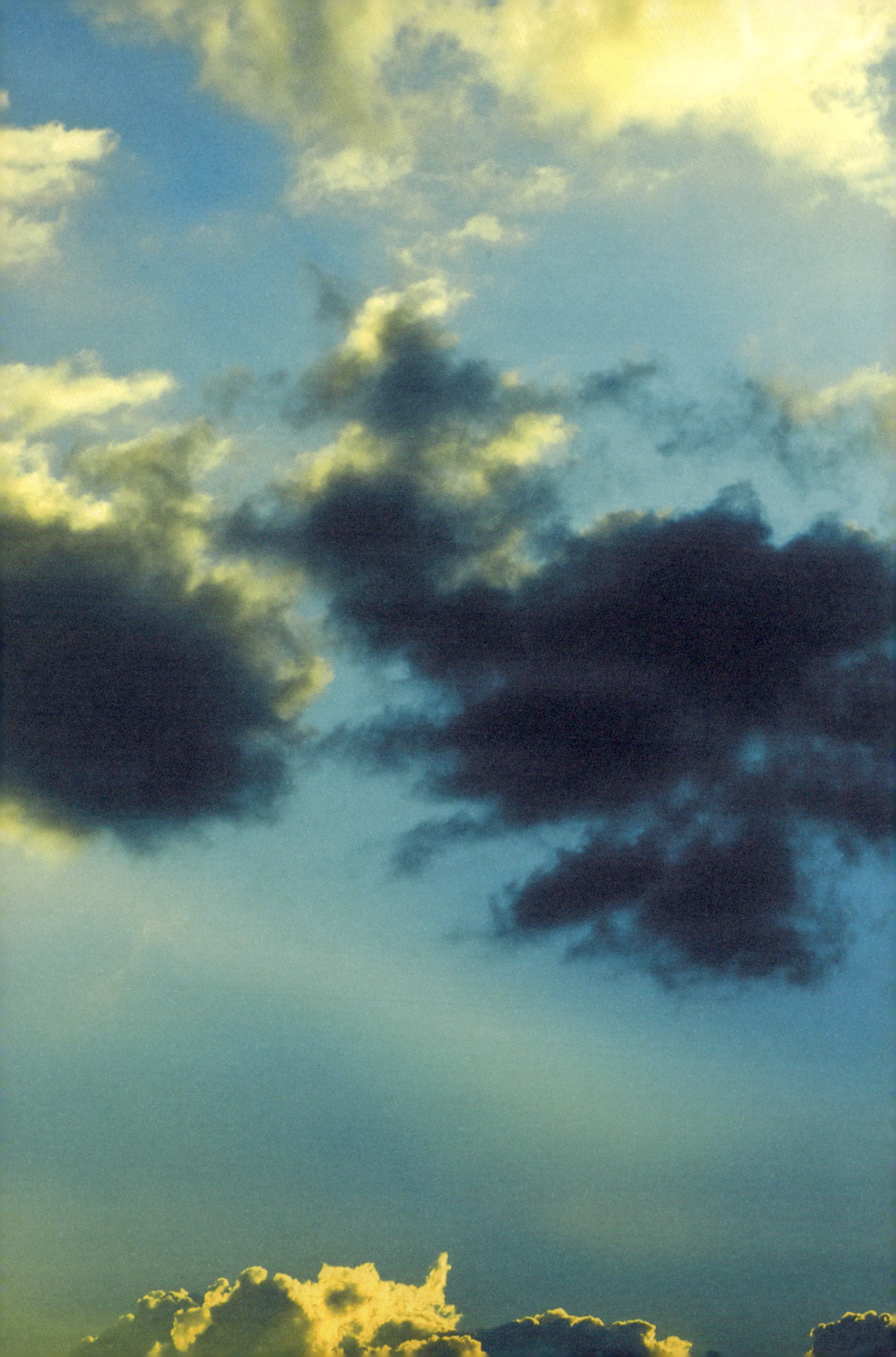

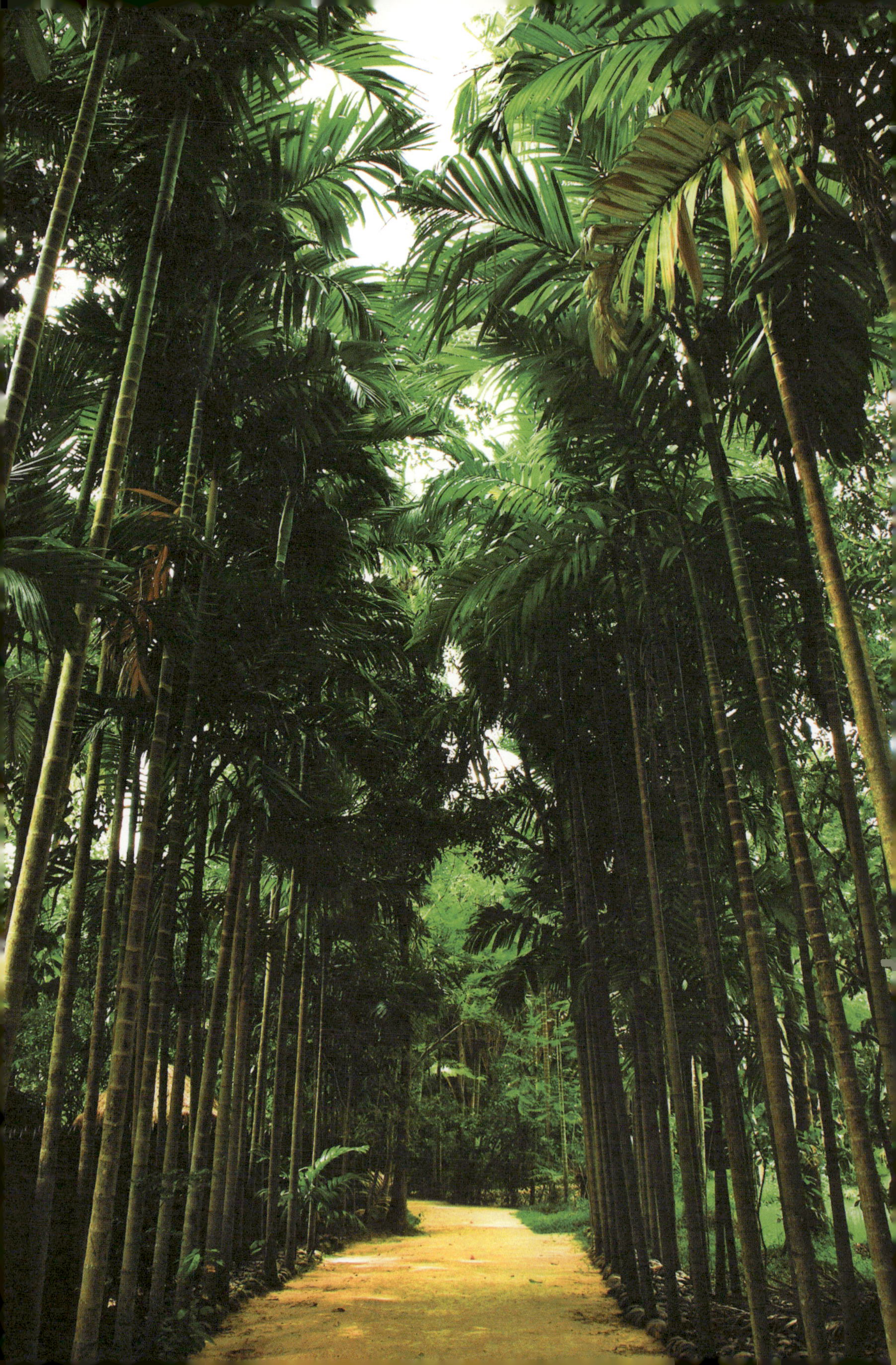

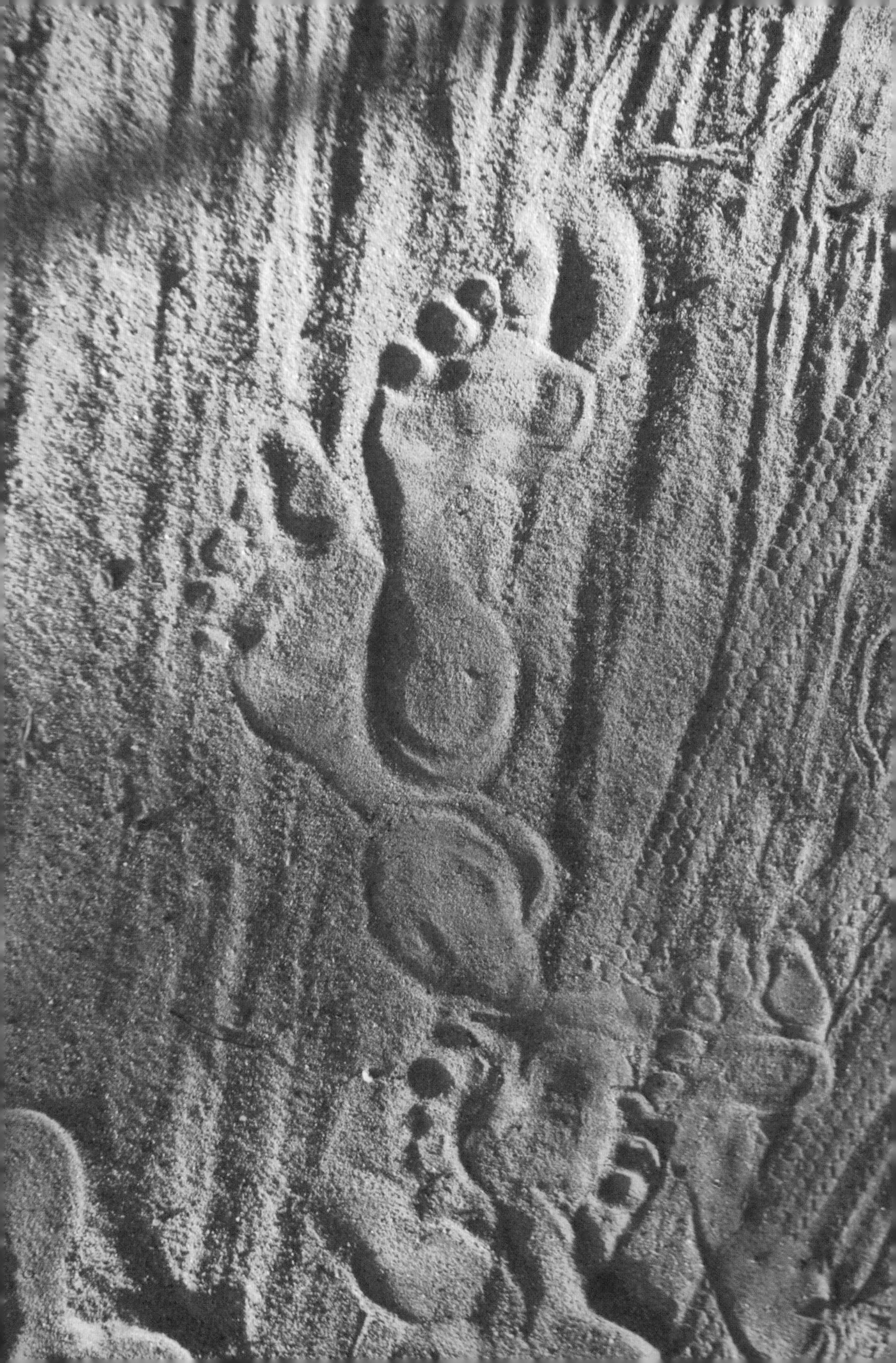

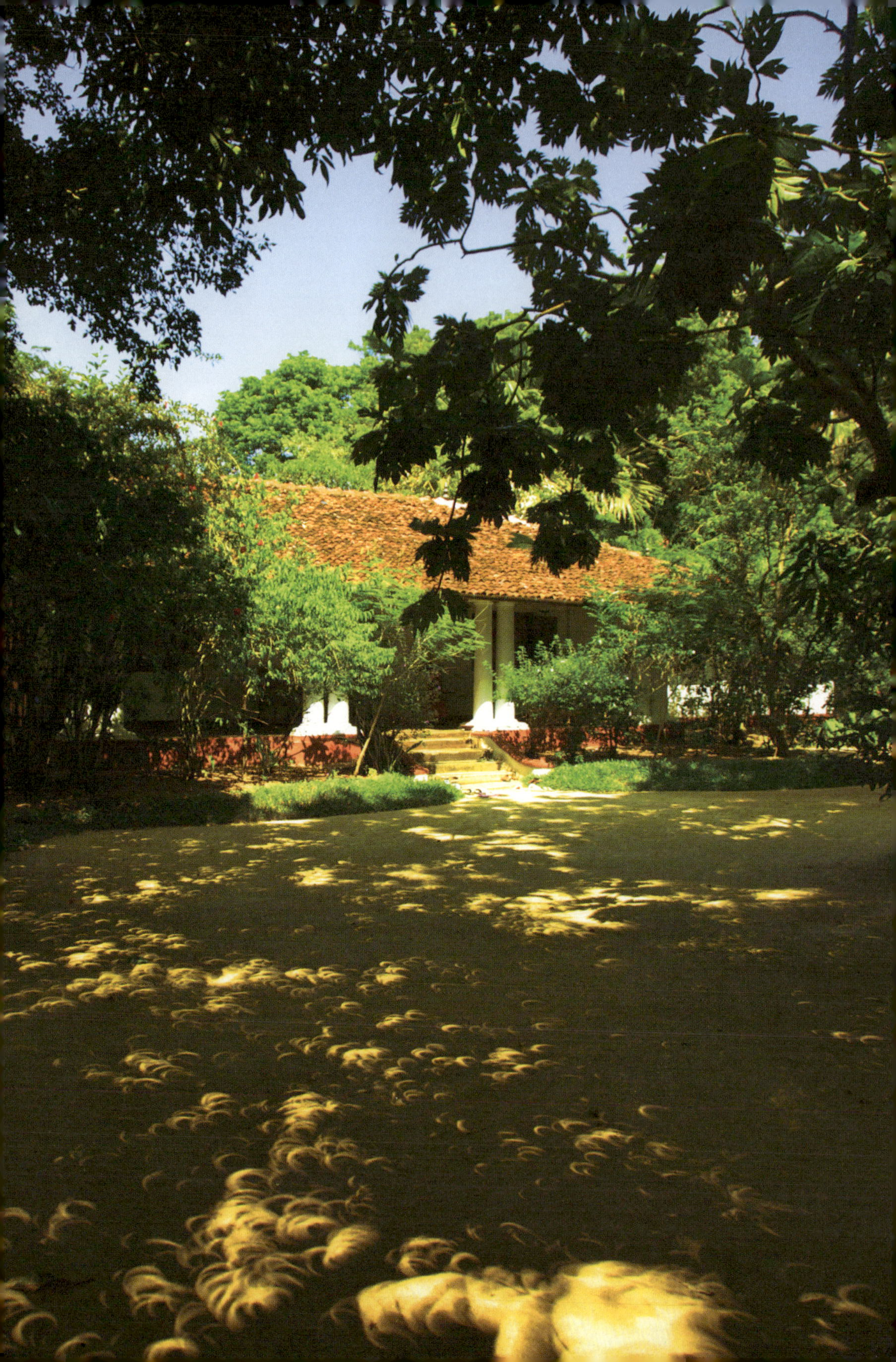

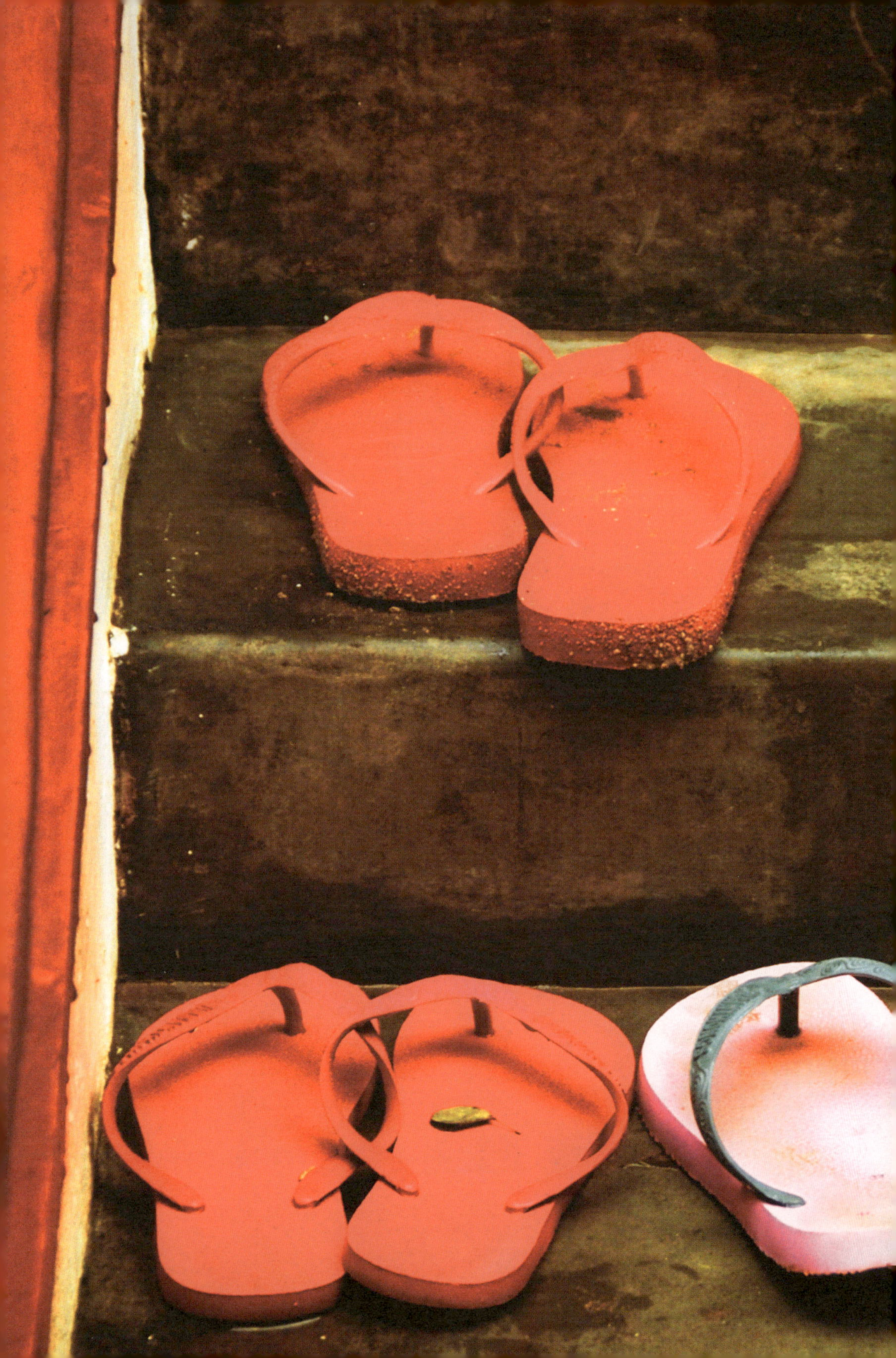

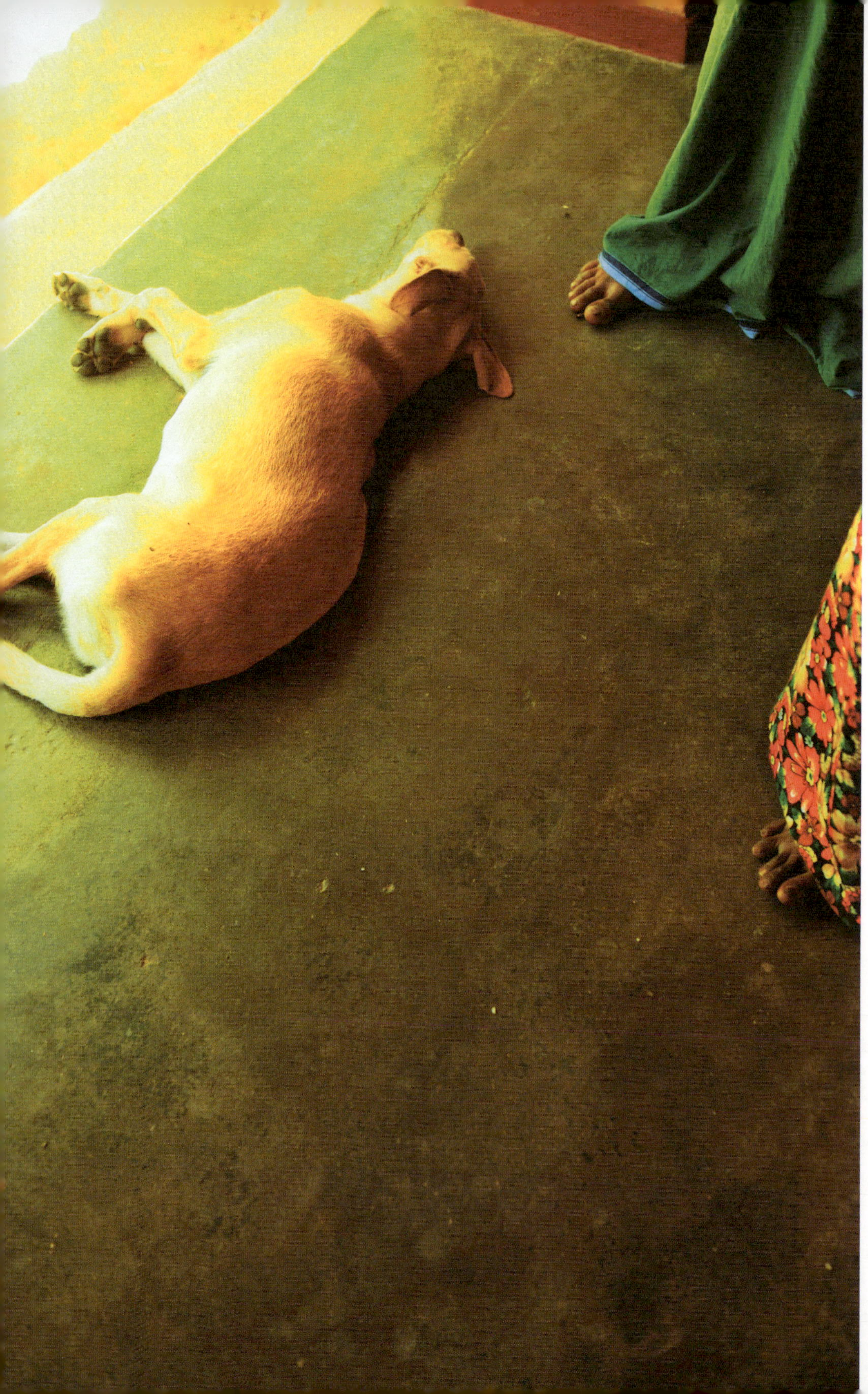

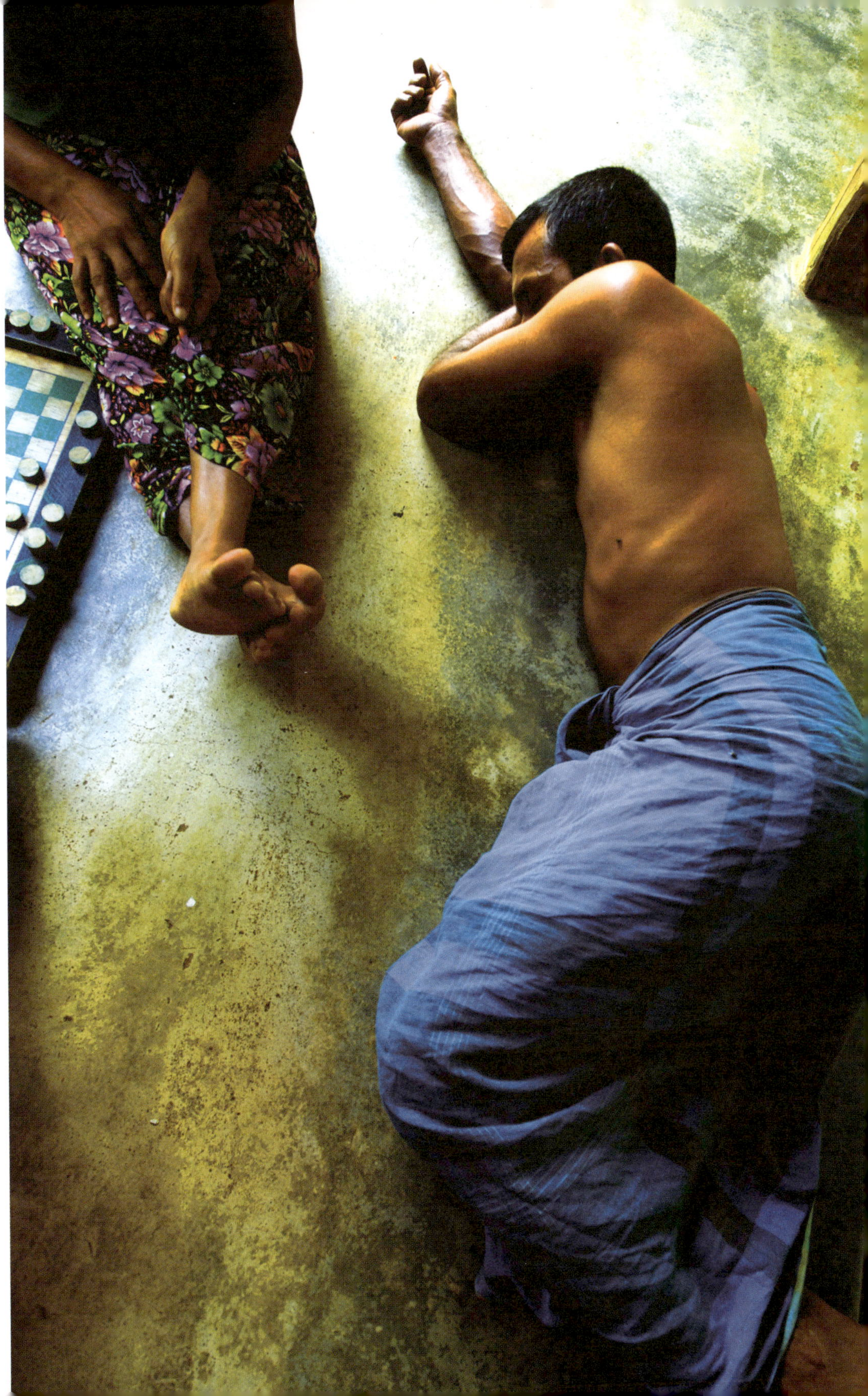

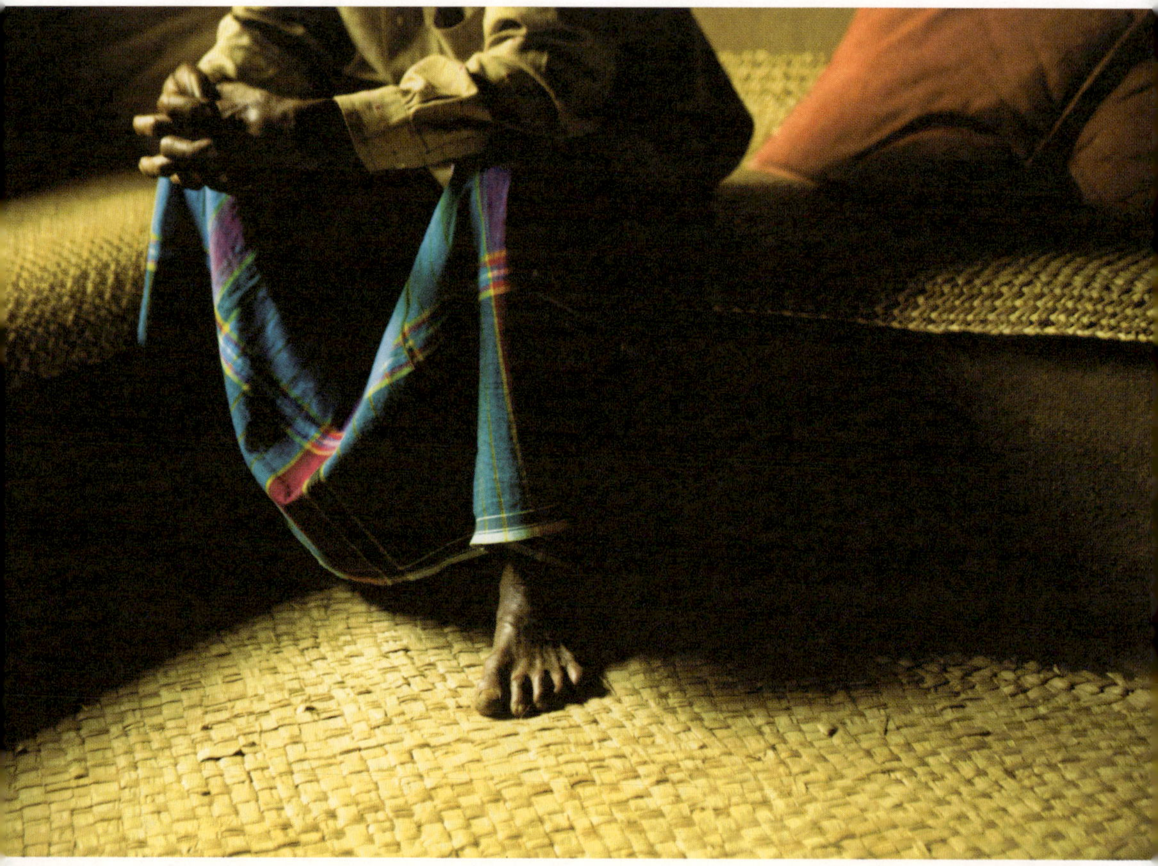

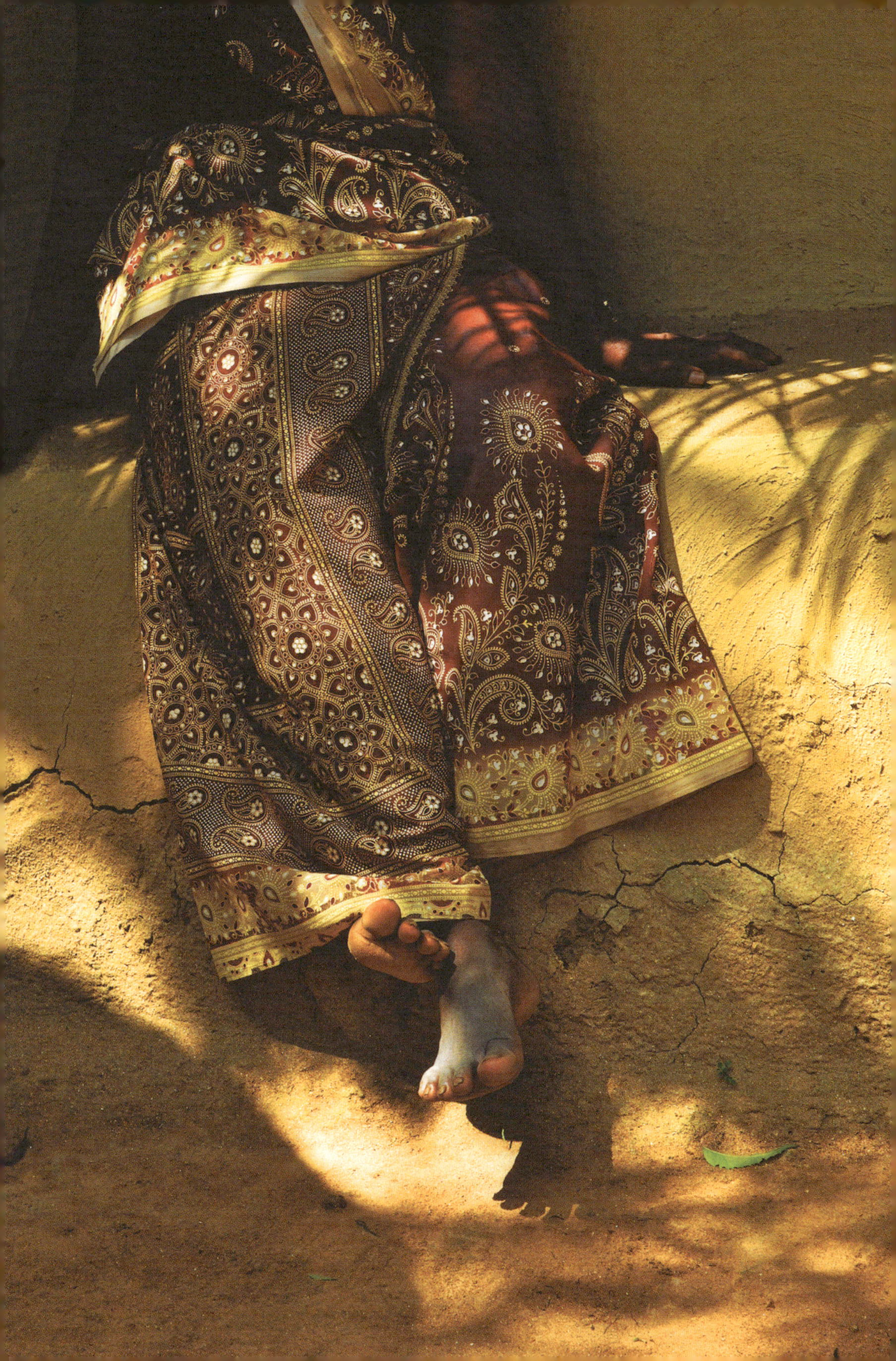

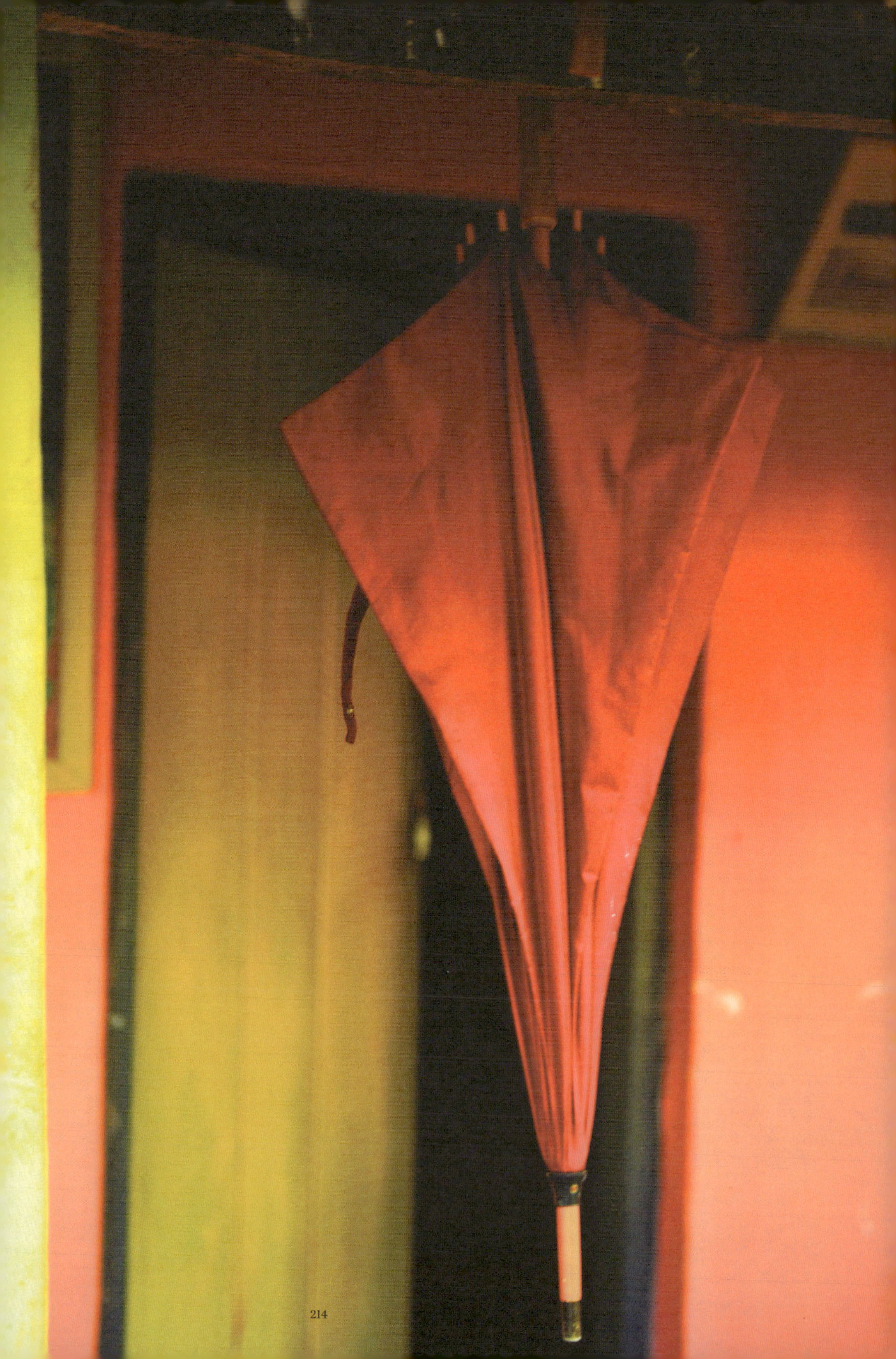

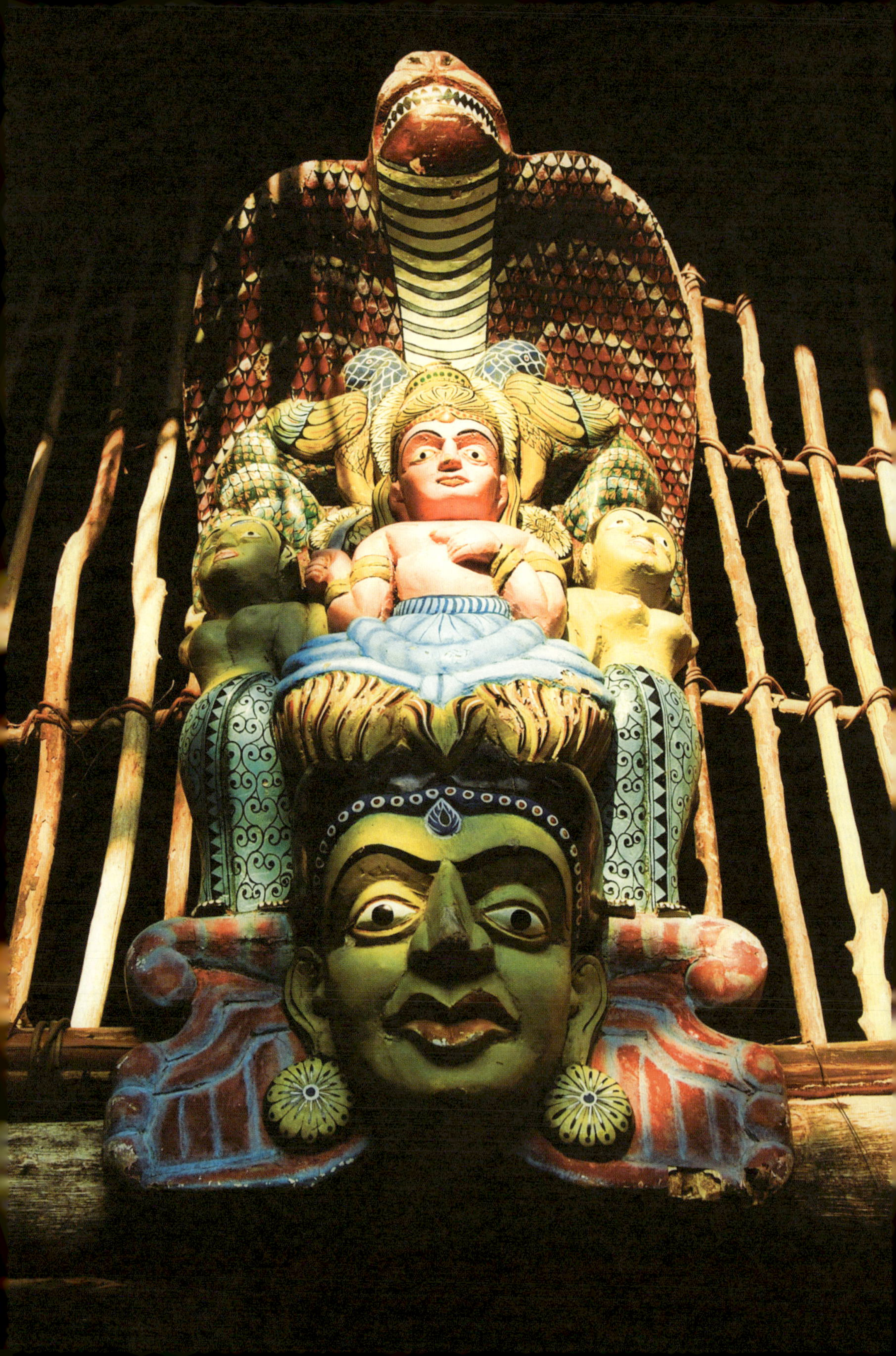

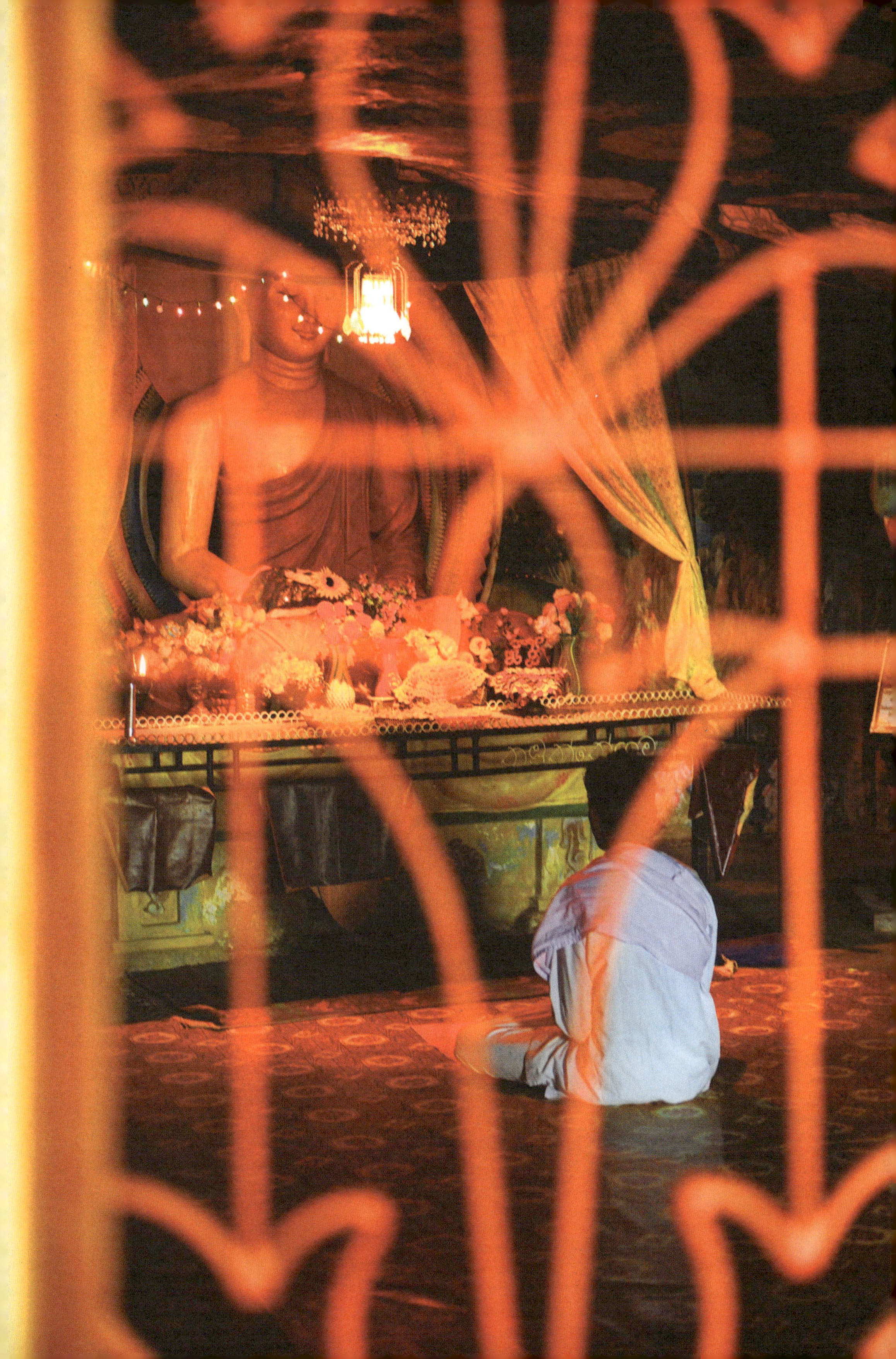

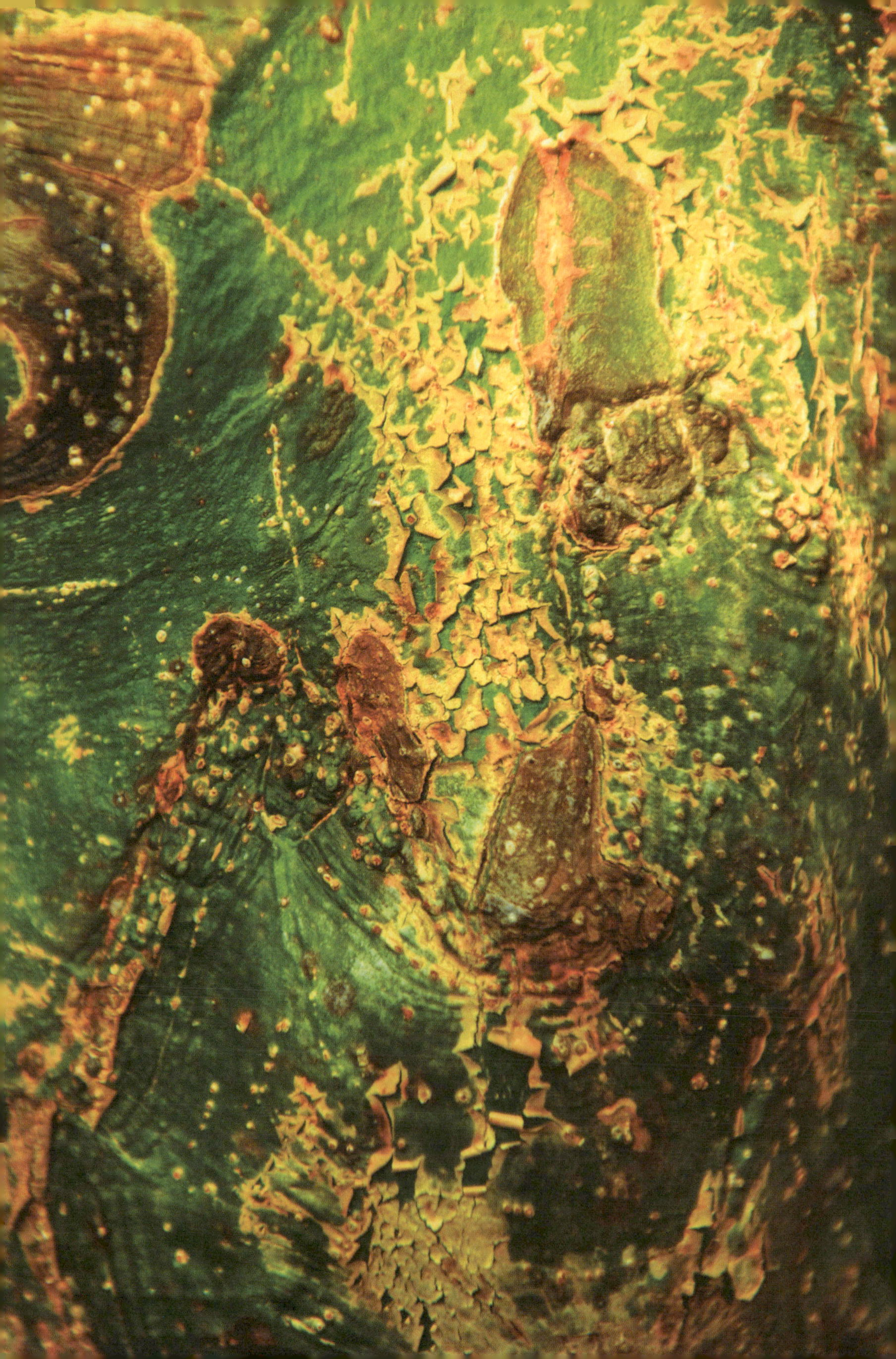

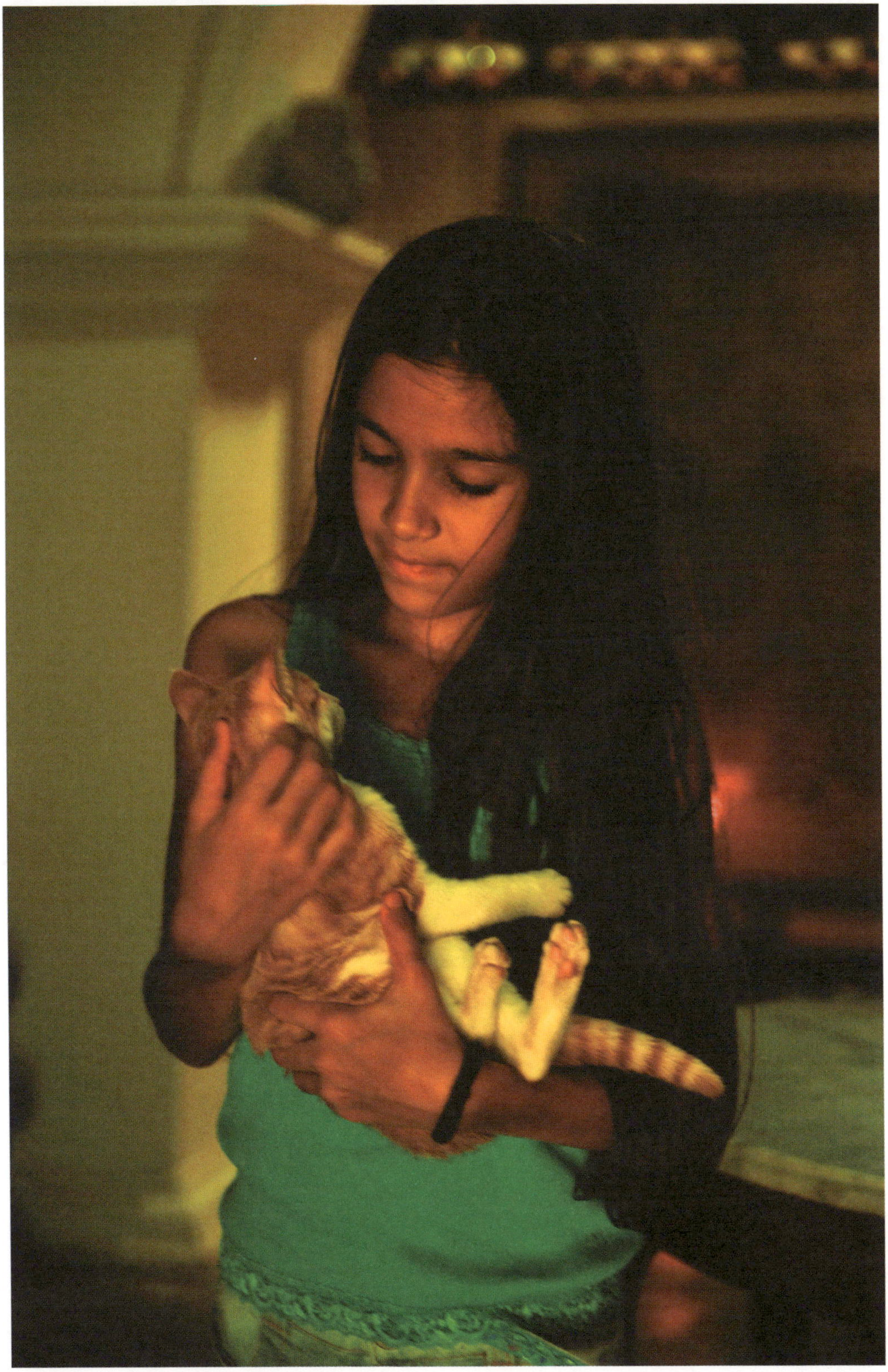

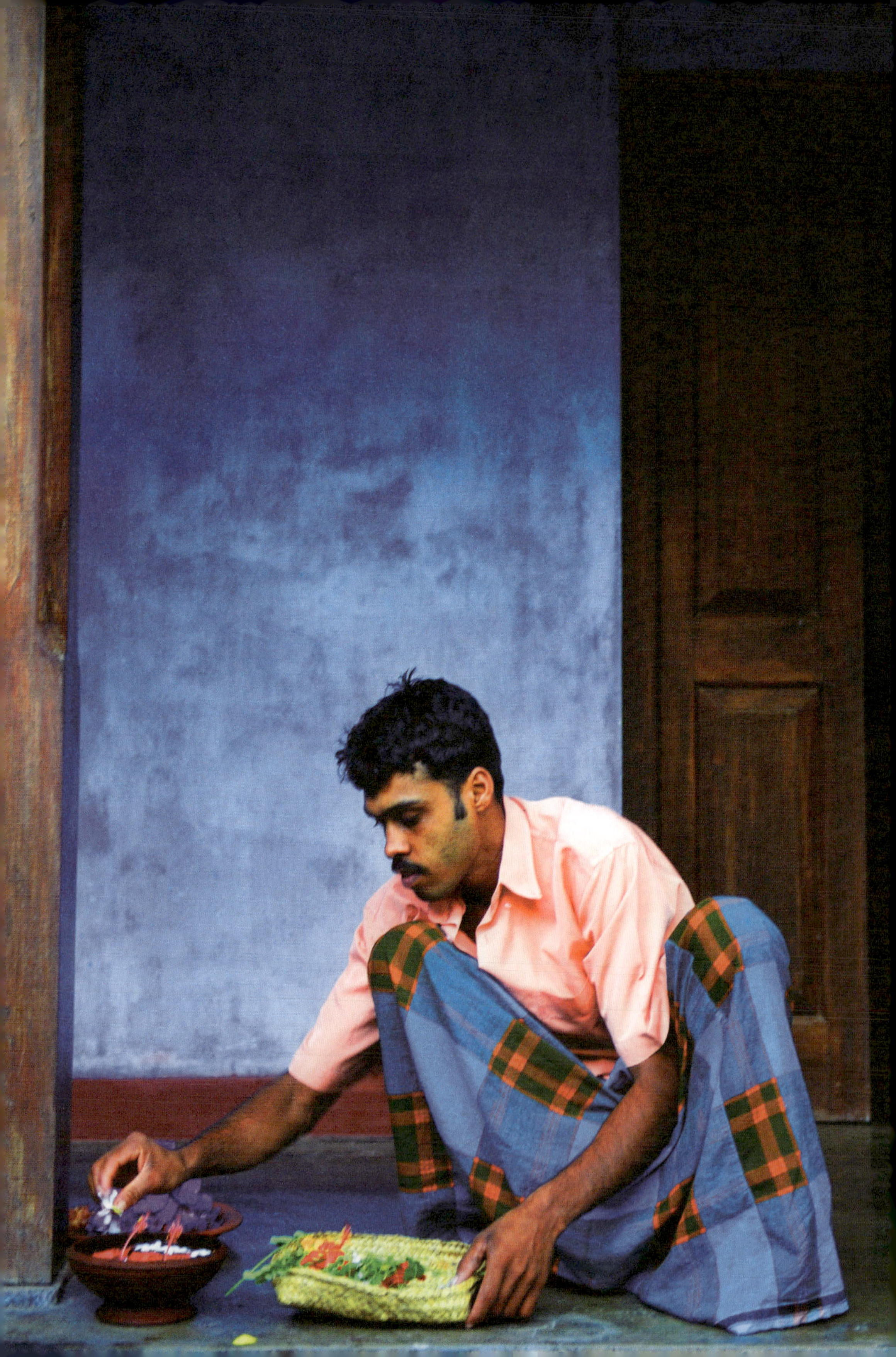

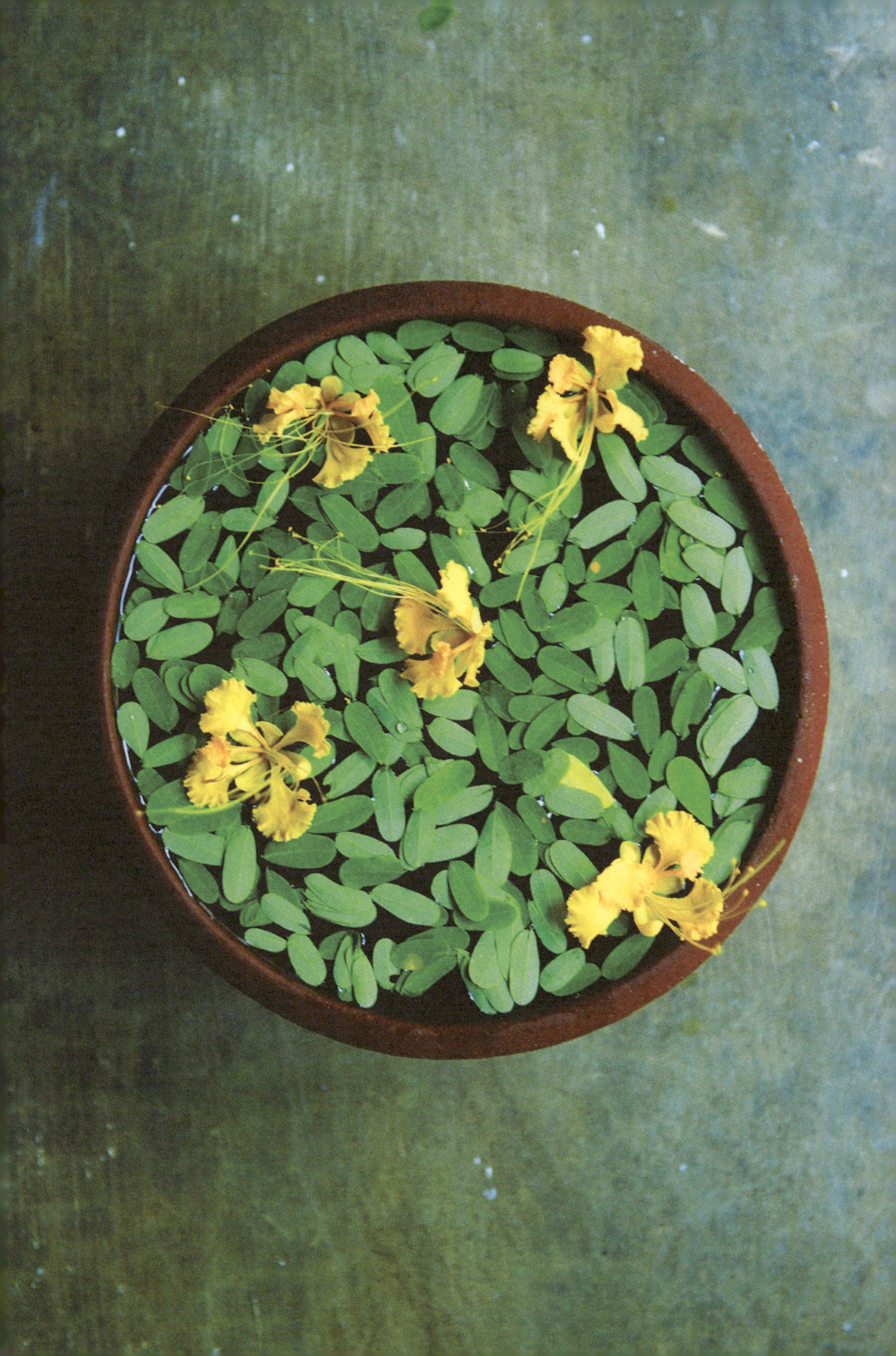

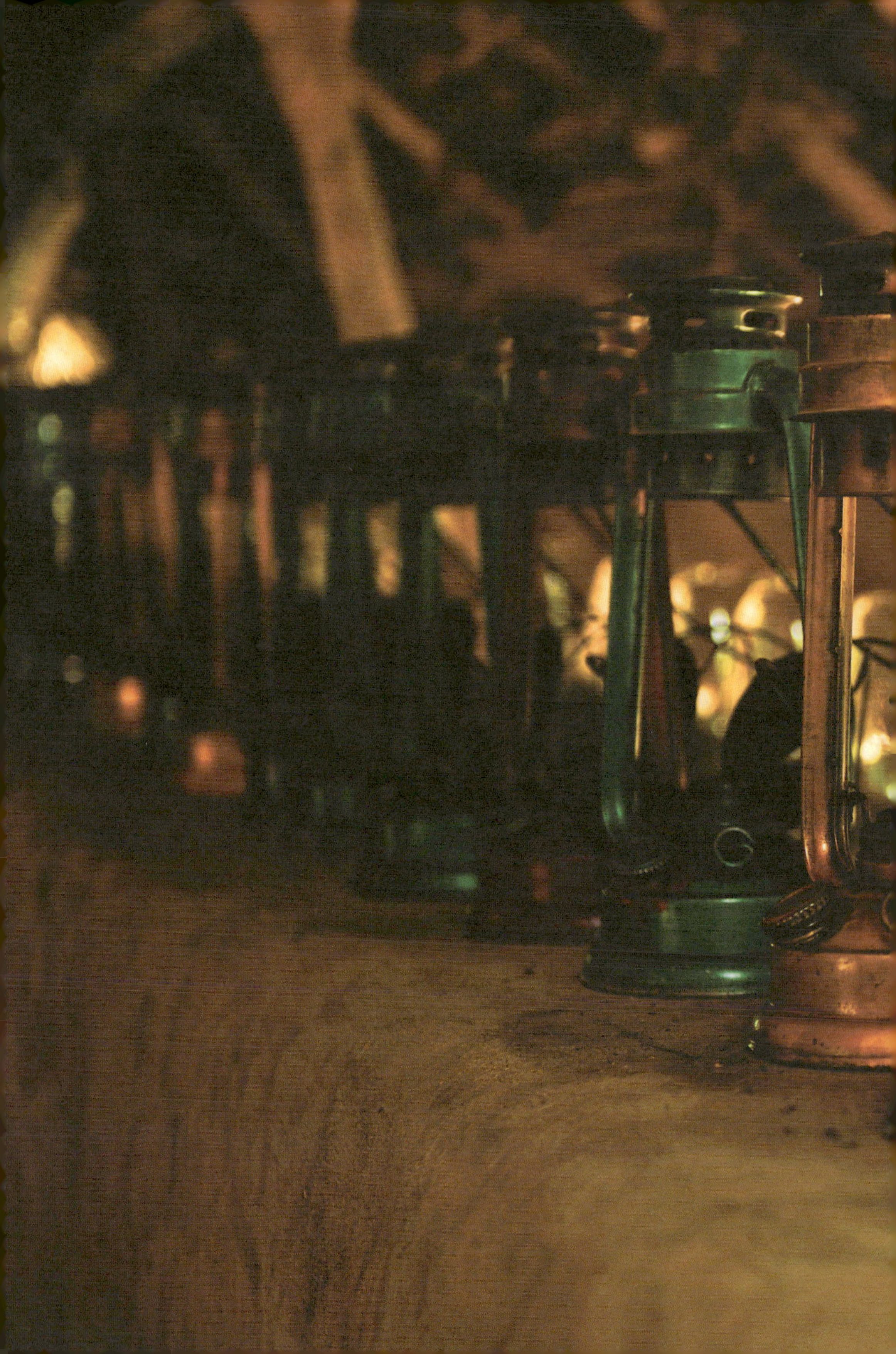

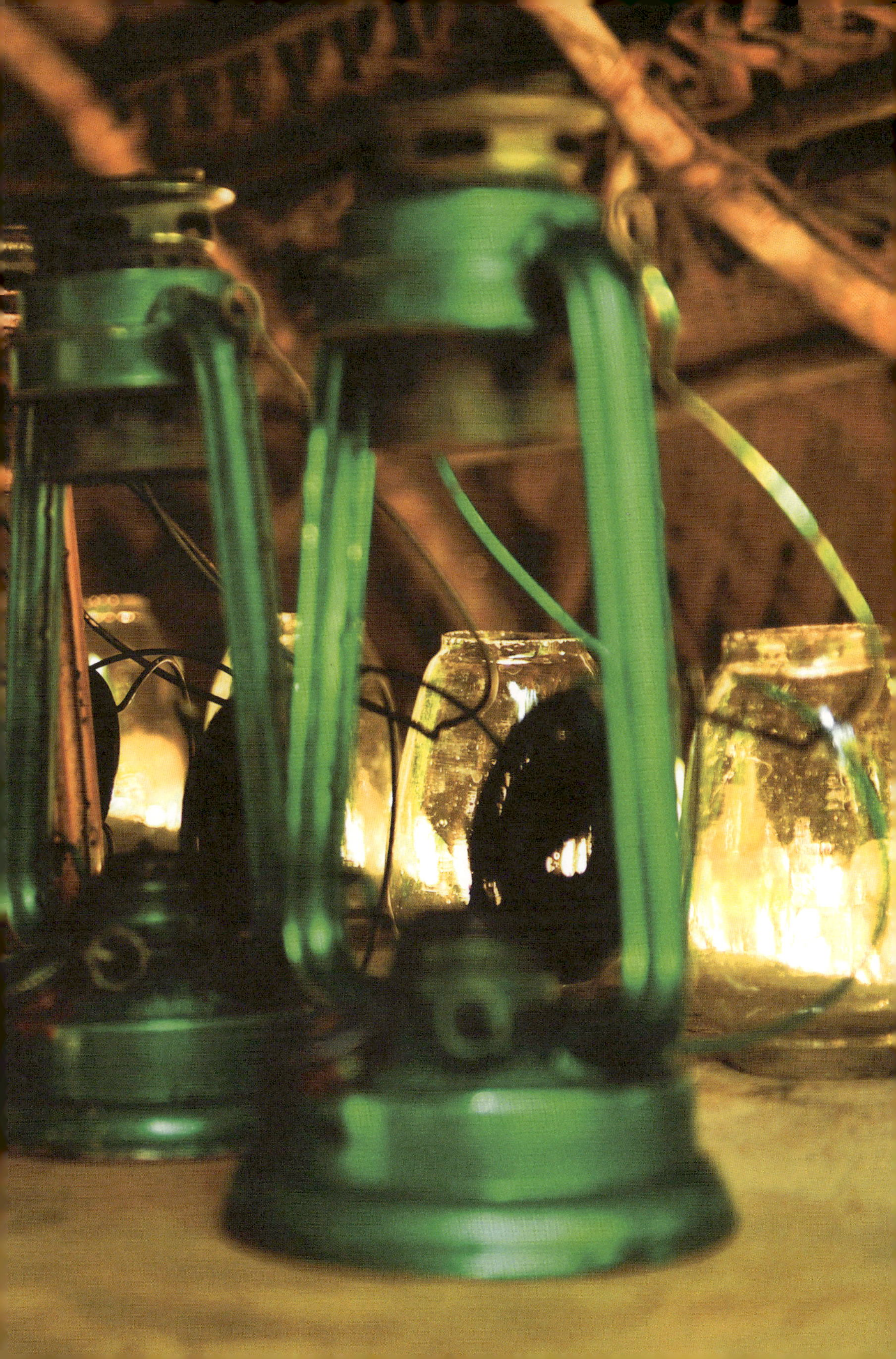

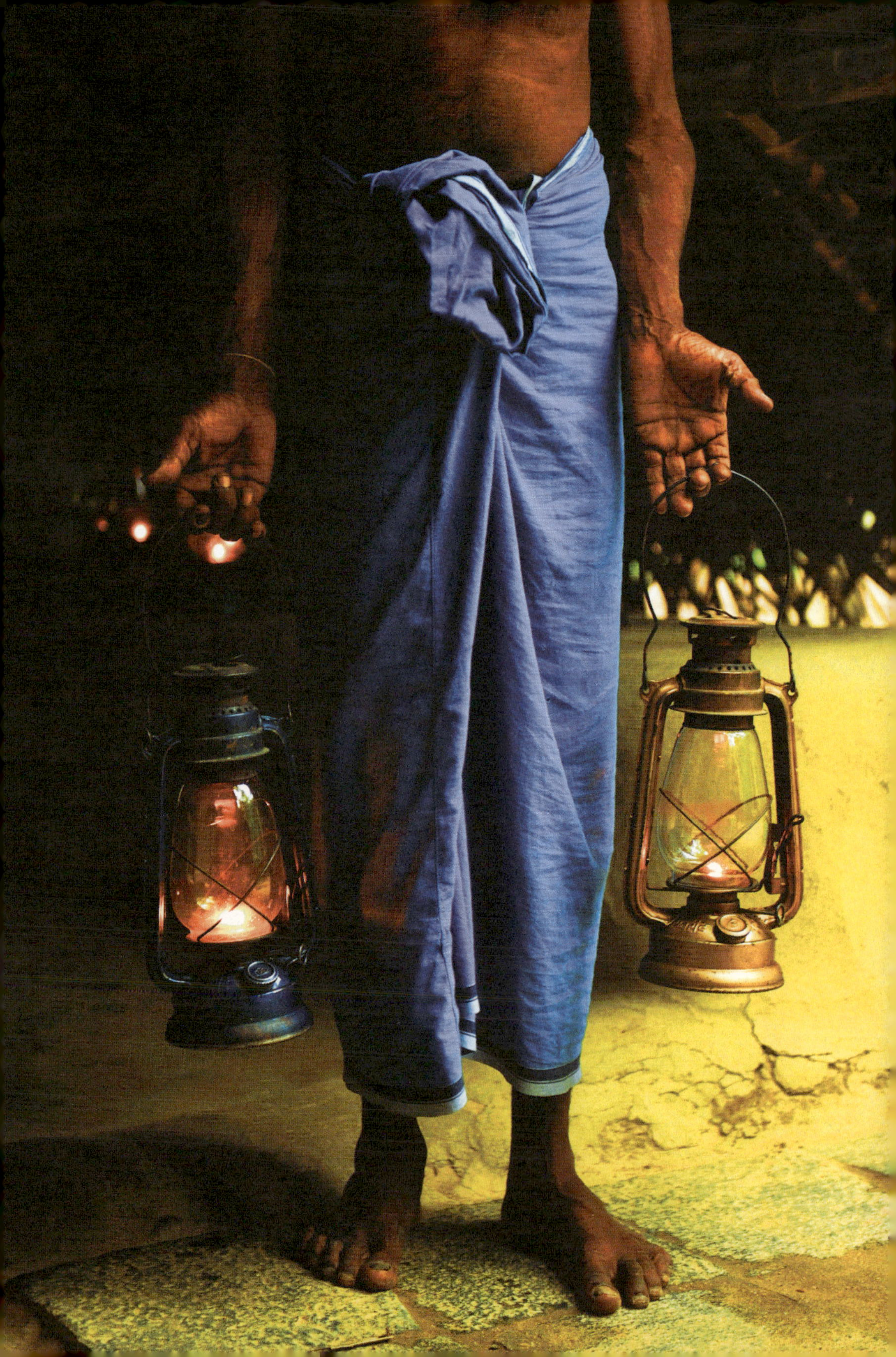

NIGHT

Daytime, when the sky is a deep Madonna blue, is like a curtain that separates us from the greatest show in forever.

Staring into the canvas of colour, piercing through to what I only know to exist from experience and could never imagine to be, is the eternal universe or multiverse, which allows us to look into the infinite. It's a strange paradox that to see into the furthest reaches of forever you need not light… but dark.

The Sri Lankan star-scape is crystal clear. There is minimal light pollution, with the South Pole being the nearest landmass to the south, India to the north, Africa to the west and Indonesia to the east.

The night sky is the only thing that is almost exactly what our ancient ancestors would have witnessed as we do. Even dinosaurs were bathed in galactic light. When I'm in Ulpotha, I find it to be the most precious of luxuries to lie on the large slab of granite known as Telephone Rock, still warm from the day's sun, feeling contented as a lizard as I star bathe, star gaze and drink in the diamond-studded ever after.

In the west we like nightlight to match daylight. In big cities we might get a glimpse of Venus on a rare night but with it brings a sense of loss from our natural heritage.

Here in the tropics, I feel I have to brace myself for night and to be aware of a new sensation.

The sun sets more often than not in a fanfare of reflected fire and exquisite colour, which leaves a golden afterglow that gently winds down the mind and body and leads one into the most impenetrable inky pitch for the next twelve hours.

In Ulpotha people use minimum illumination, often only palm oil and a wick, so night exudes mystery and magic and everything takes on an altered state. Once the countryside rests in slumber and goes into darkness, especially with a waning or waxing moon it becomes a different landscape. I feel Gaia is happy to have a rest and have the velvet blanket of nigrescence pulled over her form.

The jungle arena turns from the purple gloaming into hues of dark blues, most clearly resembling a Rousseau painting.

Huge fruit bats glide between the trees like black ghosts.

The shadowy forms of the jungle plants sit calmly with graphic outlines, and there is a sense of diva spirits emerging from the darkened landscape.

Fireflies flash through the air like little sprites seducing one to follow their sparky trails.

The bullfrogs are wind instruments giving deep plaintive mating calls with their bassoons, baritone belches and burps. The cicadas scrape their back legs incessantly, bringing out their maracas and become the percussionists to this all night cacophony of an orchestra.

At 3.15am the train to Trincomalee shrills like a ghost train in the distance...

Darkness begins to recede as dawn breaks and the bird song becomes excited and wilful. The Buddhist temple, perched on its rocky mount, sounds the bell to awaken the monks.

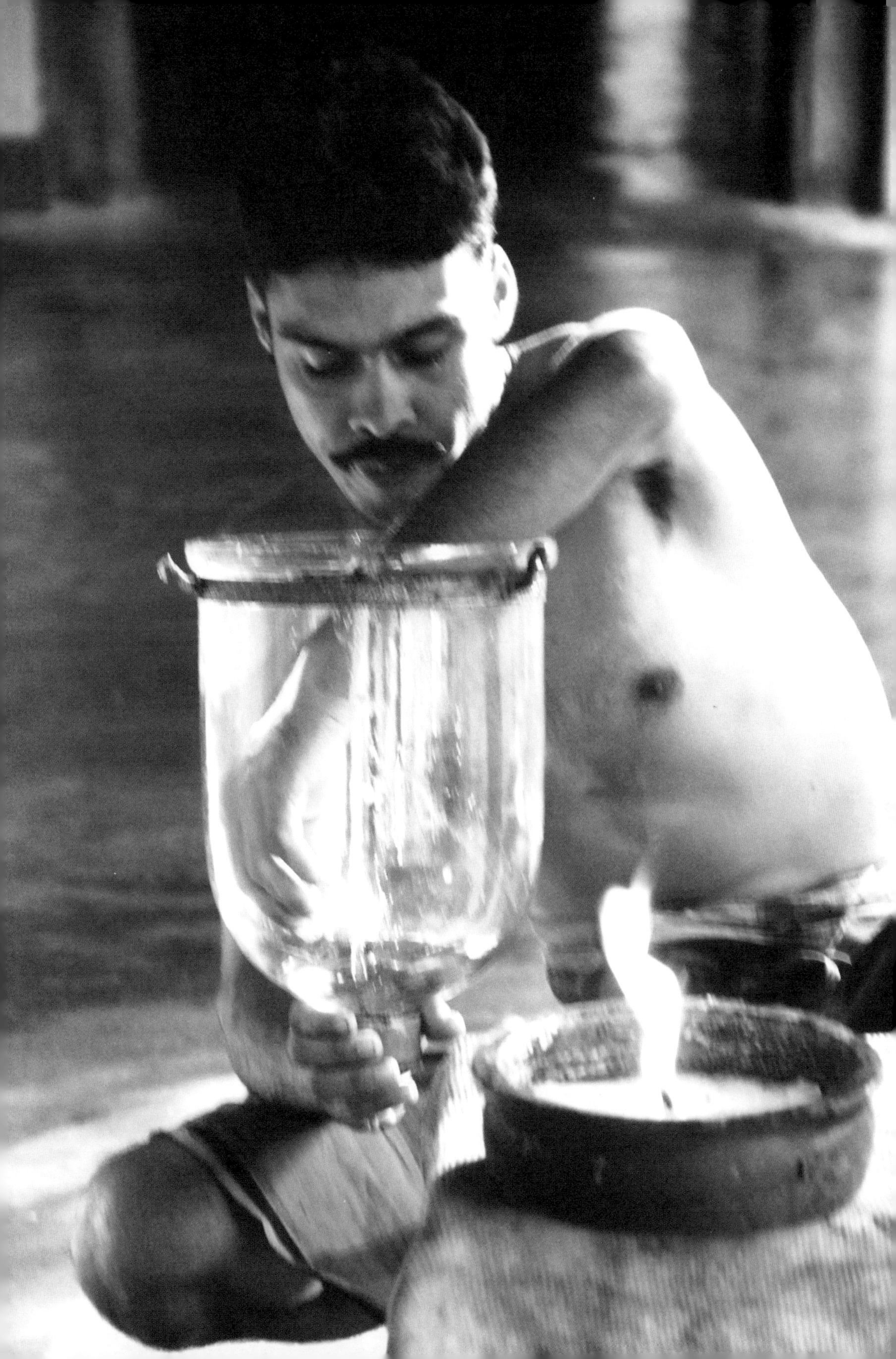

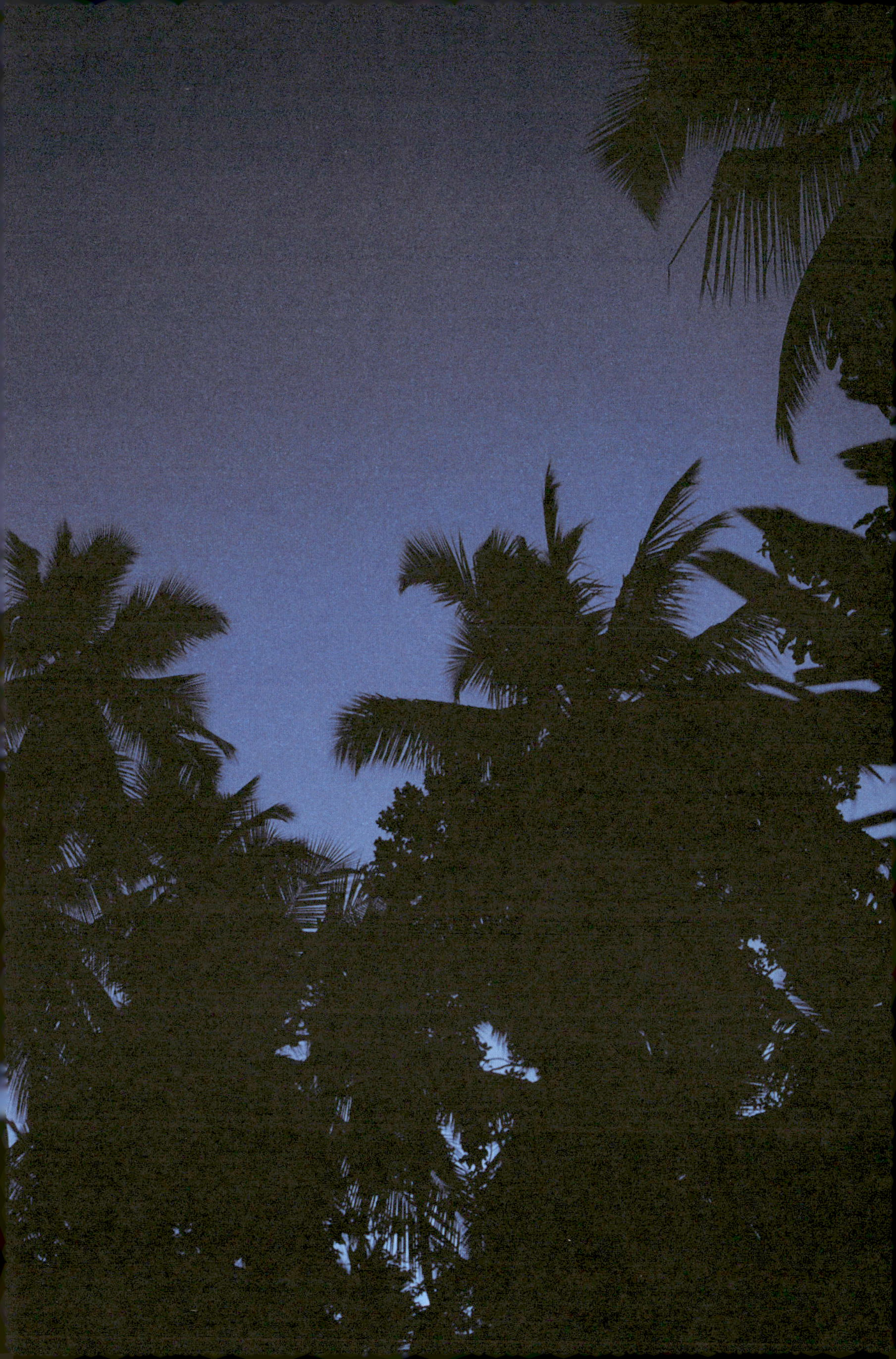

THANK YOU

CHANDRAWATHIE    DR SRILAL    SAMPATH

KAKULI    ATHULA    NALIKA    SUMEDHA

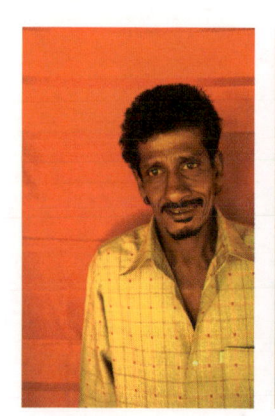

EDWIN    THARANGA    GILES    SUJATHA

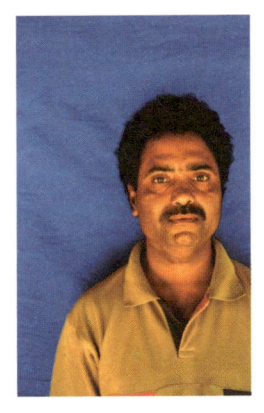

SUNIL    PODIMENIKE    THILAKARATHNE    CHAMPIKA & RESHAN

RAJA    NIROSHA 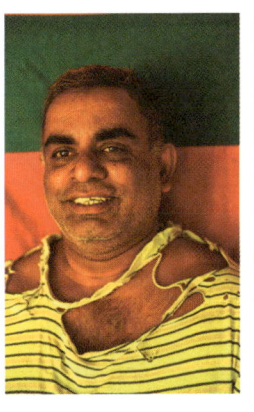   AJITH    DIMUTHU

TOFU    NALAKA    AMARAWATHIE 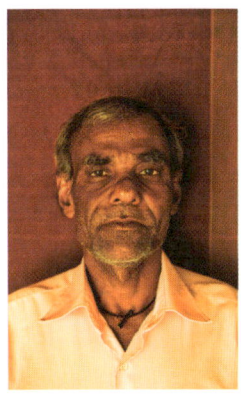   GUNARATHNE

231 THANK YOU

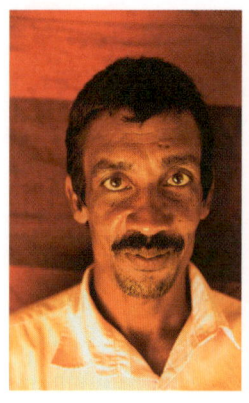

WANNINAYAKE	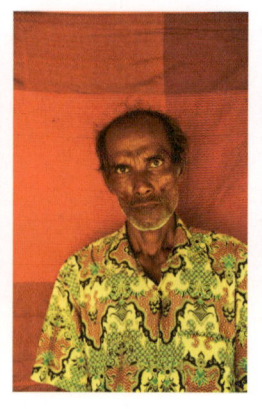 KARUNARATHNE	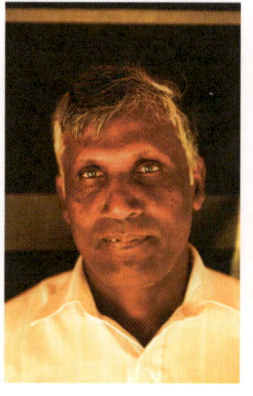 RANBANDA	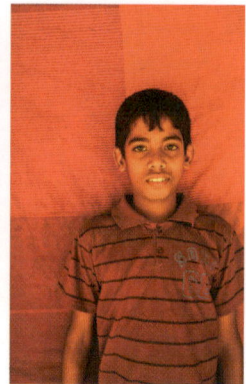 ROHANA
 RATHNASIRI	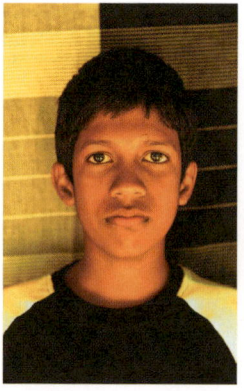 THARINDU	 SUZI	 NILUSHI
 RANJI	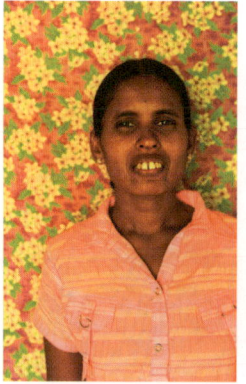 RANEE	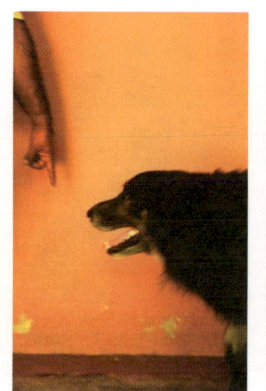 COKKOO	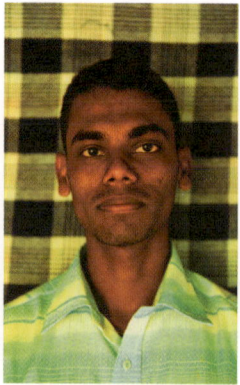 ISURU

232 ULPOTHA - A KITCHEN IN PARADISE

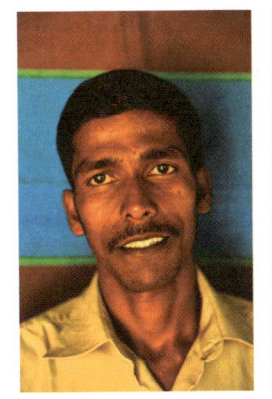

SAKUNTHALA	POTHANA	SAMITHA	PRIYANTHA
NANDAWATHIE	WEERASIRI	ANTHE & ZINDZI	BANDARA
RAJAKARUNA	DAYAWATHIE	VIREN	ROHANA

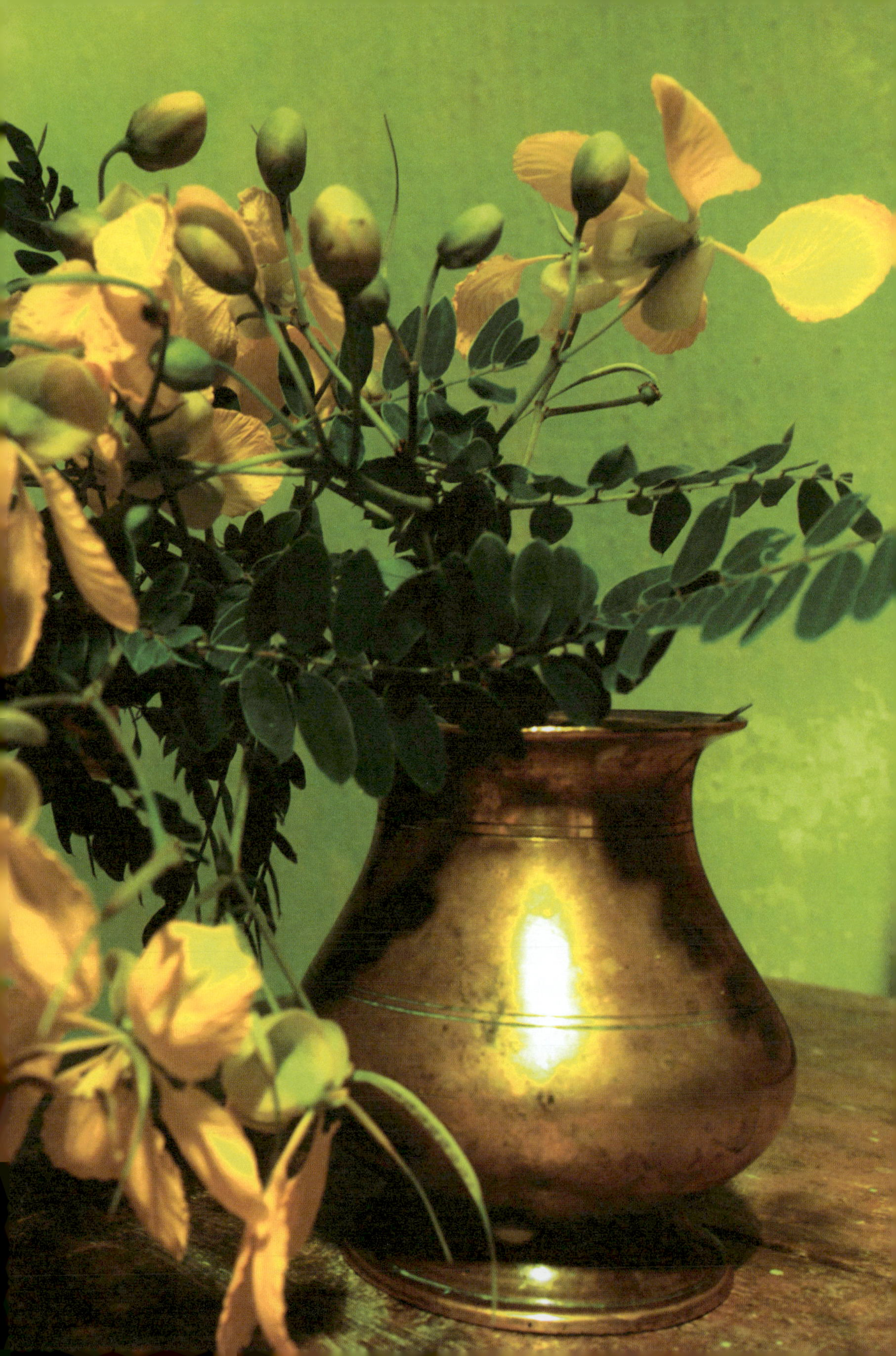

CARINA COOPER
Author

Carina Cooper is the author of three cookbooks including *The Notting Hill Cook book* and *The Working Cook*. She wrote a daily recipe column for the *London Evening Standard* newspaper and a monthly column for *Harpers Bazaar* and has contributed to *Australian Vogue Living, Italian Elle, Red* and *The Saturday Times*. She was introduced to Ulpotha when she first cooked at the *Galle Literary Festival* with Rose Gray from the *River Café*. She has four daughters and lives between London and Devon where she tends her biodynamic kitchen garden and regularly forages the hedgerows and fields around her small holding. Carina is a regular visitor to Sri Lanka.

INGRID RASMUSSEN
Photographer

Ingrid's first book *'Takeaway'*, a celebration of multicultural London and inner city diversity, was published in 2002 by Booth Clibborn Editions. Since then she has had a further 7 books published. She was the original photographer for Thames and Hudson's hugely popular *'STYLE CITY'* series, working on the launch issues of London, Paris, New York and Barcelona. She has photographed 3 interior and lifestyle books; *'New London Style', 'New Country Style'* (Thames and Hudson) and *'Ibiza Style'* (Merrell). Her travel work has appeared in *Conde Nast Traveller, Vogue* and *The Sunday Times* and her interiors photography in *Elle Decoration, The Telegraph Magazine* and *the Guardian*. She lives in London but travels extensively for her work. Ingrid first collaborated with Carina in 2000 on *The Notting Hill Cook Book* and they have worked together on various projects since. See more of her work at www.ingridrasmussen.com

THANK YOU

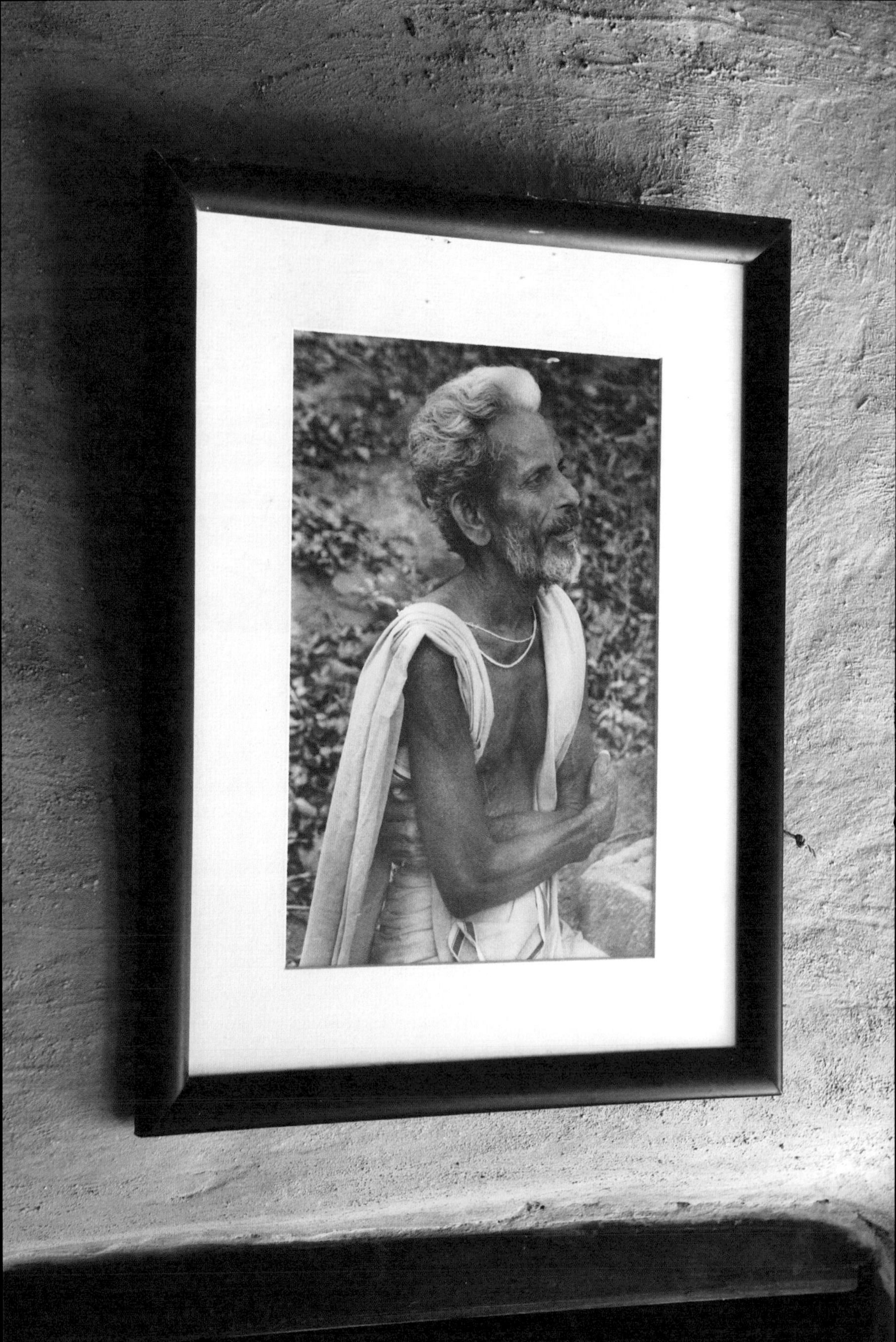

AFTERWORD

An un-aimed arrow never misses its mark is a Zen saying that was reflected back to me by a journalist who came to write about Ulpotha some years ago, after having heard the story from me of how Ulpotha came to be. It's stayed with me ever since because I thought it was a great take on Ulpotha – it was never meant to be anything in particular but seems just about perfect for whatever anyone might take it to be.

Ulpotha was created for the love and sake of it – there was never any specific intention, though of course there were many, many plans. Most were vague, some were good and a few were acted on – sometimes in a manner that might have appeared random to an outsider.

If it can be said that any one person's vision and spirit is reflected in Ulpotha, it's Tennekoon's. Called a 'Philosopher Farmer' by Teddy Goldsmith, he stayed true to his principles throughout and was an inspiration and pleasure to have as a partner and a friend.

Manik played a vital role in the beginning by introducing me to Tennekoon and organizing the road trip that brought me to Ulpotha for the first time. One would be very hard pressed to come across a better or more entertaining raconteur than he. Together Tennekoon and Manik made a captivatingly eccentric and irrepressible combination.

After the first couple of rather impractical but idealistic years, it took Giles' involvement in Ulpotha and Manik's decision to move on for things to take a more practical turn in direction. Giles has been singularly responsible for attracting yoga to Ulpotha and has been the most wonderful and dependable partner-in-folly one could ever hope for.

GILES SCOTT & VIREN PERERA

I think that each of us had a benign streak of madness and that Ulpotha is the happy manifestation of the point at which those various streaks of madness intersect. Since Tennekoon is sadly no longer in this world, having passed away a number of years ago, Giles and I remain the custodians of what seems a paradise on earth.

As for Ulpotha, its specialness is in the land and in the place itself. When one visits now, one might be struck by the delicious food, or the attention to detail, or the friendly villagers, or the great yoga, or the design of the mud huts. But my experience tells me that most of the wonderful feeling Ulpotha inspires is the feeling that was there before we did anything at all – when it was just birds, rocks, gentle winds, trees, the sounds of nature and water. Our challenge now is to gently quash the urge so often found in most kinds of endeavour to make things bigger and better and, instead, to quietly focus on preserving and going with the flow of what's here.

Ulpotha continues to remain an exceptional place and I hope it does so for my lifetime. I don't know of many other places where one can drink untreated water (though what psychological somersaults I had to do before I drank the water fresh from a tap the first time) and live without doors and locks while feeling safe in nature's embrace.

I would like to thank all the villagers who collectively run and look after Ulpotha. For me, as lovely as Ulpotha might be, the villagers are lovelier. The good humour, love and care they bring to everything they do is extraordinary.

VIREN PERERA
Ulpotha
June 6th, 2012